Disclosing New Worlds

Disclosing New Worlds

Entrepreneurship, Democratic Action,
and the Cultivation of Solidarity

Charles Spinosa
Fernando Flores
Hubert L. Dreyfus

The MIT Press, Cambridge, Massachusetts, and London, England

©1997 Massachusetts Institute of Technology

This book was set in Bembo at MIT Press and was printed and bound in the United States of America.

Library of Congress Cataloging-in-Publication Data

Spinosa, Charles.
    Disclosing new worlds : entrepreneurship, democratic action, and the cultivation of solidarity / Charles Spinosa, Fernando Flores, and Hubert Dreyfus.
        p.   cm.
    Includes bibliographical references and index.
    ISBN 0-262-19381-7 (hc : alk. paper)
    1. Social action.   2. Collective behavior.   3. Entrepreneurship.
4. Social change.   I. Flores, Fernando.   II. Dreyfus, Hubert L.
III. Title.
HM281.S635   1997   96-29295
306—dc20   CIP

To Nancy
Para Gloria
À Geneviève

Contents

Acknowledgments

Disclosing New Worlds is an unusual venture. Few books yoke together entrepreneurship, citizen action, and solidarity, and few books written in a philosophical temper have three authors whose backgrounds are so diverse. For these reasons, we have depended more than most writers on the criticism of our friends and colleagues. They have tried to prevent us from making obvious mistakes and have challenged us to think harder as we tried to open a new way of looking at topics usually approached through empirical disciplines or journalistic accounts of leading figures.

We owe a special debt to Alastair Hannay, the editor of *Inquiry*, who edited and published early versions our chapters on entrepreneurship, democratic action, and the cultivation of solidarity (see *Inquiry* 38:1–2 [June 1995]). We have profited enormously from each of the writers who offered criticisms in that issue, even when we were in fundamental disagreement. We order their names in the order of their responses: David Couzens Hoy, Robert C. Solomon, Rogan Kersh, Chantal Mouffe, Torbjörn Tännsjö, Charles Taylor, Robert Grant, and Albert Borgmann.

Leaders in the Chilean government, media, and industry have also been helpful critics. We thank Andrés Allamand, Mariana Aylwin, Sergio Bitar, José Joaquin Brunner, Teresa Chadwick, Mercedes Ducci, Cristián Eyzaguirre, Arturo Fontaine, Juan Enrique Forch, Alberto Fuguet, Jaime Gazmuri, Ricardo Gonçalves, Ricardo Lagos, Cristián Larroulet, Pedro Lizana, Luis Maira, Roberto Méndez, Diego Maqueira, Patricia Matte, Verónica Montellano, Clemente Pérez, Raúl Poblete, Gormán Quintana, Alvaro Saich, Elena Serrano, Ricardo Solari, Eugenio Tironi, Mario Valdivia, Juan Agustin Vargas, and Maria Elena Wood for taking time out of busy schedules to attend a conference in January 1995 to listen to and comment on this theoretical work.

We owe special thanks to President Eduardo Frei of Chile, whose insightful response to our presentation of our work encouraged us to continue thinking about the three main constituting practices of history-making.

Our friends at Cemex, especially Lorenzo H. Zambrano and Gustavo Caballero, helped us think both about human life at its best and the nature of entrepreneurship.

We also thank the many colleagues and friends who helped us informally to shape our arguments and narrative accounts as we wrote: Thomas G. Barnes, Chauncy Bell, Pat Benner, Martha Bohrer, Judith Butler, Tony Cascardi, Chris Davis, Fred Dolan, Maria Flores, Barbara Freeman, Nat Goldhaber, Kit Gordon, David Hiley, Jennifer Hudin, Cheryl Johnson, Eric Kaplan, Oleg Kharkhordin, Steve Knapp, John Longo, Maria Merritt, Lenny Moss, Mary Reynaud, Luis Sota, Gopal Sreenivasan, Iain Thomson, Bud Vieira, Nancy Weston, Mark Wrathall, and Michael Zimmerman.

Our editor at The MIT Press, Larry Cohen, has been indefatigable in helping us bring this book to print. He saw better than we did how the book's parts formed a whole.

Last, none of this work would have been possible without the exquisite kindnesses of Nancy, Gloria, and Geneviève, to whom we dedicate this book.

Introduction: History or the End of History?

This book does not present a *theory* of entrepreneurship, democratic action, and solidarity production. Nor is it a manual that will tell you how to succeed in these domains. Rather, we hope that this book will help you develop a skill that is essential for being an entrepreneur, a virtuous citizen, and a solidarity cultivator—that is, for regularly and as a matter of course seeing yourself and the world anew. Your ability to appreciate and engage in the ontological skill of disclosing new ways of being will, we hope, be expanded when you reexamine your old experiences from the perspective of this book's descriptions and analyses. As you read, we ask you to keep the following questions in mind: Is this description true of some part of my life? In what situations have I experienced something like this? Are the authors seeing only part of a larger phenomenon whose overall shape they are missing? On the basis of experiences that I share with the authors, is what they say compelling?

We write in support of entrepreneurial practices within capitalist market economies, of citizens' action groups in modern representative democracies, and of the culture figures who cultivate solidarity among diverse peoples in modern nations.[1] Indeed, we think that these practices are so important to human life that most of the everyday, conventional aspects of capitalist market economies and modern democratic republics necessary to support them must be preserved.[2] Yet frequently entrepreneurs, citizens in action groups, and culture figures seem to be locked in venomous dispute. This suggests that the skillful way of being human that brings entrepreneurship, citizen action, and solidarity cultivation together is being lost. This book is an attempt to retrieve sensitivity to this skillful way of being. Our main goal is to show how entrepreneurial practices, the practices of virtuous citizens, and the practices of solidarity cultivation are ultimately grounded in and integrated by a crucial skill that human beings in the West have had for at least 2500 years.

We call the special skill that underlies entrepreneurship, citizen action, and solidarity cultivation *history-making*. Though this term is frequently used in a fairly insignificant way, as when we say that Hank Aaron's last home run was history-making, we nevertheless retain a sense that the term ought to be reserved for events that are recorded in the history books that nonspecialists read to find out about the nature of their country or culture. But even this sense of history-making is too weak for what we have in mind. While the dates of each presidency are found in U.S. history books, for example, the election of each new president is not history-making. Something that makes history, we shall argue, changes the way in which we understand and deal with ourselves and with things.

In the recent past, the feminist movement in the United States has been history-making. Watching a Marilyn Monroe movie made in the 1950s underscores how our perception of women has changed. However little some things may have changed—full justice for women has not been achieved, patriarchy has not been eliminated, women are not commonly seen as exemplary representatives of as many skill domains as men— watching a woman defer to a man's authority simply because of his gender evokes distaste in most of the West, a distaste that generally crosses gender, class, and race lines.

We are not saying that feminism has been history-making because it has changed the reflective judgments we make about women, though it obviously has. Rather, feminism has changed the way we see women *prior to* our reflective judgments. Such changes at the heart of perception are the ones we designate as history-making.

History-making also occurs on a national scale. Many still vividly remember President John F. Kennedy's attempt to articulate a historical sense of the American people in the 1960s. In instituting a "space race" with the Soviet Union, setting a goal of sending a man to the moon and returning him safely before the end of the decade, President Kennedy was changing our sense of our national identity—of how we felt about and saw ourselves. In schools throughout the United States, classroom instruction stopped during blastoffs and touchdowns. Students and teachers gathered around radios and televisions to follow events that were determining who they were as U.S. citizens. At best, U.S. citizens felt that the space program expressed their understanding that life was an exploration of frontiers.

John F. Kennedy retrieved the identity of the pioneer by joining it to a technical engineering education. Science studies replaced religious studies as the endeavor that was expected to produce new futures. Astronaut cool became a style of American masculinity. Instead of being a God-fearing people, we became a space-race people. Even more important, Kennedy set in motion a way of understanding ourselves that put our sense of our national identity at risk. If we did not put a man on the moon and return him safely by the end of the decade or if the Soviets did it first, we sensed that we would have failed to fulfill our vision of who we were. History-making acts such as Kennedy's—which we shall call acts of *articulation*—help us retrieve a way of dealing with ourselves that has lost its prominence and relevance—in this case, the pioneering way— and find a new way of making it worthwhile.

But articulation is not the only way in which history is made. President Kennedy articulated by statement, action, and example an understanding of how U.S. citizens could call on pioneering practices left over from the past. The women's movement never articulated a single project that gathered and focused its diverse energies the way the space race did for U.S. citizens. Specific groups within the movement did support significant actions such as the Equal Rights Amendment, but the attempt to pass the ERA did not define either the women's movement as a whole or the identity of women as individuals.

The story of how the feminist movement has come to recognize the differences at its core has been covered extensively in the media. Here is small part of Alice Echols's account of the divisiveness of the early movement:

The first wave of radical feminism was, as Ann Snitow observes, characterized by the belief that "we are one, we are woman." But by 1970, the rhetoric of universal sisterhood had given way to wrenching discussions of women's differences, as lesbians and working-class women challenged the assumption that there was a uniformity to women's experiences and interests. From 1970 onward, excoriations of the movement as racist, classist, and heterosexist became routine if not obligatory at feminist gatherings.[3]

These early divisions are found in the quite different groups of women who constitute the feminist movement of today. Following Echols again, women's groups divide over three main questions.[4] (1) Is feminism about gender equality or about the affirmation of a particular understanding of the category feminine or female? (2) Does patriarchy construct the pleasure of heterosexual sex for woman and prevent sex (which for women is egalitarian) from being consensual? Or does women's sexual pleasure, like men's, necessarily involve power and fantasies of dominance and submission? (3) Are oppressions of race and class interlocked with sexual oppression in such a way that sexual oppression cannot be seriously addressed without addressing the other forms? With different groups of women coalescing around combinations of answers to these fundamental questions, one may well wonder how the feminism of the last 25 years has so successfully transformed the way in which we deal with women and "the" feminine. Women clearly have not simply retrieved practices available for dealing with women and found ways of introducing them to the center of our lives and interests.

Rather, women have adopted practices from various groups according to each practice's use in specific situations. By proceeding in this ad hoc manner, the women's movement has developed a whole new body of practices for dealing with women. We call this bringing of practices into contexts that could not generate them, but in which they are useful, *cross-appropriation*. For instance, in considerations of work-related hiring, promotion, and compensation, women have cross-appropriated practices applied to men. But in matters such as sexual harassment, rape legislation, child care, health, ecology, peace studies, legal reform generally, and moral theory, women have borrowed, mainly from women's groups, practices that reflect sexual and gender difference. In these areas, practices that previously enforced general patriarchal submission have been carried from the general social arena into particular contexts where they can resolve dilemmas arising out of patriarchal rigidity. Perhaps the best-known case is Carol Gilligan's claim that women's standards of situational care enable negotiation in contexts where men's standards of universal justice produce stalemates. In certain matters such as abortion, feminists tend to borrow practices from socialist politics and link together all forms of oppression. Consequently, feminists resist any attempt to make obtaining abortions more expensive or bureaucratic, even if they cannot defend such resistance in pro-choice rhetoric. For many feminists, then, abortion is not just a matter of choice like education but a matter of equalizing resources for bringing the female body under the control of all individual females. Consequently, in thinking about abortion, women treat racial and class liberation as part of feminism. But in other situations, such as writing academic studies, women have adopted the practice of treating sexist oppression in isolation from other forms of oppression.[5]

Our general point is that feminists have cross-appropriated practices from the regime of patriarchy, from relations among men, from socialist politics, and so forth to form a new body of practices for women. If the old model of femininity was submissive with various inflections—as in old Marilyn Monroe movies—the current model is one that we might call *subversive adaptation*.[6] This style identifies how today's feminists confidently cross-appropriate into new contexts practices that formerly marked their oppression as well as practices that were reserved for white men. As cross-appropriated, these practices now become materials for redesigning women's lives and consequently all our lives. Old conventions of the business, family, entertainment, or other domains are abrogated as the most unlikely practices are cross-appropriated back and forth. Even the practice of women bringing along their children as they shop, pick up the dry cleaning, and so forth has been drawn into the context of business travel: as women increasingly bring their children on business trips, hotels compete with one another by offering child-care services during the business week instead of only on weekends.[7]

So far we have tried to recall what understanding ourselves as history makers feels like. Westerners, however, no longer seem to see events from the perspective of a grand mission that we are carrying out. In the absence of nation-state history-making and in the absence for most people of committed membership in a political movement, people live in one of two nonhistorical ways: on the one hand, we live as modern subjects in control of an objective world; on the other, we are becoming postmodern and ending history. In order to see more clearly who we were and one additional way we still may be as history makers, we need to understand these two tempting escapes from history—one left over from the end of the seventeenth century and the other that we are inventing now.

Galileo turned thinking away from trying to attain a wisdom that would deepen and enrich a person's connections with the cosmos. Instead, he promoted a desituated understanding of people and things by attempting to explain all physical phenomena in terms of fundamental laws. By the late seventeenth century, the revolution in thinking introduced by Galileo was incorporated into common everyday practices. Descartes generalized Galileo's achievement, and through the dissemination of Descartes's thinking by such philosophers as Locke, people learned to focus on and bring to prominence whatever similar practices they already had in their everyday lives. For this reason we designate as *Cartesian selves* or *subjects* the kinds of people who arose through this transformation of everyday lives. It will be helpful to us to look more closely at the aspects of the Galilean approach that influenced the way a large part of everyday life was led.

The Galilean habit of thought that Descartes drew into prominence was *detachment*. For people interpreting themselves and things with detachment, the best view of anything would then be the spectator's distanced view. Detachment enables us, first of all, to obtain a wider view, by extracting ourselves from the immediate pressures of the moment, and to see what is before us in terms of its relationships to other matters. To understand what is happening, say, in a bustling port or on a battlefield, a port supervisor or a general who seeks detachment would find high ground from which to view operations below in their interrelations as a whole.

Detachment also enables us to extract ourselves from the passions of the moment so that we can be objective—that is, think and speak out of the composed mood that characterizes both our normal life and those moments when we feel ourselves to be thinking most clearly. The idea here is that we want neither to be bound by words spoken in heat nor to allow another to take advantage of our passionate words. This form of detachment is highly valued in everyday life: hearing that someone is motivated by an intense involvement automatically leads us to discount his or her claims. Our appreciation of this Cartesian form of detachment is epitomized in the way we evaluate newscasters. A passionless appraisal, no matter how dimwitted, generally is preferred to one driven by a clear passion, even if the latter's facts are trenchantly organized.

These two aspects of detachment—detachment for seeing all the relevant interconnections and detachment from passion—combine to form a third. We may seek detachment from our traditions and habitual forms of life—from, in short, our past. We experience this kind of detached observing when we return home after spending a significant time abroad living among people with very different customs and manners. At our homecoming, we understand what our friends and family members are saying and doing, but we see their actions with foreign eyes.

That is, we can't help but see our native practices as a spectacle and note their instrumental effectiveness for achieving what it seems they are deployed to achieve.

Detachment reaches its nearly final form when we privilege the instrumental view that comes when we look at things with foreign eyes. When we can see things as odd and evaluate them instrumentally, we can detach ourselves from the things we encounter and begin noting only the features of the things that most clearly serve the instrumental purpose at hand. We may begin evaluating a spouse by asking which of his or her features bring us happiness. Likewise, we may start asking which features of a business bring us profits (*as though* exploring worthiness in either a marriage or a business were about maximizing either happiness or profits). We reach the ultimate form of detachment—pure theory—when we isolate the features of things that we uncovered in our instrumental investigations and investigate how the elements are interconnected. As science shows, such a theoretical approach—reducing phenomena to the relations of context-free elements—produces great insight and power when it comes to understanding the physical world.

Theorists now claim that the basic building blocks of each domain are among the features detachment finds. For instance, atoms are the building blocks of physical nature, and profit is the building block of business. Using such features, we can account for events in a domain in a regular or lawlike way. Such an account is called a *reductive explanation*. So we can say that heat occurs when atoms start moving faster, or that a business produces increasing profits when the cost of inputs decreases or when more outputs are produced from the same inputs. In the domain of work, one might in a detached way determine that some particular tasks are the basic building blocks of a factory and then, in the same reductive attitude, create an environment where those tasks are best deployed and most carefully supervised. Such acts of design would shape the important functions of management: supervisors would not be craft masters who produce work to be imitated but instead would disengage from the production tasks and monitor the workplace in order to increase productivity by eliminating distractions. In education, if the basic building blocks of teaching are determined to be information retention, then the teacher analyzes a subject matter in a detached way to discover those pieces of information that students will need to retain given their future tasks, then disseminates the information efficiently, and finally develops a test to see how well the information has been retained.

Part of the problem in facing up to the pervasiveness of Cartesianism in our practices is that it no longer seems focused by an admired institution (as the institution of apprenticeship focused the Medieval order). So we no longer all share the fact that we share Cartesian practices. But we remember the days when theoretical science was considered the highest human endeavor, when Einstein was one of the most admired men in the West, when we hoped that the brightest among us would develop theories about how things happened in both the natural world and the social world that would lead to vast improvements in our lives. In those days scientists could make pronouncements about virtually any aspect of human life, and people assumed that their dispassionate, detached position and their working familiarity with the fundamental building blocks of whatever domain they studied gave them insights into how life worked as a whole. But the scientist heroes of the 1940s, 1950s, and early 1960s have become the benign, slightly warped figures of today's television sitcoms or the insensitive, inquisitorial bureaucrats of movies like *E.T.* Indeed, our attitude toward disinterest today is often vexed. People in the United States and much of Western Europe and Latin America admire such disinterested Cartesian fantasy figures as Spock from the television show "Star Trek" and the Terminator from the movie of the same name, but they are puzzled as to whether human emotions would enhance or diminish these fantasy characters.

Still, despite a certain vexation with regard to our Cartesian ambitions and despite the lack of a single institution that focuses our shared admiration for Cartesian practices, these practices, even in their dispersion, exert enormous influence on us as individuals. We can find Cartesianism going strong in our personal wills to be right, our individual sense that what others say in heat is not to be trusted, our individual sense that we should be responsible for knowing the facts of the matter in any discussion we undertake, and our admiration of certain science-fiction types. We still think that we ought to have an orderly picture of our lives as a whole and to distinguish the essential from the contingent. Muddling through is deficient. We wish for the architect's plan of the whole before we build a building, write a book, begin a career, or raise a child.

Institutions also perpetuate our sense of responsibility for having orderly pictures of the world. To talk about the institution of power, for instance, brings to mind notions of power elites that control what people do in business or public life or even in their everyday activities. We develop pictures in our minds of powerful people with enormous data banks containing financial, personal, and professional information about all those whom they control. And we even worry that we are being manipulated by this advertiser, that teacher, this company or financier, that political leader, and so forth. In short, we fear that we may be treated as objects controlled by some nearly invisible subject, in all aspects of our lives. The economic power elite that controls the means of production, division of labor, work rules, and so forth; the political power elite that makes the laws and controls the judges; and the cultural power elite that determines which imaginative works structure our aspirations and self-definitions—all these elites, we may fear, together control the structural aspects of our lives. The notion of such an elite grows precisely out of the Cartesian notion that a domain of activity *can* be controlled by those who understand its basic features and the laws governing their association.

Large portions of our political and productive lives are ordered according to worries about power elites. The separation of powers in the U.S. federal government into three main branches, and then between the Senate and House of Representatives in the legislative branch, was instituted precisely in order to prevent any power elite from achieving total control. We hear of similar worries regarding powerful elites in the call for laws to protect us from both entrenched legislators and the special interests that write laws and prevent competitive elections.

People with large resources are influential: they are in a position to train, govern, focus the interests of, and inflect the views of large numbers of people. Also, in the business world, companies may worry that competitors will obtain control of certain markets or that executives will gain control of divisions of a company or of whole companies, while employees may worry that a boss will be "in control" of them. These are all cases where a Cartesian notion of control that works well for handling machine tools establishes itself in such a way as to hide from us what it is like to work with people. In fact, no one is sufficiently detached from working conditions to stand outside them and control them, as fantasies concerning power elites would suggest. The fear that an executive or politician will learn the hidden rules of manipulating objects in a domain and then control things in that domain from a detached position is a paranoid fantasy made possible by Cartesianism.

While Cartesian practices produce scientific triumphs and rules to curb power elites, they hinder adaptation to change. The only way a Cartesian can adapt to change is to try to develop an analytic explanation of the new domains opened by historical action. But whenever history is changing and people are seeing things in a new way, developing such explanations, which should then give one mastery over the domain, always leaves the Cartesian behind the curve because what counts as facts is changing. Consequently, we find in the halls of business and of politics many people living in a state of profound resignation. They feel themselves losing touch with the world, and after failing to develop analytical explanations of ever new domains, they begin building protected niches for themselves. Cartesianism today has developed into a series of techniques for hedging losses in life, in politics, and in business.

Cartesianism, otherwise called *modernism*, is not, however, the only set of practices we have for living in a nonhistorical way. A second, postmodern set of practices for living is developing today. The newer kind of self that develops from these practices embraces change as the supreme good.

To see what is happening, we need to note two different aspects of how change itself is coming to be experienced. First, we are developing practices for enjoying change for its own sake. We seek the experience of being in a flow of events, improvising so that we use our skills to their best advantage in whatever situation comes along. Second, since such an improvisational way of being—or "surfing," as some call it—would overwhelm anyone whose practices depended on having a stable identity (that is, an identity that always preserves enough continuity for any change to merit either celebration or grief), we are also developing wholly different practices for dealing with and therefore for having selves. We can see this in the way people shy away from life plans or, if they have life plans, include a great deal of room for changing virtually all the commitments they make within them. We no longer expect careers, employers, spouses, or communities to remain constant throughout our lives. Even those who still think life at its best has these constants do not live in the expectation of them. More and more, we give up trying to arrange relations among our various roles of spouse, parent, employer, employee, friend, and so forth in order to achieve a sense of integrity or overall purpose. And as we move beyond feeling the stresses of our different roles' demands, we find ourselves not expecting to have an important connection between ourselves as spouses, parents, and workers. Instead, we try to make the most of whatever situation we are in while we are in it. When we return from a business trip, we try to put aside the concerns of work and wholly adopt the concerns of the family. In short, we are developing flexible ways of dealing with ourselves and with things. As we try to get the most out of every situation, things shift identities as much as we do. The function of the cellular telephone, fax machine, computer, and photocopier that we use at work shifts as we move from dealing with clients and reports to dealing with familial concerns. Everything becomes a resource.

We have so far listed two sets of practices—home and work— that embody the flexible style of life. Another practice—our involvement with the Internet—is representative of all the flexible, interactive networking capabilities that are being invented and discovered. Here we can see the new antihistorical future arriving in its most attractive form. By detailing how the Internet is pervading our lives, we can see, in this possibly last historical change, the third Western skill of history-making beyond articulation and cross-appropriation—*reconfiguration*.

During our lives we engage in many nonserious activities such as playing with our children, looking at the night sky, taking walks, reading fortune cookies, or playing with gadgets. Usually we cannot offer serious justification for these practices, or we justify them in a way that is overly serious and therefore misses the point—as in the claim that we play with our children to further their emotional development. Immersing oneself in the Internet has until very recently fallen into this nonserious category (although people also use the Internet in serious ways). In the academic world, a scholar may search for books in distant libraries for no good reason at all, or just to see the title of her own book listed in a university library in a distant country. For our purposes, the slimmer the reasons, the more honest because such practices are in fact marginal. They do not promote productivity, truth, maturity, quality, or fall under any of the other terms that signify seriousness to us. Our motives for playing on the computer simply run contrary to our motives for following serious pursuits. We play with guilty consciences.

Those who have been surfing the Net for a nonserious reason, however, may end up as our teachers because this marginal practice could become a central practice in our lives. Sherry Turkle has usefully described how the Net is changing the background practices that determine what kinds of people we can be. In *Life on the Screen* she details "the ability of the Internet to change popular understandings of identity." On the Internet "we are encouraged to think of ourselves as fluid, emergent, decentralized, multiplicitous, flexible, and ever in process."[8] Thus "the Internet has become a significant social laboratory for experimenting with the constructions and reconstructions of self that characterize postmodern life."[9]

Turkle's interviews show something more complicated than that we are living in postmodernity. Her work unintentionally reveals that we are in transition in the way we understand ourselves. Turkle speaks of "using virtual spaces to construct identity,"[10] but the idea that we construct our identity is not new. As Turkle notes, it goes back at least to Shakespeare. The crucial question is, What sort of identity does the Net encourage us to construct?

There seem to be two answers, which Turkle does not clearly distinguish. On the one hand, the Net can be used for self-exploration and articulation. As she notes, "On a MUD [multi-user dungeon, a virtual space popular with adults that has its origin in a role-playing game popular with teenagers] one actually gets to build character and environment and then to live within the toy situation. A MUD can become a context for discovering who one is and wishes to be."[11] Thus some players are exploring various roles in order to become more clearly and confidently themselves. The Net then functions, as Turkle says, "to facilitate self-knowledge and personal growth."[12] But, on the other hand, although Turkle continues to use the modernist language of personal growth, she sees that the computer and the Internet promote something totally different: "MUDs make possible the creation of an identity so fluid and multiple that it strains the limits of the notion. Identity, after all, refers to the sameness between two qualities, in this case between a person and his or her persona. But in MUDs, one can be many."[13]

MUDs lend themselves, then, especially to playing at being many selves, none of whom is recognized as who one truly is, and this possibility is not just theoretical but actually introduces new social practices: "The rethinking of human . . . identity is not taking place just among philosophers but 'on the ground,' through a philosophy in everyday life that is in some measure both proved and carried by the computer presence."[14] The MUDs' disembodiment and lack of commitment enables people to be many selves with no attempt to integrate these selves or to use them to improve their single identity. As Turkle notes: "For most people such self-transformations are difficult or impossible. They are easier in MUDs where you can write and revise your character's self-description whenever you wish. On some MUDs you can even create a character that 'morphs' into another with the command '@morph.'"[15]

There have always been possibilities of changing one's identity on the far-off margins of our practices. As Turkle goes on to say: "In modern times, there was the con artist, the bigamist, the cross-gender impersonator, the 'split-personality,' the Dr. Jekyll and Mr. Hyde."[16] Now such possibilities are becoming available to everyone. Turkle notes that the Net encourages what she calls "experimentation" (a confusing term covering both exploration and morphing) because what one does on the Net does not normally have consequences. Sex confined to the Internet does not lead to pregnancy or AIDS. But the Internet, in its creation of worlds that have a kind of disembodied reality, reflects and focuses many marginal practices of flexibility. Real teenagers can change identities by cross-dressing and so forth at today's Goth clubs. In a world that follows the values of the MUDs, the body becomes as flexible and endlessly modifiable—through surgical interventions, implantations, prostheses, and genetic engineering—as the Net itself. One can have endless identities and indulge the postmodernist dream of change for its own sake in every domain. We see here how the transition from marginality to centrality of one set of practices, such as virtual-space morphing, can bring other marginal practices, such as sex changes, along with them and transform a whole way of life. This kind of transformation is what we mean by reconfiguration.

In the age of the Net, if such an age comes, we shall have many different skills for identity construction, and we shall move around virtual spaces and real spaces seeking ways to bring out these skills, powers, and passions as best we can. This is different from saying that we will seek to bring out our selves as best we can: to have a self in the terms in which we still think about selves means to have an identity that generally remains stable over the course of a life. Instabilities are either celebrated as conversion experiences or mourned as pathologies. But to imagine people who join in an activity with a particular identity for so long as the identity and activity are exhilarating and engaging and then move on to new identities and activities is to imagine people who thrive on having no home community and no home sense of self. Like Transformer toys and cartoons, they morph flexibly. Many teenagers live a version of morphing. They do not have a stable sense of whom to love, what career to have, where to live, what kind of life to have. They try one lover, discipline, residence, and life style after another. Because settling down is a distant concern, they often play with the multiple ways they can be.

Our society could not endure if we all had the low skill levels of teenagers, but the promise of the Net is that it will create new forms of social survival skills by enabling people to do one kind of work intensely with one set of partners and then move on to do some other kind of work with other partners. Such a society would be characterized by intense, but short, involvements and by flexibility. Communities of such people would not seem like communities by today's standards. They would not have a core cadre that remains living in them over time. Rather, they would live and die on the model of rock groups: there would be an intense effort among a group of people and an enormous flowering of talent and artistry, and then that activity would get old, and the members would go their own ways, joining different communities.[17] If one thinks that today's rock groups are a special case, consider how today's businesses are fostering work by so-called hot groups. Notoriously, the Apple Macintosh was the result of the work of such a hot group. More and more products are appearing through such efforts. The structure of the hot rock and business groups, the hot clubs, the hot restaurants, movies, models, resorts, cafés, and so forth of today will become the structure of the communities in this possible future.

Have we already entered the age of flexibility so thoroughly that we can look back on our former history-making age and stable selves only as an attractive myth? Perhaps such lives and such commitments were always anomalies, but people made themselves believe that they could imitate those anomalous lives. If so, then this book, which aims to show how the history-making produced by reconfiguration, cross-appropriation, and articulation still play important roles in our lives and in our polities, would be an exercise in nostalgia.

We do not think that history-making has declined that far. We think there is a phenomenon that the media promote where we still recognize history-making practices. This phenomenon consists of our relation to our generation. In general, we relate ourselves to generations in two different ways. First, we see our identity tied up with that of our generation. For instance, most so-called baby boomers did not go to Woodstock, to Vietnam, or even to antiwar protests. Some did not spend their time listening to the Beatles or the Beach Boys. Many may not have tried alternative medical treatments, hired personal trainers, eaten arugula, drunk bottled mineral water, bought Armani wardrobes, carried cellular phones and laptop computers, or built mutual fund portfolios. But boomers nonetheless identify (and cope with) themselves with reference to all these activities or others like them—even if only to divorce themselves from them. Being a member of a generation and living through its events colors lives as much as the dyer's trade leaves its marks on the dyer. In this respect we still understand ourselves as having developed relatively fixed historical identities.

The second way the phenomenon of generations reveals that we are still concerned with history-making is that members of each generation care about what mark their generation will leave and how they can be part of leaving such a mark. Not everyone in a generation seeks to be a leader, and members of a generation don't always keep a watchful eye on their generation's trends. Rather, members of a generation are sensitive to what other members of the generation are doing, and they try to express what they and their friends of the same age care about. This activity of focusing a pervasive style is a further aspect of what we have called articulation. Generations seek articulation; it can be a person like Jerry Rubin or Bob Dylan or even a television series like "thirtysomething" or "Friends" that plays this articulating role.

We argue that, although sensitivity to history-making and history-making practices is now focused only in the way people relate themselves to their generation, there are still many micro-occasions when we engage in the skill of history-making. Indeed, we claim that we engage in reconfiguration, cross-appropriation, and articulation whenever our lives are at their best.

The choice for us now is between the style of flexibility toward which we seem to be drifting and a resuscitation of our historical skills. Almost every action each of us in the West takes draws us one way or the other. We need to develop sensitivity to where we are going if we are to make choices instead of simply following the drift. We hope that this book will refocus attention on the way we make history both in our everyday lives and when we act as entrepreneurs, virtuous citizens, or cultivators of solidarity. We hope thereby to encourage a retrieval of history-making skills from dispersion by showing how in our personal and family lives at their best we still engage in reconfiguring, cross-appropriating and articulating and how in business, politics, and solidarity cultivation at their best we can and should still be making history.

1

The Ontological Structure of Everyday History-Making

Since most of our commonsensical ways of thinking depend on either Cartesian or flexible postmodern categories and distinctions, we are ill prepared to describe or even notice our own culture's history-making activities and skills, even when we find ourselves enacting them in the restricted domains of our life projects. For this reason, we devote this chapter to developing the distinctions and categories appropriate for noticing these activities and skills. Since we claim that our lives are at their best when we act in accord with these skills, these categories and distinctions should yield a sharper view of such important moments than that provided by either the Cartesian or postmodern categories and distinctions. Our task is thus twofold. We flesh out a large set of categories and distinctions, developed from the ontology of Martin Heidegger, and in doing this, we try to show how they clarify what is going on when we are living life at its best. For that reason, our examples draw on simple everyday-life situations that, we assume, are both easily recognizable and held in high regard. In a general sense, we try to counter the tendency to look at human experience from the point of view of individual agents who generate action and instead look at common human practices and skills into which we are socialized and that in turn produce people, selves, and worlds. The basic intuition, then, is that shared human practices tend to gather together into organizations that we recognize as worlds, people, and selves. Once those organizations gain consistency and effectiveness, we as people and selves bring them into sharper focus and organization, by means that we describe in detail.

1. How Everyday Practices Ground History-Making

We call any organized set of practices for dealing with oneself, other people, and things that produces a relatively self-contained web of meanings a *disclosive space*. To see what is essential to a disclosive space we can turn to Heidegger's account of "worldhood" in *Being and Time*. A *world* for Heidegger has three characteristics. It is a totality of interrelated pieces of *equipment*, each used to carry out a specific task such as hammering in a nail. These tasks are undertaken so as to achieve certain *purposes*, such as building a house. Finally, this activity enables those performing it to have *identities*, such as being a carpenter. These identities are the meaning or point of engaging in these activities. Cultures are obvious candidates for worlds, and normally when we use the term "world" we are referring to cultural worlds, but we can also think of professions as worlds. Thus we speak of the worlds of medicine, business, academics, the theater, politics, sports, and so on. Families can also be worlds in this sense; following Heidegger, though, we call such worlds *subworlds* because their practices presuppose the shared practices of the larger world of which they are a part. Worlds can interact, and where several worlds interact without presupposing a common world we speak of *local worlds*. Examples of local worlds are the Greek polises and those native American tribal nations such as the Algonquin that had close ties to other tribal nations. The webs of practices and meanings, from cultures to tribal nations to individual families, are disclosive spaces.[1]

How, then, do we ourselves, other people, and things appear in average, everyday human activity? By settling this matter first, we direct our thinking away from the mistake of starting where philosophers are inclined to start—that is, with our Cartesian preconceptions of *what* we and things are—and begin with *how* we, in fact, deal with ourselves and things in our everyday coping. Here we must begin by noticing that we do not, for the most part, encounter mere stuff to which we then assign some sort of meaning. We do not first encounter something metallic with a flat surface facing upward that we subsequently treat as a desk. Rather we directly encounter desks, chairs, and lamps. In other words, when we start by looking at our activity, we find, in the first instance, that we encounter meaningful things.

When we say that things are meaningful, we mean that they fit with the practices we have for using them. If we did not have practices for working at desks or eating at tables, we would not encounter desks, chairs, and tables as meaningful. We would encounter them as mere artifacts, requiring explanation. This was presumably the reaction of traditional Japanese when they first encountered European tables and chairs. We can test this observation ourselves by visiting museums. We encounter an oddly shaped flat piece of metal as an artifact. Our grandparents, when they were young, would have seen it immediately as an ox shoe. Most of us would have the same reaction to a laser or cyclotron. We see them as odd artifacts until we become familiar with their use, and then we become virtually incapable of seeing them as strange. Try to recapture the feeling of being overwhelmed by your first sight of a computer. It is virtually impossible. Our practices now simply include many skills for dealing with computers. We may be able to recapture something of our earlier experience in our frustration when our computer does not work. But even our current frustration depends on already being familiar with the way the computer should work.

Things show up for us in terms of our familiar practices for dealing with them. The same is true for people. If we are behind a counter in a store, we see those entering the store as customers, other employees, the owner, perhaps the city inspector, or people asking for change. Unless we have been specially trained, we don't see people entering the store as thieves until it is too late. Thieves, in fact, take advantage of the fact that what we see is determined by the familiar practices in which we are engaged. For the Greeks, beautiful things, slaves, and heroes were what people encountered, while for the medievals, what mattered, and so what was encountered, were tempting things, sinners, and saints.

Finally, we don't show up for ourselves very much at all. When engaged in walking, thinking, driving, or conversation, we do not notice ourselves as agents, as people, or as any thing. What needs to be done, said, or thought straightaway draws an appropriate response from us. We respond to a situation that appears in terms of the actions *we* can take. We respond to the ongoing solicitations and not to the facts a detached observer would notice. As we drive, for instance, we don't observe how far we are turning the wheel. The road constantly requires adjustments, and we are simply involved in adjusting. We understand this involved coping as normal and secure. Only when there is a disturbance of some sort do we appear to ourselves as agents, with beliefs and desires directed toward goals that require some particular action.

There is more to the organization of practices, however, than interrelated equipment, purposes, and identities. All our pragmatic activity is organized by a *style*.[2] Style is our name for the way all the practices ultimately fit together. A common misunderstanding is to see style as one aspect among many of either a human being or human activity, just as we may see the style as one aspect among many of a jacket.[3] Our claim is precisely that a style is not an aspect of things, people, or activity but, rather, constitutes them as what they are.

To understand the importance of style for a disclosive space, we turn from the way we, other people, and things show up in terms of our everyday instrumental activity to how our familiar actions and inactions are coordinated. We distinguish two aspects of a disclosive space: its organization and its coordination. We have already specified that a disclosive space is organized as an interrelated set of equipmental relations, plus roles that give a point to the activity of using that equipment. But in order for things, people, and selves to show up as *meaningful* (as opposed to merely effective), this organized activity needs a further level of organization, which we call *coordination*. To be coordinated is more than to be interconnected. Changing our driving laws so that everyone is required to drive on the left would require a massive reorganization of equipment and practices, but it would not change the way people drive—let's imagine New Yorkers—and so it would not change what it means to be a driver. Changing the way driving practices are coordinated among themselves and with other practices so that what coordinates drivers is cautious, considerate comportment rather than aggressive, quick reflexes, would, however, produce a change in driving style and thus in what it means to be a driver.

That all of our disclosive spaces are organized in a more-than-equipmental way becomes apparent if we consider the everyday phenomenon of familiarity. Sometimes finding a situation familiar means simply having an appropriate set of dispositions and having them respond on cue. No doubt people do form habits and find situations familiar, but there is another feature of familiarity that is different from, indeed opposed to, this sort of habituation. One can find a situation familiar even when one has never experienced its like before. In such a case what makes a set of practices feel familiar is that they share a style. Thus someone familiar with our culture's first-come, first-served style of handling telephone calls to businesses will also be familiar with our culture's style of lining up or merging, even if that person has never had to wait in a line or drive a car.

Moreover, when people change their practices in meaningful ways, they do so on the basis of the style they already have. Style acts as the basis on which practices are conserved and also the basis on which new practices are developed. Thus style is the ground of meaning in human activity. A style, or the coordination of actions, opens a disclosive space and does so in a threefold manner: (1) by *coordinating* actions, (2) by determining how things and people *matter*, and (3) by being what is *transferred* from situation to situation. These three functions of style determine the way anything shows up and makes sense for us.

One can see these three functions of style in a simple case that highlights the way style coordinates actions. Sociologists point out that mothers in different cultures handle their babies in different ways that inculcate the babies into different ways of coping with themselves, people, and things.[4] For example, Japanese mothers tend to place babies in cribs on their backs so they will lie still, lulled by whatever they see, whereas American mothers tend to place babies on their stomachs, which encourages them to move around more effectively. Japanese mothers tend to be soothing and mollifying, whereas American mothers tend to encourage passionate gesturing and vocalizing. In many different ways, in short, Japanese mothers promote relative passivity and sensitivity to harmony in the actions of their babies, whereas American mothers situate babies' bodies and respond to their actions in such a way as to promote an active and aggressive style of behavior. The babies, of course, take up the style of nurturing to which they are exposed. It may at first seem puzzling that a baby can successfully pick out precisely the gestures that embody the style of its culture as the ones to imitate, but, of course, such success is inevitable. Since *all* our gestures embody the style of our culture, the baby picks up that pervasive style no matter which ones it takes up.

One may easily see how, starting with a style, various practices will make sense and become dominant, and others will either become subordinate or will be ignored altogether. So, for example, babies never encounter a bare rattle. An American baby tends to encounter a rattle-thing as an object to make lots of expressive noise with or to throw on the floor in a willful way in order to have a parent pick it up, whereas a Japanese baby tends to encounter a rattle-thing as serving a soothing, pacifying function. What constitutes the American baby as *American* is its style, and what constitutes the Japanese baby as *Japanese* is its quite different style.

A style thus governs how anything can show up *as* anything, and the style of a culture therefore governs more than its babies. Adults in a culture are thoroughly shaped by it. Thus we do not just feel that each of the practices of another culture is unfamiliar; they all seem to have the same sort of unfamiliarity even if we handle some of the culture's practices better than others. For example, it should come as no surprise to us, given the caricature we have already presented of Japanese and American culture, that Japanese adults seek social integration, whereas American adults strive willfully to satisfy their individual desires. Likewise, the style of enterprises and of political organizations in Japan aims at producing and reinforcing cohesion, loyalty, and consensus, whereas what Americans admire in business and politics is the aggressive energy of a laissez-faire system in which everyone strives to express his or her own desires and the state, business, or other organization functions to maximize the number of desires that can be satisfied without creating destructive instability. In both the Japanese and American cases, the activities of the culture are all familiar because they share a style.

To see more clearly how a style makes certain kinds of activities and things matter and be worthy and other activities and things not matter and be petty or unworthy, consider two kinds of driving styles—the aggressive Parisian or New-York-City style of driving and the calm, all-too-happy-to-please driving that can be found in the Midwest of the United States. Anyone who has driven in Paris or New York knows that it matters to drivers in these places whether someone passes, whether someone pulls in front of them (which must as a matter of pride be seen as being cut off), and whether they can snake through lanes of traffic around the unfortunates who are less opportunistic. Every other car on the road and every driver is a challenge to be surmounted. The cab that passes them on Seventh Avenue in the forties blocks is one that they will seek to pass at least by the sixties. In New York, drivers feel themselves to be in a race, and all obstacles in the way of winning show up as irritating.

Midwestern drivers, on the other hand, see no reason for any tension in driving. What counts in driving is what they notice happening along the side of the road. A long detour is a joy if it affords some new perspective. Other cars are not noticed unless their drivers request an act of kindness, which drivers are happy to perform. A Midwesterner in a New York cab for the first time will see no slick moves, just a blur of terrifying motion. A New Yorker driving with a Midwesterner will not see acts of politeness but only wasted opportunities. Clearly, not only do the two styles allow different things to appear; they make different things significant and worthy of notice.

We can now also see that the style of any particular culture enables practices in that culture to be transferred from situation to situation. A style of self-assertion or of peaceful integration that allows one to shift from situation to situation in childhood also enables the shift from childhood to business and political situations. All are experienced as extrapolations of the one constitutive style that governs the culture. The baby who throws down a rattle to make a parent pick it up may become the fighter pilot who tests the limits of an aircraft, while the baby who uses the rattle to produce peaceful effects may become the CEO who offers employees lifetime job security.

Finally, when people change their practices in meaningful ways, they commonly do so on the basis of the style they have. People who are very sensitive to the style of some domain are particularly good at making such adjustments. In fact, it is this characteristic that allows us to see a mastery in what they do. Really good cooks show us this capacity when they take a cupboard full of unpromising ingredients and turn out a tasty meal. Surely this is not because they have practices for working with unpromising ingredients. It happens because they remain true to their style and not their habits, which in this cooking situation would have meant purchasing other ingredients. Our sports heroes are like great cooks in this way. They show their mastery of the game when they win by doing something that we would not have expected could be the reasonable thing for them to do given what we have seen before; but when it works out, we see, in hindsight, that what they did was to respond to the new situation by staying within their style and doing something new that the style called for.

2. The Phenomenon of Historical Disclosing

We call the general everyday kind of disclosive activity we have just described *customary disclosing*. We now turn to several ways in which disclosive activity can change the style of a disclosive space. We call this type of activity *historical disclosing*.

There are two kinds of skills required for historical disclosing. First, one has to be able to sense and hold on to disharmonies in one's current disclosive activity; second, one has to be able to change one's disclosive space on the basis of the disharmonious practices. Since both skills are displayed in daily life when human beings are functioning at their best, we describe a case of each type of skill in the life of an individual before taking up our main subject, which is the functioning of such skills in business, politics, and culture.

Disharmonies are practices in which we engage that common sense leads us to overlook because they are not well coordinated with our other practices. We should beware of the Cartesian tendency to imagine the skill of noticing and holding on to disharmonies as primarily intellectual, as noticing a problem in one's life and stepping back to analyze it, to puzzle through it, in one's mind. Rather, the skill of uncovering the tension between standard, commonsense practices and what one actually does is a skill of intensified practical involvement.

To clarify the difference, consider two ways of handling a perturbation in a romantic relationship. The reflective approach is to treat the sense of a disharmony as a problem to be solved. One meets one's partner over coffee and talks about the relationship. Or one may even try introspection, asking such questions as, Is this love or just infatuation? Have I changed, or is it my partner? If there is some clear, specific, persistent problem, this approach may succeed; when it fails, then the relationship fails.

The trouble with this approach is that it allows one to ask only the standard questions—standard given the categories in terms of which one understands the relationship—and thereby receive the relationship's standard answers. If the disharmony is not one that is standard for the two people involved, then this approach will never resolve the problem. In the same vein, one could consult a therapist who has an account of human relationships and why they sometimes fail; but this too, since it is based on a general theory, can result only in standard answers. Generally, when meaningful change is needed, the disharmonies will be of the nonstandard, situational kind that is usually passed over by both common sense and theory, and so uncovering it will require a different approach.

To see such a skill in action, imagine a husband and wife (or any two life partners) who both have successful and exciting careers but who are beginning to feel "out of sorts." They could ignore their feelings since common sense tells them there are bound to be rough moments in a relationship, but they resist common sense and the resignation it entails. They confront the disharmony not through solitary introspection or an intense conversation over coffee—which would lead to the typical solutions of the past such as going somewhere together or investing in a local vineyard—and not by going to a professional who has a theory of the nature of couples and their problems. Instead, they seek to make what is perturbing the relationship manifest itself. To do this they throw themselves into the activities that have always made the relationship seem most alive and worthwhile. But this time they do it with a special sensitivity and alertness for what is unusual because they know that focusing on what is unusual can reveal what is different now from the times when those activities worked. So the couple goes off to a favorite resort. There they find themselves talking to other couples with children. They watch children on the beach. The old standard ways of resisting having children do not seem to make sense. If they do not willfully persist in the old standard way of thinking about children (which they will not do if they are acting with sensitivity to what is unusual), they will suddenly find the old warmth coming back into the relationship as they talk over dinner about having children. Indeed, such talk will have the intensity that talking about seeking a new job or investment used to have. And with this change, the whole relationship will be readjusted (*regestalted* in psychological terms) so that what before was a disharmonious loss of warmth now seems to reveal the inner truth of the relationship. The couple will begin producing a family with the conviction that this is precisely the right thing to do. The point of this example is that a reflective approach, because it is dispassionate, could not have produced this conviction; it would not have made the world look different. The life of skillful disclosing, conversely, is a life of intense engagement. The best way to explore disharmonies, in other words, is not by detached deliberation but by involved experimentation.

The skill for dealing with a disharmony is more complex than the skill for noticing and holding on to it. There seem to be at least three ways one can change one's disclosive space in response to the realization that one's practices are not in harmony; these are articulation, reconfiguration, and cross-appropriation.

Articulation

We introduced articulation in a general way in the introduction in our discussion of the space race. We now want to reframe the concept in terms of the categories and distinctions we have just developed. Articulating is the most familiar kind of style change. It occurs when a style is brought into sharper focus, and it is easily illustrated at the level of the family. Many families exhibit intensely caring styles. Such families can be deeply concerned that each member have a strong work ethic, strong family loyalty, personal security, the best education possible, and so on. Frequently, such families start out caring about all of these and many more aspects of life. In pursuit of these goals, children are enrolled in all sorts of activities, from after-school jobs to caring for younger siblings to martial arts to foreign language instruction. But frequently something upsets this distribution of activity. Financial resources decrease. A special talent reveals itself. The many activities become too demanding. When this happens, the family finds out what is most important to it by focusing on its mode of caring. In doing this, the family might come to see that it cares most about safety—and then the martial arts classes will trump the foreign language lessons— or about communicating around the world—and then the language lessons will be retained and the martial arts dropped. If the family has indeed focused its style, then after the narrowing of interests its members will generally feel more at home with themselves, feel more integrity and less dispersion in their lives. We call this gathering from dispersion *articulating* because the aspect of the family's caring that has been driving it all along is revealed in a particular visible practice, which comes to dominate other family practices. In an articulating change, the style keeps its core identity but becomes more recognizable as what it is.

There are two forms of articulation. All articulating makes what is implicit explicit. If what is implicit is vague or confused, then we speak of *gathering from dispersion*. If it was once important and has been lost, then we have the special kind of articulation we call *retrieval*.

Reconfiguration

Reconfiguration is a more substantial way in which a style can change. In this case some marginal aspect of the practices coordinated by a style becomes dominant. This kind of change is less frequent in everyday life than articulation. We can identify it most easily when the change is large-scale. For instance, in our introduction, we mentioned the marginal practices around morphing that could become central and end history-making. The advent of machine technology also illustrates this kind of change in style quite clearly. In the days before machine technology, people used animals for transportation and for power, and the style for dealing with them was governing them. One tried to bring their wills into accord with what one wanted done. Horseback riders will recognize this style of dealing with animals. Before machine-powered tools, this was also the style of working wood and of dealing with most things. One had to bend to one's will as much as possible the tendencies in the thing one worked with, whether the grain in the wood, the shifts and power of the wind, the will of the horse, or even one's own desires.

Once machine tools took over, however, the dominant Western style changed from governing to controlling. No one governs a car. People control their cars, or they are in trouble. People control electric saws, power plants, chemical reactions, and so on. Rather than govern their sexual desires, people now control birth and the transmission of disease. Controlling manifests a different stance toward things and people and amounts to a different way of seeing them. It is a different style. We can see this in the difference between managers who try to govern their employees by having them join in the process of determining how goals will be met, and those who try to control them by simply setting work schedules and output requirements. Although in governing there always is an element of control (the manager controls the establishment of the goal), the shift from a governing style to a controlling style preserves little of the governing style (although employees may still help plan company picnics). Consequently, we designate the change from governing to control as a change of styles and not a change within a given style.

Everyday cases of a reconfiguring change of style are not so obvious, but we can describe two such situations. We find reconfiguration sometimes when women follow what was traditionally a male career path and become successful managers, stop working to have a child, and then discover that staying home and nurturing the child is as rewarding as working was. We might think that this is a full-scale change in personal or family style, and in some cases it may be. But if the woman feels some continuity with her former life—feels, that is, that the shift produced a development in meaning as opposed to just a new world imposed by listening to the biological clock—then it is likely that nurturing was a marginal aspect of her managerial style that became dominant in her maternal style. When men change careers, they may make a similar discovery. In cases of reconfiguration, a greater sense of integrity (as experienced in articulation) is generally *not* experienced. Rather, one has the sense of gaining wider horizons.

Cross-Appropriation

In the introduction we approached a third form of change—cross-appropriation—in an informal way through the example of the feminist movement. Cross-appropriation takes place when one disclosive space takes over from another disclosive space a practice that it could not generate on its own but that it finds useful. These disclosive spaces can be at the level of whole cultures or societies or nation-states, which we designated worlds, or they can be at the more restricted levels of professions, industries, companies, and even families, which we designated subworlds.

We can see cross-appropriation taking place between subworlds, for example, at the level of exchanges of practices between families and businesses. Family practices are good for establishing roles like mothers, fathers, children, husbands, wives, brothers, and sisters, and these practices also are generally coordinated by nurturing styles that bring out love, respect, loyalty, self-confidence, and a generally warm way of life. Business practices establish such roles as technicians, salespersons, engineers, project leaders, coordinators, supervisors, line managers, staff managers, senior managers, presidents, and the rest. These practices are generally coordinated by styles that bring out efficiency, invention, aggressiveness, and so forth.

We see fairly easily why the practice of carrying and using a cellular telephone has become standard in business. The cellular phone improves efficiency by making one constantly available to one's clients and to one's boss. Frequently, though, as soon as one member of a family starts using a cellular phone for business purposes, its use expands into the family. A wife with a cellular phone will find that she can schedule a last-minute lunch with her husband. When they go out to dinner, they can call the sitter from the car. Dead time spent in an airport waiting area can be used not only for calling customers but for calling children and spouses. Soon the practice of using the cellular phone has been appropriated by the family. The whole style of the office does not come with it, but what primarily enhanced efficiency in the office furthers togetherness in the family. In this case, cross-appropriation has an effect similar to articulation. But cross-appropriation can also produce massive changes in style, as when feminists cross-appropriated masculine practices and changed the styles according to which men and women understood gender identity.

Such massive changes in style generally occur when there is cross-appropriation among subworlds.

Sometimes, meaningful historical changes occur through the cross-appropriation of subworlds. Sometimes, however, the disclosive spaces between which cross-appropriation occurs do not have even a style in common. Such cross-appropriation between local worlds does not produce something as substantial as a change of style of a whole cultural world but only a change of style for the local worlds involved. True multicultural societies have this kind of relatedness of local worlds. But even more obviously, many of today's new social movements (such as the ecology movement) consist of many related organizations, each with its distinct style.

Articulation, reconfiguration, and cross-appropriation are three different ways in which disclosive skills can work to bring about meaningful historical change of a disclosive space. All of these types of change are *historical* because people sense them as continuous with the past. The practices that newly become important are not unfamiliar. We contrast, then, our notion of historical change with discontinuous change. When, for instance, a conqueror imposes a whole new set of practices on a people or a people is dispersed and must adopt wholly new practices to survive, such change is discontinuous and is beyond our range of interests.[5]

Having introduced the three ways in which disclosing may be historical—that is, may produce changes in the coordination of practices—we now introduce the notion of being sensitive to the disclosing that one is carrying on in one's life, which we call *disclosing that one is a discloser*. It should be clear that disclosing that one is a discloser will amount to more than just engaging in disclosive activity. We engage in disclosive activity all the time, whether we are aware of it or not, whenever we deal with things or people in a way that makes sense—that is, whenever we deal with things or people (disclose them) *as* the things or people that they normally are in our culture. But we are *only* sensitive to this disclosing as our way of dealing with things and people when we are engaged in articulating, reconfiguring, or cross-appropriating. When we engage in these history-making activities, we are engaging in changing the coordination in the practices of some domain we inhabit, and then we are dealing with ourselves as the kinds of beings who can disclose things, people, and selves in various ways, coordinated by various styles. Normally, we simply deal with ourselves and the people and things around us according to the role we happen to have. On reflection—of the sort in which we are engaging here—we may be able to deduce that we can deal with or disclose ourselves in a variety of ways, but only in history-making do we actually deal with or disclose ourselves as disclosers and not, for example, as Cartesian subjects with a substantive nature.

3. Why Our Role as Disclosers Is Forgotten

If we are right that human beings in the West are most in touch with themselves and the way things are when they are disclosing that they are disclosers, why has this phenomenon remained hidden from so many for so long? There are three distinct reasons. First, there is something about the way common sense works that covers up our role as disclosers. By common sense, as we said earlier, we mean the widely accepted, taken-for-granted way of dealing with things and people in any domain. And as we noted in talking about the socialization of babies, by the time people come to self-awareness, shared commonsense practices determine how things and people show up and what it makes sense to do. Even the kinds of moods we can have have already been decided. We are indebted to this commonsense understanding, for without it our practices would lack coordination and our lives would lack meaning and direction. But the commonsense practices that make our lives intelligible cover up the fact that everyday common sense is neither fixed nor rationally justified. A Westerner cannot help thinking that the sensible (healthy, civilized, natural) way to sit, for example, is on chairs, at tables, and so forth and not on the floor. Our way seems to make intrinsic sense—a sense not captured in saying, "This is what we in the West just happen to do." What gets covered up by the taken-for-granted aspect of common sense in everyday understanding is that the ultimate "ground" of intelligibility is simply shared practices—that there is no *right* way of doing things. Traditional philosophers raise the stakes by arguing over what the principled grounds for their shared ways of doing things must be.

Second, there is a structural reason why it is not already well known that we are disclosers. Once we become habituated to a style, it becomes invisible to us. We do not look at our contemporaries and see in them the style of the nineties. Nor do we look at a person from our company or university and notice about them our company's or university's style. At least, we do not notice such a thing while we are engaged in our everyday activities. We simply cope with things in similar ways, have similar concerns, and see similar possibilities. We all are simply in tune with the dominant style. And we can easily discover when someone does not fashion him- or herself according to our style because he or she will fail to express concerns as we do, fail to handle things as we do, and fail to see the possibilities we see.

Moreover, when people behave in a way that does not fit in with the dominant style, we are able to fashion their behavior to fit with ours. For instance, we have such people explain themselves in terms we understand. We encounter them continuously in our fashion. And they learn—in the same way children learn—to walk, talk, resist authority, think, eat, show respect, and so forth, as we do. In this way, our very concern with coping successfully with things (which always includes coping with other people) motivates us to bring others under the dominance of our style. We thus unwittingly inculcate others in that style while remaining focused on coping with everyday life.

Third, because we do not cope with our culture's or company's or generation's style directly—we simply express it in our coping with things and with each other—we have no *direct* way to handle it or come alive to it and transform it. This incapacity is not just a peculiar circumstance of our current situation. Our practices are designed for dealing with things, not for dealing with practices for dealing with things and *especially* not for dealing with the coordination of practices for dealing with things. We do not normally sense that we are disclosers because we are interested in the things we disclose and not in the disclosing.

Through these three ordinary tendencies to overlook our role as disclosers, we lose sensitivity to occluded, marginal, or neighboring ways of doing things. By definition an occluded, marginal, or neighboring practice is one that we generally pass over, either by not noticing its unusualness when we engage in it or by not engaging in it at all. Special sensitivity to marginal, neighboring, or occluded practices, however, is precisely at the core of entrepreneurship, citizen virtue, and drawing people together into a community. This sensitivity generates the art, not science, of invention in business, interpretive speaking, not persuasive speaking, in politics, and the courageous acceptance of cultural circumstances, not utopian hopes, that creates solidarity.

4. Methodological Considerations

In our treatment of entrepreneurship, citizen virtue, and solidarity cultivation we focus on one perspicuous case of each. More case studies would enable us to sharpen distinctions with further variations. In fact, much of the literature on entrepreneurship in particular and on citizen virtue and culture figures more generally is made up of one case study after another. Such studies assume commonsensically that entrepreneurship, citizen virtue, and solidarity cultivation are fairly rare practices, not something that most people experience, and that therefore the way to understand them is to gather together a large set of cases and try to find what extraordinary features all the entrepreneurs, virtuous citizens, or culture figures have in common.

This commonsense intuition and the practice that stems from it are among the things that we think have gone wrong in earlier studies. On our view, nations structured by civil democracies and free markets do not have the kind of historical persistence and attractiveness they have proven to have because they enable the fairly unusual skills of a few to flower. Rather, these kinds of nations are as attractive and persistent as they are because their structures are grounded in skills that are accessible to everyone and that, when exercised, make Westerners sense that they are living life at its best. What people broadly call entrepreneurs, virtuous citizens, and solidarity figures thus cover more types of skills than we discuss; but we care only about those skills that we believe people brought up in the West have some access to when they feel that they are living their life at its best. Indeed, we take it that people like market economies, democracies, and social solidarity because they sense that these social formations solicit what is best in both them *and* their fellows. For these reasons, other types of entrepreneurship, citizen virtue, and solidarity cultivation that depend on talents and skills that are not shared and do not give us the sense that we are living life at its best we from here on treat as nongenuine.

So far we have been speaking as though there are two camps: traditional humanist or metaphysical philosophers who have missed the fact that human beings are disclosers,[6] and we who instead have managed to grasp this slippery notion that has great clarifying power. But this map of the territory is incomplete. There are other thinkers, descending from Nietzsche, who oppose both the philosophical tradition and the notion of disclosing. A few thinkers and activists on the radical right and many more on the radical left deny the view that human beings are disclosers, claiming that all ways of being human are configurations of power. On the radical right, we are thinking of a few European neofascists and a few Latin American military dictators. On the radical left, we are thinking of those, mostly in the universities, who have been influenced by the political radicalism implicit in some of the work of Michel Foucault. Thinkers of both the radical right and the radical left endorse the notion that we should see things in terms of coping, which means (1) that the world is composed of sets of skills for getting things done—with no necessary reference to the identities of individual people who are the loci of these skills—and (2) that whenever some particular thing is accomplished, it is because a certain set of skills has dominated another set of skills.

To simplify matters just short of caricature, according to these radical accounts, if one gets up and goes to work in the morning, it is because one's workaday skills have taken priority over one's nurturing, staying-at-home-with-the-children skills. These sorts of priorities show the power of one skill in one situation in opposition to another skill in the same situation. Both the left and the right go on to claim that this power regularizes itself. The workaday skill would thus *in general* take priority over the nurturing skill. Only by taking such a priority over the nurturing skill is the workaday skill able to express itself as fully as possible and so become sharply defined. The radical right says that this is just what should happen. Identities of any sort, even the identities of skills, come to be defined only in opposition to other identities, and therefore these kinds of oppositions need to be developed. Thus the radical right supports an identity politics that embraces exclusion.

The more pacific radical left, in contrast, notes that there is nothing essential about power that causes it to tend toward regular configurations that produce identities. Indeed, power is at its best when it is fully situational, when it works to prioritize one thing in one situation and another in another situation, and there is no general ordering of situations. Situational power would then disrupt the formation of stable identities. And such identities, whether they are of practices, skills, nations, or individuals, tend to constrain situational power. Stable identities tend to prevent power from producing new configurations. In other words, these identities get in the way of allowing the differences of different situations to show up and thus block human sensitivity to the way life and situations are changing all the time. So the radical left calls for eliminating stable identities (not identities altogether) on the grounds that they set up nonnatural exclusions, hierarchies, and vilifications.[7]

In our account, we try to undermine the ontologies of power of both the radical right and left without losing track of the genuine phenomena both the right and the left use to support their respective arguments. We want to grant to the right the notion that life only becomes focused and worth living when identities are important. But we want to grant to the left the notion that human practices are always transforming themselves to some degree or another and that long-standing configurations of identity structures do block sensitivity to what is happening in particular local situations. (For example, we can all note how most people who have grown up in earlier generations seem to miss distinctions that are important to those growing up in the present generation.)

We seek to show that human beings respond most sensitively to local situations neither just by reacting as their identity dictates nor by responding differently to each situation, but by changing themselves in order to preserve continuous but developing identities. That is, they respond to each local situation by elaborating a current stand on who they are by reference to past or related stands they have taken. In order to have such a response, people must have identities—senses of what their lives as a whole are about. But they must not have identities of the kind the right imagines—that is, identities that are to be forever strengthened and sharpened—for then their responses to local situations would be defensive and reactionary. But they cannot go over to the left's view of identities that develop in wholly contingent ways. Rather, they must have identities whose change will be dictated by the style of practices with which they are familiar. This is precisely the kind of historical identity and change we advocate and describe.

2

Entrepreneurship: The Skill of Cultural Innovation

Entrepreneurship is beginning to be recognized as the greatest source of productivity in both Western and many nonwestern cultures. Few, however, have recognized the crucial historical dimension of entrepreneurship. We summarize and criticize the three views that currently determine most studies of entrepreneurship. Using a composite case of entrepreneurial skill, we then extract our account of genuine entrepreneurs as people who make historical change by producing both a product that solicits people to change the style of their everyday activities and a company that instantiates the new way of life the product establishes. Next, we compare entrepreneurship to business as it is customarily conducted and show how the theoretical understanding of business, developed in business schools and economics departments, impedes the development of entrepreneurial practice. Finally, we argue that genuine entrepreneurial skill—the skill of changing disclosive spaces—is identical to one of the skills we exercise when we are living our lives at their best.

1. Current Accounts of Entrepreneurship

Few people who write about entrepreneurs would doubt that their crucial effect is the production of radical social change. But two groups of writers draw very different lessons from this fact. One group, which writes mostly for a business audience, has as its goal a description of entrepreneurial change that will either encourage executives to establish research and development departments that perform entrepreneurially or that will allow people with entrepreneurial inklings to explore them. Another group of writers, mostly economists along with a few sociologists, believes that the production of cultural change is an activity too radical for analytical description. Consequently, these writers try to produce models that capture the characteristics of entrepreneurs and the *effects* of the entrepreneurial process. They look at the entrepreneur as someone who reallocates—or, even better, coordinates—resources. They therefore focus on models that show how such reallocation or coordination can be optimized to provide the greatest social or corporate benefit. We argue that such a theoretical stance devalues and is sometimes injurious to the history-making skills of entrepreneurs. We return to economists and other social scientists when we discuss the dangers of theory. However, since we agree with the hope of business writers in thinking that the skill of history-making *can* be usefully described, we begin our account by distinguishing ourselves from those who describe how change is made.

Among those who write about business and describe change there are three widespread ways of thinking about entrepreneurship. Each may usefully be represented by a paradigm case. The first way of thinking about entrepreneurs, represented by Peter F. Drucker, follows the Cartesian model of seeking a *theory* of entrepreneurship.[1] "Every practice rests on theory,"[2] Drucker says. The assumption behind such accounts is that entrepreneurial innovation is a particular way of dealing with the facts of the world. Innovation is, as Drucker puts it, "organized, systematic, rational work."[3] Again, he says, "Entrepreneurs need to search purposefully for the sources of innovation, the changes and their symptoms that indicate opportunities for successful innovation. And they need to know and apply the principles of successful innovation."[4] Thus innovative entrepreneurship would amount to a disciplined search for symptoms of change or opportunity followed by the application of principles to these signs of incipient change in order to produce actual innovations. We can see the shape of entrepreneurial activity as Drucker understands it by comparing it with the practice of medicine; it involves a disciplined and systematic search for symptoms, followed by the application of principles of diagnosis and cure.

Drucker also says that the practice of entrepreneurship is to "create something new, something different; [entrepreneurs] change or transmute values."[5] We agree with Drucker that entrepreneurs change values, but it is precisely because they do this that his method of understanding entrepreneurship is inadequate. Drucker thinks of the entrepreneur for the most part as the person who simply notices changes that are already happening and then exploits them. Indeed, theorists like Drucker are compelled to think something like this because of their Cartesian presuppositions. They think of a world of facts and of organizing minds. Innovation amounts to an anticipation of a change in the physical or mental facts. In general, the person who gets the first adequate representation of the occurring change will see what new needs are developing and then be able to develop specifications for various kinds of equipment required to satisfy those needs. Thus, an entrepreneur could see that the baby boom generation is aging and that, at a certain time, there will be a strong need for increased medical services for the elderly. A business like Citibank might notice that, because many women see themselves differently from the way their mothers saw themselves and are entering the work force, there is an increasing pool of talented women that it can hire while its competitors are still competing for the best male job candidates. Both of these examples involve responses to change but not innovative ones, at least not as Drucker describes them.

True, we may be fairly sure that the aging of the baby boomers will cause a large proportion of U.S. citizens to reach old age in the coming years. That is, we may assume that they will neither emigrate nor be killed off by a plague. But it is not clear that any particular needs of these aging baby boomers will be predictable. Many of the diseases that now send the elderly to hospices may be cured by then. Playing golf in sunny Arizona may become anathema to baby boomers. Other booms of babies did not produce sexual revolutions, support enormous music industries, or pioneer illicit drug dealing on a grand scale. We list these events not to characterize boomers but to note how little we can predict what they will do. According to our view, the innovative entrepreneur is not someone who can predict the physical or mental needs of aging people and invest in satisfying those needs. Once the needs are determinate, an average businessperson can catch on and try to catch up; the entrepreneur is the person who determines which needs will seem important.

Citibank is deservedly celebrated for hiring large numbers of talented women at the moment when the feminist movement had prepared the way for large numbers of women to seek to work as equals to men. But it would be a retrospective illusion to think that Citibank simply saw that the feminist movement had prepared the culture for women to work with men as equals. The feminist movement always understood its goals in many different ways. Much of what it understood was inchoate. Those who remember without retrospective illusions the time when many women were going to work in the late 1960s and the 1970s will recall that feminists were also thinking that the general capitalistic market structures ought to be transformed. They sought radical changes in the law that would strike at the patriarchal core of most institutions. Citibank acted entrepreneurially not because it was able to see a particular change already happening but because it played a leading role in making the change occur *as it did*. If no businesses had acted as Citibank acted by hiring scores of women, the change in perception of women would likely have been political, with successful women looking more like egalitarian champions with government jobs than like enterprising executives.

In addition to changes in demographics and perception, Drucker cites other sources of change—the unexpected, incongruities, process need, and fragile industry and market structures. In all these cases, Drucker thinks that the entrepreneur does not need a representation of the overall change but needs only to do good market research, which amounts to asking people carefully and persistently about their needs. As we have already shown, however, people experience needs only once these needs have been articulated. No teenager in the early 1960s could have said that he or she needed to hear the music of a group of four young British musicians who were developing a new tight harmonic sound and gently ironic lyrics that would eventually change the way teenagers felt about seriousness and joy and hope for the rest of their lives. It is unlikely that anyone could have come close to guessing the size of the need for this new kind of music. These sorts of changes—where whole new markets and interests develop and new kinds of concerns appear—are, we contend, paradigm cases of entrepreneurial change.

Not all change is entrepreneurial, of course, and the changes that Drucker and other theorists of entrepreneurship describe are precisely the sorts of change that various kinds of research can produce. A research department may review the numbers on the aging of the baby boomers and set out to develop a new fabric that keeps people warm, on the view that older people get chilled more easily. But this does not "transmute values." It does not open a new space for human action. The entrepreneur is the person who develops a cold weather activity that elderly people subsequently seek out and that changes the way the elderly see themselves, their bodies, and their lives.

We have described Drucker and other theorists as devising nothing more than methods for chasing change. And that is what a good many executives think they are doing. But have we been unfair to Drucker? He does recognize one kind of change—he calls it knowledge-based innovation—that creates a new want. He even recognizes that market research would be of no use in such cases.[6] But even here, when he analyzes these cases, he misses the entrepreneurial action. In attempting to categorize knowledge-based innovation as one of his procedures, Drucker claims that the first thing such an innovator does is look at what she is trying to innovate, divide it into the kinds of "knowledge roots" it will require, determine how much development of the various knowledge bases is needed, and then determine whether the project is feasible. The Wright Brothers, for instance, required both knowledge of light gasoline engines and knowledge of aerodynamics developed in experiments with gliders. The first entrepreneurial bank also needed two kinds of knowledge—knowledge about venture capitalism and about banking.[7] All of this is no doubt true. But Drucker and other theoreticians fail to see that the innovator needs a very concrete vision of the new invention that she thinks will succeed before she can go about acquiring the necessary knowledge. The real question, then, is how one can obtain such a concrete vision. It is good to know what to do once one has the vision, but the heart of innovative entrepreneurship is in achieving the concrete vision itself.

The problem with thinking that innovative entrepreneurship can be reduced to a number of fairly stable and regular procedures is that this view claims that interesting change can be represented by something stable such as procedures. The procedures would give us a place to stand virtually outside of change. Such a view is profoundly antihistorical, at the very least. When we are not holding to Cartesian prejudices about reflection, most of us acknowledge that we change when the world around us changes. We do not have any special part of ourselves that remains separate from the change. We only have to watch movies that were produced when we were young to discover that things that interested us in earlier decades hardly make any sense now. We cannot go back and feel the way we did before, and, consequently, we cannot go back and see things the way we did before. When human beings produce change, they change themselves as well.

In what follows we discuss how human beings, in particular entrepreneurs, produce change, but we do not represent the process in principles or procedures. We do not set out a theory. Rather, we look closely at what happens when change is being produced. For that reason, we do not state a procedure and then show how many businesses succeeded when they followed it either knowingly or unknowingly. Instead, we evoke occasions where we think most readers have experienced the production of change and show how an entrepreneur acts in similar situations. This book, then, is attempting to develop sensitivities, not knowledge. Once one has a sensitivity to something such as good food, decency, certain kinds of beauty, or even the pleasures of hiking, one is already on the path of refining and developing that sensitivity. One sees food, decent behavior, beauty, and hiking trails in a new light. They draw one to them in a way they did not before. As one is drawn, time and time again, one then continuously develops one's skills for dealing with what one is sensitive to.

In stressing historical change, we are not simply objecting to theoreticians such as Drucker; we are also taking issue with a more pragmatic kind of thinking about entrepreneurship. This second approach is empirical and classificatory. Writers of this type describe many different cases of entrepreneurial success and failure, classify different types according to the way their examples seem to cluster, and finally offer general rules of thumb that work a large percentage of the time but have clear exceptions. Perhaps the best in this tradition of thinking about entrepreneurs is Karl H. Vesper. Vesper's work compels interest because he is so clear about what he seeks to do for his readers. He does not wish to give them a theory about how innovation and entrepreneurship occur. He does not see human beings as theory-driven creatures. Rather, he seeks to give readers as many cases of the various kinds of entrepreneurship as possible so that they will develop a wide array of distinctions for thinking about and dealing with the subject. In short, he wants to give readers many, many experiences in a particularly intelligible form:

The aim here is to acquaint the reader not with a comprehensive theory but rather with a spectrum of possibilities illustrated by real-life experiences. . . . The reader should become sensitized to a variety of types of opportunities and thereby more likely to recognize any that may come his or her way and to be able to act on them before someone else does.[8]

A few sentences later, Vesper explains how his examples should be read:

The examples are not intended only as something to be skimmed while the text is carefully read but rather should themselves be read with care for the experience they contain. . . . The collective experimentation and experience they represent for the entrepreneurs who lived them represent an enormous investment of living, doing, and learning that the reader may share.[9]

Vesper sees human beings as practical creatures who become competent at various activities not by abstracting theories and guiding their actions to conform to them but by doing, failing, and doing again until they become sensitized in their habits to what is worth considering and what is not. The accounts he gives are to substitute for life experiences and develop our sensitivities just in the way talking to many different people sharpens our skills for making discriminations about what is discussed.

We can begin to see where Vesper fails us, however, when we look at the connections among the various items on the lists that he provides. Vesper gives us eight sources for the ideas with which to begin a new venture: (1) invitation by a delegation of venture capitalists, creditors, and so on to begin producing the new widget that they desire, (2) venture ideas from prior employment, (3) obtaining rights from companies to produce and market inventions they are not currently interested in producing or marketing, (4) self-employment, (5) hobbies, (6) social encounters, (7) pedestrian observations, and, least important of all, (8) deliberate search.[10] The first of these sources generally pertains only to people who are already respected entrepreneurs, so it may be understood as dependent on one or another of the other seven sources. But what about entrepreneurship gives consistency to these other seven sources? Vesper does not say. He does recognize that many people wish things were different but that that does not make them entrepreneurs:

Many people may have been exposed to the same needs and venture opportunities; what sets the entrepreneurs apart is that they take action to do something about it, namely devise a solution for the need and follow through to make that solution available to others.[11]

What has Vesper told us here? Many people encounter the deficiencies that entrepreneurs encounter, but entrepreneurs do what entrepreneurs do; they treat the encounter as a problem, resolve it, and market the resolution. But this tells us nothing more than an entrepreneur acts like an entrepreneur. We want to know what enables an entrepreneur to hold on to a problem that others pass over and then to innovate on the basis of it. Vesper has nothing special to say about this. In other words, Vesper passes over precisely the practice that makes someone entrepreneurial.

Vesper fails here for the same reason Drucker fails. Both theoreticians like Drucker and empirical pragmatists like Vesper are profoundly antihistorical. We have already described how Drucker is antihistorical. We are now in a position to see that Vesper is antihistorical too because he thinks both that people are skillful beings and that all skills are essentially of the same genus. Vesper thus assumes that the skill for arriving at the new venture idea amounts to a convergence of (1) the technical know-how and (2) the social skill for dealing with people so as to empathize with what they would like to have. The entrepreneur can then produce some new thing or service that people want. But this convergence is not enough, he notes:

It is hard to determine to what extent entrepreneurial success was created by circumstance versus being the cause of the circumstance. Like campus fads, the basic mechanism seems often to contain a persistent ingredient of mystery.[12]

Later, Vesper gives us the name for the third thing that the entrepreneur needs in order to deal with the ingredient of mystery. It is luck.[13]

But the entrepreneurs worth thinking about are not the ones who produce fads or manage to put some slightly different spin on something that is already selling quite well—the new improved detergent that gives a whiter white. The entrepreneurs worth thinking about are the ones who are sensitive to how the problem that they sense has its roots in our pervasive way of living, our lifestyle, either in our culture as a whole or in some more or less self-contained domain. The changes they bring about are changes of historical magnitude because they change the way we see and understand things in the relevant domain. Such an entrepreneur senses that he or she is on the scent of such a problem when he or she senses that the product or service he or she will have to produce will change the *general* way we handle things or people in some domain. We call the cultivation of such a sensitivity the cultivation of the skills for making history. Such skills are quite different from our other skills. These are the skills that define the genuine entrepreneur.

It is instructive to see how close Vesper comes to noting such skills. Here is his account of King C. Gillette:

The idea for the safety razor hit King C. Gillette when he started to shave and found his razor dull. Ever since a conversation with the inventor of pop bottle caps, he had been looking for a product that people would throw away and reorder.[14]

We could hear this account as telling us that Gillette saw the success of the pop bottle top in its convenience and its disposability, which, in turn, required reproduction. He then set out to find some other product whose convenience would be enhanced by its disposability. But if his sensitivity remained limited in this way, he could have had no strong intuition that the razor was just the right thing. Indeed, straight steel razors were something of a shibboleth among men. Fathers purchased them for their sons. They were sometimes handed down from generation to generation. The art of learning to shave was one of the glories of coming of age. These considerations, and others like them, should have weighed against disposable razors. Surely something like pens, belonging to the domain of the business office where there were many fewer sentiments running against efficiency, should have seemed a far more sensible choice.

But the fact that Gillette's insight led to committed action shows that he touched more than pragmatic concerns with his dull razor. He sensed that he and other men were willing to give up their masculine rituals not only for the sake of convenience in the domain of removing facial hair but also for the sake of having a different relation to things in general. Gillette sensed that masculinity could—and would, thanks in part to him—be understood as commanding things and getting rid of them when they ceased to serve rather than as caring for and cherishing useful and well-engineered things. Gillette's entrepreneurial conviction did not rest on a skillful balancing of technical know-how and needs; he sensed the dullness of the blade *as unusual, as something to be changed in the way he dealt with things generally*. The entrepreneurial question for Gillette was not whether people would like disposable razors, nor was it whether disposable razors could be produced. The entrepreneurial question was, What did his annoyance at the dullness mean? Did it mean that he just wanted a better-crafted straight-edge razor that kept its edge longer? Or did he want a new way of dealing with things? We shall argue that genuine entrepreneurs are sensitive to the historical questions, not the pragmatic ones, and that what is interesting about their innovations is that they change the style of our practices as a whole in some domain. Vesper and the empirical pragmatists like him miss this dimension of entrepreneurship and so miss entrepreneurial ability in general.

A third approach is represented by George Gilder. He understands more clearly than any other writer on entrepreneurship that the practice of entrepreneurship is not based on practices like those that we normally engage in during our day-to-day lives. The entrepreneur's "success is . . . a thrust beyond the powers and principalities of the established world to the transcendent sources of creation and truth."[15]

Gilder uncovers three essential entrepreneurial virtues: giving, humility, and commitment. The first constituted the most fundamental attribute of Henry Ford, insofar as he was an entrepreneur:

[Ford] showed that high profits come from giving, through low prices and high wages, rather than from gouging for what the traffic will bear. This discovery is the moral core of capitalism. The policy of anticipatory pricing—making price cuts that will register losses without large and unpredictable gains in volume— is a mode of temporary sacrifice for later and undetermined reward. In the generous and optimistic spirit of enterprise, Ford *invested* in his price cuts.[16]

The second essential virtue Gilder isolates is humility. This humility is manifested in two ways. First, entrepreneurs must be willing to spend long hours in the "very material substance, the grit and grease and garbage of their businesses."[17] His model entrepreneur here is Thomas J. Fatjo, who founded Browning-Ferris Industries, one of the world's largest solid-waste disposal firms, one that saw garbage collection as a large centralized business that could articulate our new concerns about the environment. Starting out as an accountant, Fatjo gave up his job to spend years driving a second-hand garbage truck, running his independent door-to-door garbage route and learning the ins and outs of the garbage business so that he could bring together many local firms into one large conglomerate. Second, humility is manifested in listening. Here Gilder looks to Andrew Carnegie, who suggested that his epitaph should read, "Here lies the man who knew how to gather around him men who were more clever than himself."[18] Gilder writes:

Entrepreneurs can be pompous and vain where it doesn't count; but in their own enterprise, the first law is to listen. They must be men meek enough—and shrewd enough—to endure the humbling eclipse of self that comes in the process of profound learning from others.[19]

The entrepreneur must learn this practical humility because she must learn to inhabit a different domain from that of ordinary life. The entrepreneur needs "a willingness to accept failure, learn from it, and act boldly in the shadows of doubt. He inhabits a realm where . . . expertise may be a form of ignorance and the best possibilities spring from a consensus of impossibility."[20] This is to say that the entrepreneur must learn humility in order never to be sure of her know-how or of herself and to let herself be captivated by a possibility whose exploration will produce results larger than those produced by mere knowledge. The entrepreneur shows the ingenuity not primarily to create some new thing or service but a new situation or world: "The entrepreneur prevails not by understanding an existing situation in all its complex particulars, but by creating a new situation which others must try to comprehend."[21]

The third basic virtue of entrepreneurs is faith or commitment:

[Entrepreneurs] give themselves, their time, their wealth, their sleep; they give it year after year, reinvesting every profit, mortgaging every property. They leverage their lives to their . . . belief in a redemptive idea. And their long outpouring of belief and faith and funds and sacrifices, seemingly wasted and lost in the maws and middens of the world economy, somehow mysteriously coheres and collects. Beyond the horizons of calculation or prophecy, at last the mountain moves; and there unfurls a great returning tide of vindication that overflows all plans and expectations.[22]

The entrepreneur does not have faith in and commitment to herself but rather to an intuition or an idea that has struck her as requiring the giving up of the self as she knows it for a new life in a new world that everyone will share.

The special virtues that Gilder thinks drive entrepreneurs—giving, humility, and a commitment through which one discovers one's identity—are the specifically Christian virtues that our culture has inherited.[23] Understanding these virtues as religious means that these practices make other practices sensible. They are, to use a philosopher's term, second-order practices. When one takes them up, one changes the ordering and sensibleness of normal practices. Acting according to second-order practices produces metachanges, changes of the world of normal practice.

We grant Gilder that the only way to make sense of what entrepreneurs do is to think of them as taking up second-order practices to produce world-changing effects. This is what Drucker and Vesper miss.

But notice that Gilder's second-order practices all pertain to the entrepreneur's Christian ways of living and thinking. It would seem that someone could practice these Christian virtues and still not be an entrepreneur. For Gilder, the success of the entrepreneur who has all the necessary virtues is still a mystery. We seek to demystify Gilder's intuition. We contend that it is the product or service, not the virtuous life-style of the entrepreneur, that makes the world change, and it is the entrepreneur's practices for innovating and forming a company to market products and services that should be examined. Here we shall find practices that do not fall easily under the headings of humility, giving, or commitment.

2. A Composite Case of Entrepreneurship

Since we are interested in entrepreneurial skills, not in entrepreneurs, we want to show how we all exhibit such skills here and there in our lives, though without the consistency with which entrepreneurs exhibit them. We see as primary what most accounts pass over—namely, innovation, establishing an enterprise, and the connection between the two. Many people can innovate and many can manage an enterprise, but it is the ability to link these two activities that is definitive of genuine entrepreneurial skill.

Analyzing entrepreneurial ability requires a close look at how human beings work. But first we look at a representative entrepreneur. Our representative, who happens to be a composite,[24] started out as an executive-level director of national economic planning. He thought that the primary concern of a person in his position was to ensure that his office produced the best possible model of the economy, which could then be used as a guide to improve the efficiency of functioning of every economic institution in society. Though he was trained both to develop such models and to evaluate the models that others developed, he seldom found time to do this work. Instead, he was constantly talking; he explained this and that, to that and this person, put person A in touch with person B, held press conferences, and so forth. It seemed to him that he was doing nothing substantial. And if we think of work as a matter of performing certain tasks to produce certain products, little, indeed, was being done.

This entrepreneur, however, did not simply inure himself to the fact that what he was doing differed a good deal from what he thought ought to be done. Rather he retained this oddity in his life as an anomaly.[25]

Holding on to an anomaly *as* an anomaly is not an easy process to describe. It is a matter of constantly being sensitive to the anomaly as happening in one's life. In our case, the entrepreneur remained sensitive to the fact that his work was not producing any concrete or abstract thing but that he was working nonetheless.[26] Because he was sensitive to the anomaly, it eventually led him to take a course on the theory of speech acts, and in that course he found a key to the anomaly. He came to realize that this anomalous aspect of his work was actually its central feature. He saw that work no longer made sense as the craftsmanship of writing this or that sentence or the skilled labor of banging this or that widget into shape but that currently work was becoming a matter of coordinating human activity—opening up conversations about one thing or another to produce a binding promise to perform an act.

It has long been the case that producing things that are not part of an implicit or explicit promise to satisfy some request is seen as wasting time or engaging in a hobby. Work never occurs in isolation but always in a context created by conversation. Passing over the conversation and focusing on things may further the production of standard things by businesses and highly detailed things by hobbyists, but only when conversation becomes the center of attention can highly differentiated business products and activities emerge. In Western culture, which has always emphasized the production of things, this insight appears as a startling innovation.

The innovation of a new understanding of work, like many other innovations, does not, however, make an entrepreneur. It makes only an inventor. In the case of our composite entrepreneur it resulted in an academic degree and presumably could have led to an academic career. But instead our entrepreneur formed an enterprise for *marketing* his new conception. How can a new conception be marketed? Answering this question is in fact an essential part of forming a new enterprise. We tend to think that the innovator produces something for an already existing market and then establishes a more or less traditional company with traditional departments to produce and market the new thing. But entrepreneurs time and again tell us that this is not the case. The market is always being developed along with the product. Alexander Graham

Bell, for example, thought at first that the telephone would be used only in business offices. Even when the product is in its prototype stage and exists only as a subject of contemplation, the entrepreneur will be contemplating the sort of company that will be needed to market it. Listening to the inventors of the Apple Computer—Steve Jobs and Steve Wozniak—one notices that they were forming a company even before they fully understood how human beings were supposed to interact with the box they were making; the keyboard and screen came even later. We are claiming, then, that an entrepreneurial enterprise grows at first not to produce and market an already understood widget but to aid in the development of the market for an intuition or new conception.

Our composite entrepreneur had to determine how his new concept of work—essentially speech acts that open people to new possibilities and persuade them to live according to these new possibilities—was to be given concrete form and marketed. In making this determination, he had to devote a certain part of the enterprise to finding others who were also in difficulties because of their inadequate notions of work and educating those others in the new way of thinking and acting. This activity, which is conducted informally in many companies, alerted our entrepreneur to the difficulties that people had with the new conception and what needed to be done to keep the difficulties from arising. Most important of all, it provided a testing area for various platforms for realizing the new conception. The enterprise found itself offering courses to administrators who were in positions similar to the one our entrepreneur had been in when he uncovered his anomaly. By putting his idea into various situations, the entrepreneur preserved his central intuition by seeing how it worked in different contexts.

Classes—whether formal, as in the case of our composite entrepreneur, or informal—are not enough to produce an enterprise, unless the enterprise is a school. Classes can lead only to the testing of ideas and their development. What becomes definitive of an entrepreneurial enterprise as opposed to many other kinds of associations is the development of particular *products* or *services* or *business practices* around which it forms an identity. For that to happen interest in the innovative practice has to be sought beyond the small group of those already receptive to it. Here our entrepreneur sought to discover where our culture was misunderstanding work most crucially and how he could insert his thinking into that crucial misunderstanding. This kind of activity is one of those poorly understood, necessary, and very risky things that an entrepreneur does. The entrepreneur seeks to insert her understanding into that domain where she can maximize both the strangeness and the sensibleness of her product.

For our entrepreneur the domain where the nature of work was most misunderstood and where he could still respond with at least minimal intelligibility was that of computers. Computers were thought of as information processors at that time (as they still frequently are). Information is entered into the computer, the information is reshaped according to algorithms that are triggered by the information or the user, and new information comes out. The larger the store of algorithmic conversions, the more powerful the computer. These large machines were understood to be helpful to people at work because work itself seemed to have just such a structure. A business manager, for example, is presented with certain facts, such as that factory A employs M people at X dollars per hour and produces Z widgets per day but that there are backlogs of P widgets per month. The manager performs various operations on the basis of this information. She determines whether hiring more workers, purchasing new equipment for the factory, raising the price of the widgets, building a new factory, or doing nothing makes sense. But our entrepreneur discovered that this is precisely the wrong vision of work. Fulfilling tasks may be part of work, but it is no longer the heart of work. The problem was that one aspect of work had come to look as though it were necessarily work's dominant aspect, and computerization was reinforcing this mistake.

Since our entrepreneur understood that under today's conditions the heart of work consists of coordinating human activity, and since computers covered up this understanding, he developed one of the first programs for networking office computers in order to allow computers to help coordinate people rather than process information. This software called the attention of its users to how they were coordinating their actions with those of others. For those who employed it, a new vision of work emerged where tasks no longer seemed the end but merely the means to forming and building coordinated relations with clients, customers, vendors, bosses, employees, and so on. This shift in vision enabled people to focus much more on coordinating their actions, instead of treating coordination carelessly or confusedly. This shift was made all the more powerful because it was produced by a computer software program, which caused them to develop different relations with precisely the instrument that had previously reinforced the notion that work was a series of tasks. The computer became the crux for two ways of understanding work, keeping the newness of the vision alive and keeping its authority from becoming banal.

Through this particular realization of his intuition, our entrepreneur engaged in an act of reconfiguring work. The means for bringing about this transformation in the understanding of work were as important to the enterprise as its manufacturing dimensions. He met with all those involved in designing the new software product and determined how to explain it to customers, reviewers, and others so that the point of the product would become apparent—a process that ultimately determined where the efforts of company personnel would be directed. He also met with people to determine the feasibility of networking and the appropriate way to use networking—meetings that necessarily forced adjustments of the original vision. This was the point of the entrepreneur's activities even before the idea of instantiating the new vision in a computer networking program took shape. From the moment when the innovative entrepreneur, or the entrepreneur who acquires others' innovations, begins to think or to talk to people about how precisely to realize her thoughts so that they have authority, she is aiming at reconfiguration.

Finally, all this entrepreneurial activity had to be organized into an enterprise with a particular identity and particular way of coordinating its various dimensions. The way the enterprise worked had to be understood by all who worked in it and with it, as either employees or suppliers or customers or consultants or government officials, in order for that coordination to take place efficiently and without breakdowns. Accordingly, our entrepreneur did what most innovative entrepreneurs do: he staffed his company with people like himself who had found similar frustrations, had a strong interest in the way computers were dominating the understanding of work, and were philosophical in disposition. By staffing his company in this way, he was sure to cultivate a more or less intellectual style for treating problems—a style that fitted with his own style and with his conception of work becoming more and more discursive.

The way the enterprise's cultural practices are structured will determine whether its personnel are in tune with the product they are producing and also with each other. Standard business management texts now recognize half this claim—that is, they recognize that the entrepreneur is responsible for the culture of her company and that people in the company relate to one another in terms of that culture. But they see this simply in terms of management styles that are not related to the product or services that the company is providing. But the relation of the product to the style is crucial. If, for example, an entrepreneur is setting up an enterprise for producing high fashion clothing, the cultural practices of the company need to incline people to think aesthetically about themselves and the world. Otherwise, the people who make important aesthetic distinctions will feel themselves working against the grain of the company, and their manner of presenting their ideas will seem eccentric to those who live in the company's dominant culture. Clearly, keeping an enterprise's culture in tune with its product is important.

Having described our composite entrepreneur, we can enumerate the aspects of his entrepreneurial skills that we think important: (1) the entrepreneur innovates by holding on to some anomaly; (2) he brings the anomaly to bear on his tasks; (3) he is clear about the relation of the anomaly to the rest of what he does, and once he has a sense of a world in which the anomaly is central, such as the world of work, he embodies, produces, and markets his new understanding; (4) to do this, he preserves and tests his new understanding—for instance, by leading workshops or other kinds of discussions—to see how it fits with wider experiences than his own; (5) as we have claimed but have yet to argue, he must take his new conception and embody it in a way that preserves its sensibleness and the strangeness of the change it produces, seeing to it that his new understanding retains for others the authority that it has for him and reconfiguring the way things happen in a particular domain; (6) finally, he focuses all dimensions of entrepreneurial activity into a styled coordination with each other and brings them into tune with his embodied conception, so that the critical distinctions involved in appreciating the product become manifest in the company's way of life.

We are now in a position to describe the changes that entrepreneurs make, to show why these changes are more than just changes in practices, and to explain why they have a historical or meaningful quality. We are ready, then, to explain why the entrepreneur requires a maximizing of strangeness and sensibleness in the way she instantiates her innovation. The first four activities listed above are shared with inventors, philosophers, scientists, and others who innovate. They all try to make their innovations as sensible as possible so that their activity leads to changes of particular practices *in* the world. The entrepreneur, in addition, embodies her innovation in a way that preserves its strangeness. This kind of embodiment enables the entrepreneur's innovation to produce a change *of* a world or at least a subworld—that is, to produce what we sense as a historical effect. The introduction of a product that solicits new skills becomes like a social movement, whether the movement is bringing a new understanding of liberation to the West or bringing a new appreciation for tastes and flavors to a small Midwestern town by opening a café that sells cappuccino and by forming coalitions with restaurant owners who are also bringing sophisticated tastes to the region.[27]

Our composite entrepreneur brought a marginal aspect of our style of work—talking, conferencing, and the rest—to the center of our activity. Human work then comes to be understood primarily as coordinating the contexts for tasks and only secondarily as performing tasks. This is a case of reconfiguration. And with this change comes a wider sense of what we are doing during our workdays. We work with a greater concern for the commitments made by the people with whom we are dealing than we had when our primary concern was completing our tasks. Our style of work becomes more responsive, and this responsiveness gives us a sense of a wider horizon. We see now how to talk to people and how to design workflow to make a wide range of products adapted to the concerns of individual clients.

Any change in practices involves aspects of all three kinds of history-making change: reconfiguration, cross-appropriation, and articulation. For entrepreneurs, reconfiguration is the most important of these, but in reconfiguring work our entrepreneur also articulated by gathering the concerns essential for the conversations that set up contexts for tasks: making offers and requests, negotiating promises, stating conditions of satisfaction, and declaring whether these conditions have been satisfied or not. Such aspects of work conversation were already important for setting up the context for tasks, but by focusing on these aspects of conversation at work—in meetings, in conferences, and even in casual talk—our entrepreneur made conversations related to work clearer and more efficient. Moreover, recall that the entrepreneur had both to discuss his ideas with and to show his prototype to people from other subworlds to see how it could be useful to them before he put his product into final form. This was an instance of cross-appropriation.

We have not yet entered a historical moment in which products are generally understood as designed for the particular concerns of each particular user—in which, in other words, the distinction between products and services has broken down and the reconfiguration initiated by our composite entrepreneur has taken place. But it is easy to imagine what a reconfigured world would look like. We see it already in many of our practices. In such a world, we could not imagine how people got along with standardized products for standardized situations. Every product would be provided inside a service such as those now provided by lawyers, physicians, interior decorators, and so forth. From such a world, we would look back and wonder how people could purchase standard lightbulbs, standard soups, standard toothpaste, standard software. Consumers of the future, in order to imagine our current state, will have to turn to whatever margins standard commodities will have been banished to. These margins will give enough continuity for the change from our present age of standardization to the new age of individual design to be meaningful. Yet the style of a world where almost all products are purchased within services for lifestyle design would be so different from ours that we would see it as a new historical period. This is why, if it succeeds, we would call our composite entrepreneur's change meaningful and historical.

We have so far benefited from using as an example a composite entrepreneur, one whose innovation has not yet become a settled part of our cultural scene—so that we do not yet see the structure of his actions as being obvious—but for this reason we cannot call on our example to reveal one of the last things that becomes important in an entrepreneur's activity. That is, how her company as a whole gives its character to an industry or industry segment and to the way people go about thinking about the product. We cite two examples of this phenomenon. Perhaps the most famous is the way the IBM culture of the 1960s taught us how to think about computers, the computer industry, and the place of automation in the world.

In this period IBM was organized to sell big computers and programs that handled all parts of a company from payroll to inventory management. IBM employees all wore authoritative white shirts and ties. People who managed data processing all wore white lab coats. Everything was managed with the efficiency, scrupulousness, and intelligence of modern science. Just as computers and IBM employees were to take care of client companies, so IBM took care of its own employees with lifetime employment, health insurance, and most of the other benefits an employer could offer. Computers were to fix up our companies, societies, and lives by calculating everything faster than we could and getting everything that ran by calculation—and in those days everything seemed to run by calculation—to run more efficiently. One can think of this as paternalism, but IBM went further. Just as the church once took care of the world by taking care of each and every member of its congregation, so IBM took care of each employee's needs, just as it promised to take care of each company's needs. One could therefore characterize its style as pastoral.[28]

Our second example, Apple Computer, developed its product and its company image with an opposing style. Its product was a "personal" computer, not a large mainframe. It promised liberation from centralized programs, centralized data, centralized ways of organizing things. Its appeal was to renegades, and its corporate culture expressed this appeal. The company was a campus. Friday afternoons were spent with beer and pizza. In general, employees were expected to see things as brilliant, renegade college students would. Focusing the lives of employees in each of these ways helped employees to develop additional insights in marketing or design that would fit with either pastoral or renegade styles.

Thinking further about reconfiguration enables us to explain why the entrepreneur should try to realize her innovative thinking in such a way as to maximize both its sensibleness and its strangeness. In one sense, we already know why the entrepreneur would want to realize her new thinking in this way. Anyone who has had a new idea of any sort in whatever domain knows that she immediately faces banalizers who will say that the idea is really old and has already been tried. People tend to see new thinking according to its kind and not its precise content. So a case of new thinking will be categorized as of a certain type, and all the old constraints on ideas of that type will be rehearsed. The other problem with new thinking can come from the success of the thinker's own formulation. If a new thought is formulated carefully, it will seem obviously true. And this will stand in its way. For, again, banalizers will say that, if the thought is so obviously true, it must already have been taken into account. It does not make sense that an *obvious* truth would be making its appearance at this late date. These are only two of the most familiar strategies for disarming new thinking. Just disabling these responses is reason enough for someone to try to preserve the initial strangeness of her accomplishment and thereby retain a sense of how things looked before the new thought was realized. We call this reason for preserving the oddness of the innovation—the glamor of the product—the *marketing reason.* But there is also a more far-reaching reason for preserving strangeness.

We have seen that a successful entrepreneur is neither just an inventor nor just a thinker. The successful entrepreneur builds an enterprise around her new thinking, and a successful enterprise perpetuates itself by continuing along the lines of the founding entrepreneur or along the lines of a new entrepreneur who takes over the enterprise. We have also seen that the kind of thinking that leads to innovation requires an openness to anomalies in life. It requires an interest in holding on to these anomalies in one's daily activities and in seeing clearly how the anomalies look under different conditions. If people are to do this in an enterprise—and the more they do it, the more entrepreneurial the enterprise will be—then they cannot see their lives and the disclosive space in which they work as settled. Being settled, seeing things as settled, acting as though the way we do things is the natural way of doing things are the greatest enemies of seeing anomalies in the first place and of holding on to them in the second. If one is living in the natural settled way, then things happen as they should. The unordinary will appear as unnatural and monstrous, not as a truth worthy of preservation or a focus for reorganizing one's life. A company whose employees are complaisant about their work lives is a company headed for disaster. Indeed, it was one of the paradoxes of IBM's total-pastoral-care style that it produced the false belief that IBM and IBMers were invulnerable. The computers produced at IBM may at first have embodied something of the way the world looked before centralized processing made obvious sense, but neither the products nor the company culture was able to retain this strangeness, and this failure, in turn, prevented IBMers from seeing and holding on to the anomalies in their work lives and continuing to come up with innovations. Thus, maximizing both uncanniness and sensibleness serves not only a marketing function but provides for a company culture that promotes meaningful, historical innovations.

3. Involved versus Detached Business: Economic Theory and What Is Lost in the Rationalization of Business Skills

Now that we have shown how entrepreneurs develop a useful product, service, or practice whose employment involves a regestalting of all the practices of a disclosive space, we can see that entrepreneurs are in the business of changing history. They give their cultures or industries new styles for dealing with people and things. We need only think about how Ford's mass-produced car led us from a governing style to a controlling style or how Jobs's personal computer led us from a style of getting everything under control to a liberated renegade style in order to see how far-reaching these changes can be and also how different from normal business competition such entrepreneurial activity is. The first mass-produced cars were not competing with other mass-produced cars but with another way of life. The first personal computers were not competing with other personal computers but with our pastoral work habits. If this account of entrepreneurship is right, then those accounts of entrepreneurs that focus on competition for profit have at best described a constant feature of entrepreneurship but have in no way grasped its essence. But if the traditional account misses the mark, how precisely are entrepreneurs related to the market economy?

Entrepreneurs and entrepreneurial skill constitute heightened forms of customary market behavior. But to say this means that we must recast how people think about normal market behavior. Commonly, people say that profit motivates businesspeople and business activity. One thinks that this claim makes sense only if one has lost track of how market activity is tied to our way of life. In market economies, we are brought up to regard effectiveness highly. We like tools to do transparently what they are designed to do. We like people to excel at doing what they have undertaken. And we are brought up to test the usefulness of our tools and our own excellence by comparison with others—that is to say, by competition. But this does not mean that we are simply brought up to be competitive. Competitiveness is just one element of our practices. We have to be cooperative to form associations that compete. And we do not generally compete in areas where doing so cannot improve the quality of the performance. So, for instance, we know that if partners compete over who is the better parent, this will actually degrade the parenting. Indeed, we are brought up to sense many of the limitations of competition. We generally have a rough and ready practical sense of when competition is appropriate, what it means to compete fairly, and what it means to compete unfairly. We developed this sense by experiencing many different events of competition as we were growing up. By the time we are adults, most people who live in nations with market economies are proficient at acting in the appropriate competitive way to market their skills and products. (Misers and monopolists, and others who "game" the system, are out of step with, and have missed the point of, *appropriate* competitive practice.)

This all implies that we compete because we enjoy the ongoing exercise of our skills in a context where those skills make sense as components of a meaningful way of life. That is, we compete to make things and ourselves more worthy. We compete to make the qualities of products that we care about or qualities of ourselves that we care about stand out. In short, we compete to develop identities within communities. In saying this, we are also saying that we do not normally compete to make money. Such a claim will seem absurd at first to most people. Even many who find their work compelling will argue that they are working precisely to make money: "If they didn't pay me, I wouldn't be here another moment." We claim that when one thinks in this way, one is not seeing profit as part of work as a whole and work as part of one's whole life, but is breaking up what should be a gestalt into a set of steps that then appear merely as a series of means to further ends. Since every end can be converted into money, money then looks like the supreme end. We argue that this detached, seemingly rational account distorts our sense of ourselves as involved in the ongoing activity of making sense of our lives.

Business owners do not normally work for money either. They work for the enjoyment of their competitive skill, in the context of a life where competing skillfully makes sense. The money they earn supports this way of life.[29] The same is true of their businesses. One might think that they view their businesses as nothing more than machines to produce profits, since they do closely monitor their accounts to keep tabs on those profits. But this way of thinking replaces the point of the machine's activity with a diagnostic test of how well it is performing. Normally, one senses whether one is performing skillfully. A basketball player does not need to count baskets to know whether the team as a whole is in flow. Saying that the point of business is to produce profit is like saying that the whole point of playing basketball is to make as many baskets as possible. One could make many more baskets by having no opponent. The game and styles of playing the game are what matter because they produce identities people care about. Likewise, a business develops an identity by providing a product or a service to people. To do that it needs capital, and it needs to make a profit, but no more than it needs to have competent employees or customers or any other thing that enables production to take place. None of this is the goal of the activity.

We are claiming, then, that customary businesses and businesspeople exist in market economies to form identities that are recognized by others as respectable due to their usefulness or excellence. But we must be careful here. When we say *customary*, we mean so far as businesses and businesspeople act simply in accordance with the practices of market economies. But nowadays there is an exceedingly strong pull away from acting according to the practices of market competition in which many of us were raised. There is a tendency toward rationalization. Indeed, the one thing that the diverse economic and sociological views of entrepreneurs have in common is that virtually all characterize the entrepreneur as perpetuating and enhancing the rational concerns of modernity. Such economists and sociologists think that entrepreneurship took off during modernity for precisely the reason that entrepreneurs are exemplary for living the rationalized life where customs become beliefs that can be reordered and therefore exploited in many different ways. We see entrepreneurs as in touch with a certain form of history-making that has been with the culture of the West since the classical Greeks and the ancient Hebrews. On the basis of this difference, we can begin to distinguish our account of entrepreneurship from that of contemporary economists.

We start by looking at how we differ from those economists and sociologists who, one might think, are closest to us. We begin with the sociologist Brigitte Berger. In describing relatively small-scale entrepreneurs, she writes,

The social skills that [small-scale entrepreneurs] are forced to nurture are distinctly modern, rational-instrumental patterns of interaction on several levels. Chief among them are those relating to commercial activities: interaction networks have to be constructed between entrepreneurs and suppliers, between sellers and customers, between entrepreneurs and other actors on the local as well as on the more distant scene. In this way the entrepreneur not only creates and re-creates institutional structures but becomes constitutive of them. Propelled by the need to adapt to the demands of a modern economy, which can no longer be understood in terms of local needs alone, the individual entrepreneur is eager for information on larger issues of technology, economy, and politics. The entrepreneurial mind-set transcends the confines of family and tradition, opening individuals up to modern styles of consciousness and securing them a place in modern industrial society.[30]

Berger pictures the entrepreneur as transcending the engaged practical approach of the local customary person who simply does what she has been trained to do from birth. In surveying the world from above, so to speak, the entrepreneur sees people (who are producing X, Y, or Z in their own local communities) as suppliers of X, Y, or Z to her community and as purchasers of the A, B, and C of other communities. The entrepreneur, in other words, does not become entranced by the wonderful X, the curious and versatile Y, or the brilliantly simple and useful Z. Rather, the entrepreneur sees all of these items from a detached stance in which she applies the appropriate reductive analysis so that they become information, values, or commodities. Likewise, she sees the relations between others and herself as those of buying and selling. And, buying and selling are no longer practices embedded in local communities with local meanings and interrelations to other local practices. Rather, buying and selling are transactions that have rationalizable and ordered rules. What practices remain to determine the correct application of the rules are the general cosmopolitan practices of modernity itself, which is to say practices of abstracting general essences from local situations. For all her cultural embedding, Berger ends up seeing the entrepreneur in the terms developed by Israel Kirzner,[31] who characterizes the entrepreneur as someone who earns profits by applying arbitrage techniques to many different local markets.

Don Lavoie, a rare interpretive economist influenced by the hermeneutic thinking of Hans-Georg Gadamer, tries to provide a useful corrective to the common view of entrepreneurs as having detached reductive-analytic views. But his entrepreneurs are, if anything, too engaged in their local cultural situations. The picture Lavoie offers is of people so engaged in the practices of their culture that they pull ahead of others by doing in a more intense, more focused way what people in the culture already do. Whatever possibilities the cultural practices leave open, Lavoie's entrepreneurs enact by becoming so skillful at their cultural practices that they—to use the metaphor of test pilots—push the edges of the envelope. We might think of Lavoie's entrepreneurs as athletes who become so skilled at their game that they bring out latent possibilities and, in so doing, change the game's nature. Lavoie is certainly right in seeing that the entrepreneur regestalts a culture or, as he puts it, "shifts interpretive frameworks" and that such shifts are global:

A shift of interpretive framework can bring about a more fundamental change than simply adding to a stock of things that have been noticed. An interpretive framework can change in a far more profound manner: all the old opportunities will suddenly look different, indeed may no longer be considered opportunities at all, when a new one is found. And of course the circumstances one has been alert to in the past help determine the kinds of situations one will be apt to notice in the future. That is, profit opportunities are not independent atoms but connected parts of a whole perspective on the world. And the perspective is in turn an evolving part of a continuing cultural tradition, constantly being reappropriated into new situations.[32]

But, in simply understanding entrepreneurs as more engaged than others, Lavoie misses how engagement works because he misses the phenomenon of holding on to anomalies:

The really successful entrepreneurs we know are not unusually separate from others; on the contrary, they are especially well plugged into the culture. What gives them the ability to sense what their customers will want is not some kind of mysterious alertness that gets "switched on" but their capacity to read the conversations of mankind. They can pick up the sense of where their fellows in the culture stand, what values they adhere to, what purposes they pursue, what they consider beautiful, and what they deem profane.[33]

Because Lavoie sees the entrepreneur as engaged with the same cultural materials as her fellows, only with more sensitivity, his essential interpretive insights may be subsumed into standard descriptive and quantitative economic accounts. Here is how Mark Casson, for instance, takes the insights typical of Lavoie into account:

It was suggested earlier that the successful entrepreneur requires a monopoly of some item of information. Strictly speaking, however, the only item that has to be monopolized is the information that a particular profit opportunity exists. Information about the existence of a profit opportunity may be called commercial information. . . . Commercial information is typically a synthesis of other information, which may be called raw information. Items of raw information are like the pieces of a jigsaw that have to be fitted together to get the overall picture. . . . Not all entrepreneurs have the same background information by any means, but all are searching for the last few pieces of the jigsaw. . . . A better analogy would be searching for pieces of a Meccano set. Different types of synthesis can be effected with different combinations of pieces, and people with imagination may be able to achieve a synthesis with a given combination that other people would be unable to visualize. It is the imagination that dictates what kinds of synthesis are believed to be possible.[34]

For purposes of modeling, Casson wants to treat any Lavoie-type entrepreneurial interpretation[35] as a rearrangement of facts. Lavoie would want to say that Casson has no right to do this because the reinterpretation of cultural practices leaves *what counts as a fact* looking quite different after the entrepreneur's reinterpretation. This argument is usually illustrated by the change from Aristotelian to Galilean physics. Interpretive historians of science point out that Galileo's achievement cannot be understood in terms of discovering some new fact or some new arrangement of old Aristotelian facts. With Galileo the world (that is, the very nature of the facts) changed. For instance, when Aristotle listed the examples of change he would have to take into account in his physics, he listed the motion of a cart, a celestial body, and a blush. All of us who have been brought up within the Galilean ways of seeing things will find this mysterious. We may suppose that when Aristotle said blush, he really meant the motion of the blood, though we realize that this is highly unlikely. Or we might suppose that when Aristotle spoke about motion, he meant the much broader notion of change. But we soon find that substituting our notion of change does not work either because Aristotle does not include change of laws as something his physics should account for. Aristotle is really seeing things significantly differently from the way we do, and only interpretive research can enable us to understand how he did see things.

However it is that Aristotle sees things, Galileo certainly does not see things differently because he has rearranged Aristotle's facts. So, if Casson were to develop a model for revolutionary scientists like his model for entrepreneurs, including an optimization curve for determining the optimal number of revolutionary scientists searching for new facts in any domain, the model would tell us nothing relevant for two reasons. First, revolutionary scientists are not searching for new facts. Second, and more important for a model maker, the revolutionary scientist's achievement, no matter what she is actually searching for, cannot be cashed out as the discovery of a new fact or a new arrangement of old facts. The very notion of physical facthood changes with the revolutionary scientist.

But does Lavoie's account of entrepreneurial reinterpretation enable him to make the sort of argument we have just described? No. His entrepreneurs' reinterpretations are neither like shifts from Aristotelian to Galilean physics nor like our shifts from a culture with a governing style to one with a controlling style. The possibilities that Lavoie's entrepreneur exploits are possibilities that are already implicit within the dominant style's typical practices in any domain. An example that fits Lavoie's notion of reinterpretation is Mendeleev's discovery of a way of arranging the chemical elements, whose reality scientists had already accepted, on a periodic table that reveals important new possibilities for dealing with these elements.

To bring this point back to entrepreneurship, we can contrast Henry Ford's introduction of a new pervasive controlling style with the introduction of the cellular telephone. Given that it was technically feasible and also that people were already adopting a flexible controlling style in business, the cellular telephone made sense as simply intensifying current work and communication practices. So far as its primary use is in business, it simply sharpens the sense that one dwells within an environment of constant and flexible support of customers, clients, managers, and so forth. Reality changes to some degree. Employment no longer means being in a certain office for certain hours. It now means being available for service during many more hours. But availability for service was already becoming a central part of business life. Traveling for work, preparing proposals on the weekend, and going on work retreats had prepared the way for the additional commitments brought about by the cellular telephone.[36] For these reasons, the Lavoie-type entrepreneur changes practices in such a way that what counts as a fact is a clear development out of what used to count as a fact. The shift is so slight that a modeler would be justified in describing its result as a new arrangement of facts based on the new fact of constant communication. Whatever nuances the modeler misses would be trivial insofar as the model is used for the formation of general public and business policy.

It might seem that we have been unfair to Lavoie in arguing from the example of the cellular telephone. But Lavoie's form of entrepreneurial reinterpretation comes down to examples like this so long as he insists on the entrepreneur's intense embeddedness in the culture's dominant practices. His entrepreneur is someone so tuned into the possibilities already implicit in these dominant practices that she realizes them before anyone else. Are there such entrepreneurs? We are certain that there are. But we do not think that they reveal most deeply either life at its best or, therefore, the nature of genuine entrepreneurship. Nonetheless, the fact that there are such entrepreneurs as Lavoie describes enables us to see something important. The actions of these entrepreneurs are precisely the ones that can be modeled by economists such as Casson. Indeed, the kinds of innovators that Lavoie describes are probably found most frequently in research and development departments, whose managers are the most ardent seekers of aid from economic modeling. But Lavoie's description of the entrepreneur as a cultural interpreter does not account for the most genuine cases of entrepreneurship, and models that can take account of his description of the entrepreneur but not the most genuine entrepreneur are limited in an important respect. We certainly would not want to develop an industrial or governmental policy that aided a deficient form of entrepreneurship while positively impeding the more genuine and democratic kind.

To see how policies driven from economic models might advance deficient entrepreneurship while impeding genuine entrepreneurship, we turn to William Baumol's thought-provoking development of models for optimizing the allocation of entrepreneurial talent and innovations both within industries and within nations. Baumol assumes that by changing the structure of financial rewards, entrepreneurship can be reallocated from sector to sector of the economy. In particular, Baumol is interested in reallocating rewards so that legal entrepreneurship becomes less attractive and engineering entrepreneurship more attractive. For such an argument to make sense, Baumol must assume that *many* entrepreneurs are like Casson's and Lavoie's, to the extent of being in touch with general social possibilities and being able to develop one or another of them. He makes this point about entrepreneurs being able to shift their domains of activity quite clearly:

Perhaps not for all entrepreneurs, but surely for many of them, the identity of the line of endeavor that offers the most promising prospect of profits is no matter of great moment. . . . [T]he pricing arrangements that determine prospective profitability therefore can have a profound influence on the pattern of allocation of the economy's entrepreneurial resources.[37]

Since we have agreed that Lavoie and Casson do describe a kind of entrepreneur who is in touch with various exploitable opportunities, we could agree with these claims about *many* entrepreneurs, but we would add that Baumol's assumption is by no means true for the most genuine cases. Entrepreneurs who are holding on to anomalies cannot willy-nilly move from domain to domain. Someone who has noticed that working is a matter of making commitments and not performing tasks will want to embody this understanding in a device that is at the heart of task-driven work. Such an entrepreneur would not find it sensible to embody this insight in a device used primarily in entertainment, by hobbyists, or even in one or another of the professions. Moreover, such a genuine entrepreneur will not be able effectively to embody this insight in one of the old standard work devices such as file cabinets, timecard machines, or payroll systems. Entrepreneurs like our composite entrepreneur, who hold on to anomalies that can change our world, do not have a great deal of leeway in how they embody their new awareness, and such entrepreneurs, as we have said, are the most important ones because they are the ones who transform a cultural style.

Nothing would be amiss, however, if the results of Baumol's models for optimizing deficient entrepreneurial activity simply did just that, and many of them do. We could endorse, indeed embrace, many of the policy suggestions Baumol makes on the basis of his models. Some, however, would advance deficient entrepreneurship at the expense of the genuine entrepreneur. We can see this clearly in his suggestions for changes in patent laws. We quote the first two provisions, but all lead, indeed force, the entrepreneur into a situation where she can succeed in business only if she licenses her innovation to her competitors:

Provision 1. Award of the Patent to the First to File. In the United States and Canada, a patent is awarded to the party that provides evidence that it was the first to *discover* the invention in question. In Japan and most other countries, in contrast, the patent goes to the party that is first to *file* its application. This has two consequences, both of which serve to stimulate dissemination: first, the rule encourages early filing, making the technical information available sooner, and perhaps far sooner, than under the U.S. system, and giving rivals an earlier opportunity to profit in their own innovative efforts from the knowledge that is required to be disclosed along with the application. . . . Second, applications filed in haste tend to be imperfect and incomplete, making them more vulnerable to challenge and to conflicting claims. This can pressure the parties to arrive at a settlement, with the successful patent applicant precommitted to provide licenses to rivals in exchange for agreement by the latter not to challenge the application.

Provision 2. Prepatent Disclosure. In the United States, public disclosure of the technical details of a patented invention is required, but only after the patent has been granted. In Japan, in contrast, the details must be published in the official gazette where anyone can examine them, immediately after the filing of an application. The information must remain available for eighteen months thereafter, even if the patent has not been granted in the interim. Obviously, this too gives an early helping hand to rivals seeking to provide themselves with a similar invention, and strengthens their position in bargaining for a license.[38]

To the extent that these proposals are applied to innovations that, like the cellular telephone, draw on fairly well-understood and pervasive practices, forcing entrepreneurs into licensing agreements will likely have the effect of speeding dissemination and hence increase the worth of the innovation for the society. But they would be dangerous for our composite entrepreneur, since precisely the features of the product that are easily understood and have obvious applications would, if overly emphasized, prevent the product from attracting the kinds of practices and uses that would be essential for reconfiguring the culture's practices generally.

To see this, let us recall the network software our composite entrepreneur developed. The obvious use of such software at the time, and even to some extent today, would be to network various computers. That part of the software that required users to attend to their speech acts—requests, offers, promises, negotiating conditions of satisfaction, exchanging information, and so forth—would seem like a frill. But that frill was in fact the heart of the innovation. In using the software and the cues included for developing the various sorts of speech acts that lead to designing particular tasks, products, and so forth, users would become more and more sensitive to the nature of how they spent their time working. This is not to say that they would become conscious that the most important part of work now consists largely in making agreements; rather, their skills for making agreements and designing new projects would gradually be enhanced. They would then stop approaching their jobs as a set of standardized tasks and begin to see themselves as designing particular tasks, products, and services for their customers, clients, and home companies. As our composite entrepreneur's product went through generations, he could monitor how well it succeeded in transforming the way people worked, and he would make enhancements to achieve this end.

What would have happened if he had had to license out the design of his innovative product? Companies would work with the obviously useful part. They would shave off the focus on speech acts in order to add their own frills. One would network computers faster. Another would enable the networked computers to do more than one task at a time. Another would provide for privacy control. The list of such frills is virtually endless. But the effect is obvious. The exemplary innovative entrepreneur would find it much harder to reconfigure the domain of activity on which he was focusing. Indeed, with enough changes in laws and regulations like those Baumol proposes for the patent laws, the genuine innovative entrepreneur, who depends on products that emphasize both the sensibleness and strangeness of her insight, could become extinct.

What must be done to prevent this possibility? First, we must give up the counsels of despair that economists like Baumol offer us about providing a useful description of genuine entrepreneurship.[39] Baumol, for instance, thinks that since entrepreneurs change the worlds we live in, no level of description can capture what they do. We believe that precisely describing entrepreneurs as changing backgrounds and showing how they make such a change amounts to a description that points beyond the empirical and is useful. Second, to retain genuine reconfiguring entrepreneurship, we must remain clear about the limits of theoretical rationalization. The policy changes suggested by rationalizers need to be checked against direct accounts of skillful history-making in the relevant domain.

Economic modeling is only one of the ways of attempting to rationalize the supposed features of entrepreneurship while abstracting from the involvement and skills of the entrepreneur. But no economist's or any other rational system can capture the way a skilled performer copes with the solicitations of each specific situation and senses whether the coping is going well. When rationalizers try to make sense of the activities of skillful copers, they turn the diagnostic tests of the activity, such as whether it is making a profit, into its goal. Naturally, too, as soon as one abstracts the entrepreneur from skillful activity in this way, many options appear that would simply not show up within either customary or entrepreneurial ways of doing business.

For instance, one will see that one can compete by forming trusts that block competition, or by buying out potential competitors who have good ideas and then holding back the implementation of their ideas to maximize profits on products already on the market. Finally, if rationalization follows its normal course, as it does in some business school curricula and in university economics departments, one tries to work out both the theory of the domain that leads to success and the general theory for succeeding in any domain. Then, business activity looks like gaming the system to produce high indicators of success.[40] We call such activity *uprooted* because it is no longer grounded in the practices that make sense of competition in the first place. Worse, when business activity amounts to gaming the system, searching for excellence or quality or any other meaningful goal will amount to no more than further gaming techniques.[41] The notion of engaging in these activities to form an identity will be lost.

With the loss of the sense of forming identities comes a loss of the point of holding on to anomalies. Holding on to anomalies has a point only if one senses that one already has in one's practices resources for dealing with a disharmony. If one thinks instead that one is applying a system of rules, a glitch will appear not to have any truth implicit in it. Rather, it will be taken to indicate that one needs a better rule or principle. Consequently, rationalizing will block sensitivity to anomalies and so cover up possibilities for entrepreneurship. Thus, insofar as business schools have cultivated a theoretical attitude, they may be doing more harm than good.[42]

4. Entrepreneurial Skill: Human Activity at Its Best

We have already argued that the entrepreneur's activity is not a specialized activity but is based in the activity of everyday life at its best. We can now make this connection clearer by showing how being captivated by anomalies fits with our account of how things show up in everyday activity. In describing ongoing activity such as steering a car, we said that what appears for a human being in the midst of such activity is a situation that both fits the sort of action the person can perform and solicits some particular action. The structure of this ongoing activity is the basis for the structure of the innovative aspect of entrepreneurial activity, with the exception that the entrepreneur is more in tune with the *nature* of human activity. She senses with joy, for instance, that unexpected things that matter are beginning to show up and fall into place. Being captivated by an anomaly amounts to becoming sensitive to the fact that one's preanomaly understanding of what it made sense to do in the situation was more limited than the understanding one's activity now reveals. So instead of just responding sensitively to solicitations of the situation, one responds with *heightened sensitivity*.

We can recognize such heightened sensitivity in ourselves when we allow ourselves to be drawn into something to such an extent that our inhibitions or external irritations do not affect us. When people are captivated by an unusual game, for example, they just play and play, losing all sense of their surroundings, while working at the game with complete absorption and hypersensitivity but not, and this is important to remember, with the curiosity of reflective thought. This captivation happens to the innovator when she uncovers an anomaly. But the innovator is not playing a game, and the captivation lasts, perhaps, through her entire life. So the innovator captivated by the anomaly does what is normally done in being sensitive to the solicitations of the situation, but with more intensity, personal involvement, and scrupulousness.

Anyone who has been captivated by an activity such as chess or by a person who has exercised an irresistible attraction will recall that in the course of the captivation the world comes to look different. The game or the person draws out ways of acting that are disharmonious with our workaday lives, and we investigate the tensions of these new ways of acting by playing the game over and over again or by seeking every possible opportunity to be with the person. We make every effort to get the game right or the relationship right—that is, to get in tune with what it means for us. And we draw on skills we have not normally used. For example, we see possibilities for moving pawns in new ways or using the queen earlier or for taking hiking trips or going to concerts. In enacting these formerly passed-over possibilities, we not only perform them energetically but feel a mood of joyful personal involvement in what we are doing. This greater sense of involvement is part of what makes us see new possibilities in life when captivated by a game or a person. This involvement is a heightened form of the involvement we have in much of our daily coping, and it is also experienced in the three innovative aspects of entrepreneurial disclosing: holding on to an anomaly, making it appear in various parts of one's life so that its truth comes out, and seeing how others respond to it.

But what about the entrepreneur's institutionalizing level of activity? As we design our lives, we do something like this also. A person who has become captivated by chess will join or create a chess club. Or he institutes a time each week or day to meet with other chess players in the park. Other cases of setting up an institution to explore being captivated by anomalies are even more obvious when one becomes sensitive to them. Marriage is a common form of institutionalizing the exploration of a romantic/erotic attraction, but so is a life that contains a great many partners. Indeed, our marriages and our dating become stale precisely when we no longer embody in these institutions the entrepreneurial practices that they were supposed to institutionalize. When, for example, we stop bringing into our social orbit other couples whose understanding and conclusions regarding romance are like ours, when we stop talking to our friends about things to do with our families and about problems at home that we need to iron out, or when we give up celebrating the style of our attraction with evening meals or concerts or hiking trips, our institutions grow stale. There is a strong tendency to normalize the anomalous in our lives and consequently to let our entrepreneurial institutions become the customary institutions that anyone could have.

What, then, is entrepreneurship, if we look at it from the perspective of everyday activity? We have already suggested that entrepreneurs are people whose activity has the same basic structure as that of everyday coping but is "heightened," by which we mean that their lives manifest the structure of human activity more clearly. Entrepreneurs are in tune with the disclosive nature of human activity, in that they establish disclosive spaces held together by particular styles. By being in tune in this way—by holding on to an anomaly and instituting the practices by which the anomaly comes into focus—entrepreneurs contribute to reconfiguring the practices of their society. Thus successful entrepreneurs bring about social change by modifying the style of particular subworlds or the style of the society in general.

At least two other kinds of human being—the virtuous citizen and the culture figure—are also in the business of transforming disclosive spaces. To see that these three kinds are fundamentally the same, however, we need to be sensitive to the important difference among them. The entrepreneur reconfigures the style of a disclosive space by installing a new product, service, or practice in that space; the virtuous citizen cross-appropriates practices by means of his or her interpretive speaking; and the culture figure articulates important practices that we are ignoring. We turn now to the transforming activity of the virtuous citizen.

Democracy: The Politics of Interpretive Speaking

Both the increasing demand for democracy, so vividly underlined by the recent history of Eastern Europe, and the rise of multicultural pluralism in Western democracies highlight the importance of clarifying our understanding of democracy. We begin our examination of democracy with a critique of two influential models and then sketch an alternative account of citizen virtue within a multicultural, liberal democracy, drawing out its consequences for civic democracy, our preferred model. We spend most of our time elucidating in detail the phenomenon of interpretive speaking, which we take to be the paradigmatic form of democratic political action. It will turn out that disclosing skills at their best, as we have defined them, play a central role not only in enterprises but also in civic democracies. Finally, we show that such democratic activity is not limited to the nation-state but can work on an international scale as well.

1. Liberal Democracy versus Civic Humanist Tradition

Anglo-American political science has reflected roughly four alternative understandings of democracy since World War II. First, there is *majoritarianism*, based on notions of parliamentary sovereignty, which holds that sovereignty rests in the hands of those elected by the majority so long as those representatives refrain from interfering with the right of voters to vote at regularly scheduled times in genuinely contested elections. Second, there have been various forms of *popular* or *radical democracy*, which discourages stable institutions for self-rule and encourages the flexible disassembling of political and cultural institutions in order to encourage the evolution of new forms. Here one thinks of Roberto Unger, Chantal Mouffe, and followers of Michel Foucault like William Connolly. Third, there is the strain of thought (to which our point of view is most closely allied) called *republican* or *civic humanism*, which traces its understanding of democracy to the republics of the Italian Renaissance or to the Greek polis. Hannah Arendt, Robert Bellah, Benjamin Barber, Charles Taylor, and others who call themselves communitarians are frequently understood to advocate this understanding, which claims that political rule requires an expertise or excellence acquired as a skill or virtue and exercised in nondependent conjunction (or equality) with one's fellow citizens. Fourth, and by far the most pervasive way of thinking about democracy, has been *liberalism*—so much so that we tend to think of today's democratic polity as a liberal democracy.

Our first goal is to distinguish our view from liberalism and answer the main difficulties liberals have with positions like ours. Moreover, since most postwar liberal theorists assume that anyone who takes issue with liberalism is seeking radical changes in the current form of Western democracies, we try to show that this form is already a variant of civic humanism. Indeed, by examining the typical acts of citizens, we show that civic humanist practices and ways of conceiving the self are still at the core of Western democracy.

Since we see our society as a mixture of liberal and civic humanist practices, what we are seeking is not radical change but closer attention to existing civic disclosive practices that are disparaged by contemporary liberalism. The changes in political structure that we mention amount to reducing the emphasis on fundamental rights that are precious to the preservation of the liberal personality and its reflective judgments. But we list these changes mostly as a way of bringing out the logic of what is primary in our position. Our central political aim is to displace the liberal interpretation of democracy and to show that democratic life at its best is the tradition of civic humanism and that liberalism merely provides a useful floor that democratic society must respect. We need not dismantle all of liberalism for this civic tradition to thrive.

Liberal thinking about democracy starts by considering equal persons who are the self-authenticating sources of "thought, deliberation, and responsibility."[1] This understanding of personhood is Cartesian. For John Rawls, who along with Ronald Dworkin is preeminent among liberal theorists, the two primary capacities of a person that derive from these capacities for thought, deliberation, and responsibility are the capacity for a sense of justice and the capacity for a conception of the good. A person's sense of justice requires fair treatment of others and an acceptance of the fact that one cannot expect people with different experiences to seek the same goods in the same order as one rationally seeks them for oneself. This recognition grounds liberalism's defining feature—that an autonomous sphere of public life must be developed where people govern themselves and treat each other fairly, in a way that aims not to promote any particular person's or association's good. This is the liberal principle of neutrality or tolerance.[2] It concedes, of course, that the liberal state must promote certain goods; but these are the goods necessary to the perpetuation of justice, and as such they are minimal public goods that everyone in the liberal democracy will support. Liberals do concede, however, that the neutrality of liberal democracies has limits and that such societies must interdict or impede the development of goods that conflict with justice. So, for instance, ways of life that require the denigration of some individuals because of their race will be interdicted, and practices that limit a citizen's capacity for giving reasons in public—such as some religious practices—will also be impeded.

From this constrained neutrality comes a trait that most proponents see as one of liberalism's great goods: its antiperfectionism. Since the liberal state does not aim to promote particular goods, the liberal society establishes a space where citizens may freely examine and even exchange their own conceptions of the good for other such conceptions.[3] Indeed, by one account, the institution of this space is the basic point of liberalism, providing what is essential for a good life. Will Kymlicka writes:

We have two preconditions for leading a good life. The first is that we lead our life from the inside, in accordance with our beliefs about what gives value to life. Individuals must therefore have the resources and liberties needed to lead their lives in accordance with their beliefs about value, without fear of discrimination or punishment. Hence the traditional liberal concern with individual privacy, and the opposition to the "enforcement of morals." The second precondition is that we be free to question those beliefs, to examine them in light of whatever information, examples, and arguments our culture can provide. Individuals must therefore have the conditions necessary to acquire an awareness of different views about the good life, and an ability to examine these views intelligently. Hence the equally traditional liberal concern for education, and freedom of expression and association.[4]

A number of charges have been leveled against the picture of the self and of the good life that liberals say requires this particular moral space.[5] The answers liberals have given, however, suggest that they have misunderstood the charges.[6] By and large, antiliberals are attempting to paint a picture of human being, human selves, and the good life that seems truer to the way people actually live than the liberal portrayal. The issue is one of weighting. When nonliberals claim that liberal privacy cuts against democratic action and citizen virtue, they are not (or should not be) claiming that liberals support a totally unassailable right to privacy.[7] For example, nonliberals may *seem* to claim that the liberal emphasis on a private space for reflection forgets that, when one brackets off all shared public concerns, one has no basis on which to evaluate anything. And this only brings the liberal rejoinder that, of course, "'no one can put everything about himself in question all at once,' but 'it hardly follows that for each person there is some one connection or association so fundamental that it cannot be detached for inspection while holding others in place.'"[8] Or alternatively, "Liberal equality does not assume that people choose their beliefs about ethics any more than their beliefs about geography. It does suppose that they *reflect* on their ethical beliefs and that they choose how to be on the basis of those reflections."[9]

We agree with the critics of liberalism who argue that liberal privacy cuts against democratic citizen virtue and that the liberal space for reflection misses the point of how revisions in human life are made because it assumes that there is nothing so fundamental that it cannot be questioned. But by these charges we do not mean that liberals have *no* account of democratic action and citizen virtue or even of something so fundamental that it cannot be questioned. One wonders what ground a liberal would acknowledge for asserting the primacy of rationality or judgment other than one that could not sensibly be questioned?[10] The point is that liberalism puts the wrong weight on all these matters, and a different weighting of human capacities can give a better account of what we really care about and find good in democratic culture as we know it.

Before we turn to our picture of what is fundamental to democracy, we want to consider one of the core examples that drives liberal thinking, even that of liberal theorists who oppose the main line of thought deriving from Rawls and Dworkin.[11] Here it is from Dworkin:

Someone who accepts the challenge model [understanding life as a challenge to be skillfully managed] might well think that religious devotion is an essential part of how human beings should respond to their place in the universe, and therefore that devotion is part of living well. But he cannot think that involuntary religious observance, prayer in the shadow of the rack, has any ethical value. He may think that an active homosexual blights his life by a failure to understand the point of sexual love. But he cannot think that a homosexual who abstains, against his own convictions and only out of fear, has therefore overcome that defect in his life.[12]

Liberal thinking of all colors returns again and again to this and other similar examples to bolster its claim that only those virtues or actions that are not coerced count ethically or morally. This notion leads to the claim that ethical acts are those that accord with our considered, reflective, or even intuitive judgments. That is, no coerced action can count as a good for us, unless our considered judgment approves of it. This means not that each of our acts must be subsequently reflected on and pass muster but that, if we did reflect on the action subsequently, we would approve of it. Actions are judged ethically according to the criteria of reflective reason. It follows that neither a national government nor any other institution should be permitted to control or inhibit this space for self-determination. (Dworkin allows for compulsory education because it is short-term, endorsed after the fact in a genuine way, and—for reasons that are not clear—noninvasive.[13]) The panoply of liberal rights and institutions follow from this type of example. It will be our task to show that these compelling examples are woefully misleading.

While liberal democracy begins with the intuition that it must minimize governmental paternalism in ethics (as opposed to economics) so that individuals may go their own way in forming their own communal associations to seek their own goods, our version of democracy begins with the intuition that democracy is, in fact, the joining together of all to promote the diverse goods of all. We do not assume that, because people discover that they cannot come to agreement about their goods or the ordering of their goods, they *must* generally exclude such questions from political or public reason. Rather, in our view, given that none of the goods endorsed is repugnant to the others (liberal democracy has a similar qualification), people with different orderings of goods *must* work together to produce a space where each *with the help of others* can develop his or her own good. We hold the production of this civic space to be a necessary instrumental and structural good without which no other goods can be effectively pursued.

To see the relation of our claim to that of the civic humanists whose claims are closest to ours, we consider J. G. A. Pocock's account of the civic humanism of the fifteenth through the eighteenth centuries:

Any republic could be presented as a paradigm of human association ... in which all types of men combined to pursue all human goods, their nature being such that they could be pursued only in association. Since association was in itself a good, and intelligent activity another, it followed that the highest form of active life was that of the citizen who, having entered the political process in pursuit of his particular good, now found himself joining with others to direct the actions of all in pursuit of the good of all; *the attainment of his private good was not lost but must take a lower priority*. It was possible to distribute responsibility in decision-taking in such a way that each citizen was enabled to direct his activity and that of others—who in turn directed his—towards the general good, while being subject to no lesser authority that that of all, in which he was himself a participant.[14]

Civic humanists see that the pursuit of diverse individual goods requires that everyone work together. But civic humanists think that the good of forming a political organization so that people can work together is of the same type as pursuing individual goods but is higher because it makes such pursuit possible. Civic humanism is a humanism precisely because it questions the validity of any transcendent good and substitutes for it the pursuit of the immanent good of taking part in the political life. This immanent good then becomes the highest good. Thus, civic humanism falls victim to the standard liberal criticism that it subordinates all private goods to the political life and thereby produces unending conflict. Political activities that are supposed to enable the citizen to realize individual goods subordinate those goods in the name of the higher good of political activity. On occasion this political good even imposes the requirement that the citizen sacrifice individual goods. For example, civic humanism seems to require that, given our political nature, on some occasions, the philosopher or scientist must subordinate doing philosophy or science to party recruitment.

To distinguish our view from that of civic humanism, we call ours *civic activism*. For us, political activity is a unique ontological dimension that always already pervades and supports the pursuit of our individual goods. It therefore cannot conflict with them. So, for us, there must always be some political space in a society, though the space may be impoverished.

Liberals have serious objections to civic humanism. Principal among these is that it cannot deal adequately with the diversity of goods and orderings of goods that are present in today's nations. They also think that people only rarely want to be politically active in a deeply committed way and that liberalism protects them from government incursions while allowing them to exercise their powers when the spirit moves them.[15]

Civic activism turns much of liberal democratic theorizing on its head. Where liberal justice tries to distribute resources so that each person can pursue her own good without governmental interference and without having cause to feel envious of her fellows, civic activist justice seeks to enable the effective participation of each individual so that each may pursue her good with the maximal governmental support consistent with all the other goods being pursued within the state. Where the liberal looks, then, for the fair distribution of resources or primary goods (property and talents), civic activists look for fair distribution of participation and participatory skills. Where the essential feature of the liberal self is the ability reflectively to judge and then to choose on the basis of such reflection, the essential feature of the civic activist self is to act skillfully in concert with others to perpetuate or change the republic.

The essential objection that liberals have against civic humanism, which applies as well to civic activism, is that it insufficiently protects individuals from governmental coercion to adopt certain goods—for example, the state-sanctioned prescription of religious practice. In a civic humanist or activist state, citizens are obliged to promote each others' goods only insofar as some association has brought them into recognition as goods in the public discourse. If a given religion is not recognized as a good, the government can use its coercive power to curtail the practice. But then it looks as though a bare majority might disestablish certain goods.

Our general answer is that this objection is based on a misunderstanding of the Western way of life. Thus, to the extent that this problem exists, it is an artifact of liberalism itself. This answer leads us beyond the more traditional accounts of civic humanism. Recall that the picture of the individual in the liberal accounts is that of an individual who has been inculcated into the goods of her culture. She has, on this account, a fair number of the virtues. And on the basis of her personal experiences and the best experiences that have been transmitted to her by inculcation, she reflects both on the practices and beliefs she has been brought up in and on the life options that are currently available to her. On the basis of this reflection, she may alter her current practices and beliefs as she chooses among the cultural options available. Curiously, according to the liberal account, religion and sexual orientation would be among the current practices or cultural options. We say "curiously" because if this story is suited to anything important, it seems most suited to the choice of a college or graduate school, perhaps even a career. For many, a religion is not chosen; God chooses the believer. Religious people do not decide to convert or to reaffirm their faith. They are called to. The notion of endorsing God's choice on reflection would seem as sensible, meaningful, and doable as endorsing physical reality on reflection. (Skeptics have shown that once one finds a kind of reflection that enables one to doubt physical reality, one cannot use that reflective mode to endorse physical reality and answer the skeptic.) To be fair, liberals do not usually claim that we choose or alter our sexual orientation, but they do claim that on reflection we choose whether to continue engaging in some sexual practice. As in the case of religion, in the sexual case many would probably contend that desire overcame whatever resolutions they made in moments of reflection. Given this unrealistic picture of a society of reflective individuals choosing what they consider the best way of life that has been handed down to them, each individual could, as the liberal claims, arrive at choices that were entirely reasonable but depended so much on personal experience that she could not make them seem reasonable to more than a few of her fellow citizens.

Civic humanists and activists do not think that choices are made or even ratified on the basis of reflection as depicted in the liberal account. Like the liberal account, the civic activist account begins with everyone inculcated into the practices and beliefs of the culture. And the civic activist also starts with an individual who has a fair number of the culture's virtues. (Education is important on both accounts. Civic activists need not be squeamish about the invasiveness of education, though. For them, education makes participating citizens.) But for civic activists one virtue that is architectonic, and thereby inextricable from all the others, is participation in public institutions. Indeed, for the civic activist choices are not made by closeting oneself. Rather, the civic activist makes her most important choices by engaging with others.

As we have seen, civic humanists of the past have thought that such public engagement counted only if it was explicitly political. Such a limitation made civic humanism seem obviously inadequate to human life.[16] The basic point for the civic activists, however, is that politically important choices are made in conversations with others in relevant institutions, where the relevant institution is also the one that is likely to be coercive with regard to the practice under discussion. Thus, we may address some of our most important concerns by speaking with other members of our family. For other concerns, we may need to speak with our colleagues at work. For others, we may need to speak to various members of the medical profession. For more vexing concerns, we may need to speak with lawyers, judges, and members of the clergy.

Whomever we speak to in whatever institutional setting, the speaking is in most cases not going to be experienced as producing a judgment in which we say that, on the basis of evidence collected from these reliable sources, including our own experiences, such and such is the best course to follow. Rather, talking to people will bring out concerns that we will come to see as related to the concern we were initially addressing in isolation. We might discover whole bodies of experience and tradition that suggest we should approach the matter in some other way. We will find different weightings of particular experiences that define the concern and make it look different. In this talking, we do not just hear about other ways of seeing things; we try them out, at least imaginatively. But even such imaginative trying out requires that we take into account practices we have previously ignored.

We keep talking until we see things in a way that resolves the initial concern or resolves it nearly enough for practical life. As we have seen, this resolution may take the forms of a reconfiguration, a cross-appropriation, or an articulation. We later seek to show that, where talking is central, cross-appropriation is most likely to resolve the problem. But notice that this is not a resolution solely for the individual who began the process of talking. It is a resolution for all those in the institution who took part in the conversation. If the conversing and institution have been well designed, then the institution will adopt the resolution. This accords with our sense that ideas generally are adopted in institutions if a small cadre of people share some concern and then start talking to more and more people unofficially until the concern takes a certain official shape that enables it to be acknowledged widely, discussed widely, and finally resolved with a consensus.

We have said nothing so far that a liberal need deny. A liberal would simply ask, What about the person who cannot carry along others to produce a shift in the institution? What about the person whose experiences are genuine but too unusual for him to be able to articulate them clearly and bring others to see things as he does? Does this position, this point of view, get eliminated? Our response is twofold. First, since, for the civic activist way of thinking, we come to know our points of view only through discussion or other expressive activity,[17] we would deny that, except in extremely rare cases, a clear point of view can be produced in a closet. It is more likely that the "inarticulate" individual has certain strong intuitions that have not had adequate venting. Perhaps he engages in some practices that he has not been able to make others credit as related in a clear way to the concern under discussion, though he feels quite strongly that they are related. These practices may even in some way be suppressed, but if they are, the suppression will look like a nonadoption. But it could hardly be said that a way of life is being suppressed or not adopted, since the view has never come forth with the clarity of a way of life.

Second, sometimes we must grant that a fairly well-articulated way of seeing things does not carry the day. This often happens in appellate court cases. Two goods compete to define some region of life. People on both sides acknowledge the goods and acknowledge separate places where those goods rule. But people of good will can acknowledge that the community in general would be well served by having one or the other good rule in the domain where the goods compete. People, however, passionately and articulately argue for one good in this domain over the other. What happens in such cases? The parties on both sides are brought to see and experience the legitimacy of both their claim and the opposing claim, and coming to experience this through discussion broadens their range of relevant experience, even if it does not change their minds about which is the top good. When a hard decision must be made for the sake of public order, both winning and losing sides ought to see it as decision that, because it was hard, could be reversed in the future. They both, however, are likely to abide by it if they are convinced that their goods were fairly acknowledged and that order should be preserved.

What about the liberal's extreme case of people criminalizing the other's good? As long as we are describing cases where what is being criminalized is already understood as a good by those who seek it and is therefore a putative good for those who seek to criminalize it, there must have been public articulation of the good already, especially among the group that cherishes it. Criminalization might then occur only when the group that enjoys the good seeks to export it. We might imagine, for instance, the Amish trying to impose the good of farm work over high school education in the larger communities where they live. In most cases, discussions will follow that will strengthen the hold of the good over the restricted group in which both sides recognize it already rules. The whole community's support for it will grow, even though it will probably not be given a high position in the wider community. Indeed, this is precisely what has happened in the case of the Amish and education. Most people value the Amish way of life but would not want their whole community to adopt it. Thus, civic activism normally satisfies the liberal premise that *under no conditions* may we coerce someone with settled convictions to do something against her will so long as her acts are just. Civic activism satisfies this premise *normally* simply by virtue of the way in which engaged democratic discourse works. The liberal examples of unjust coercion depend on someone holding a clear view that has not drawn an association of conversational partners who are able to make a public case.

Of course, liberals would be better off than we are if they could say: "You civic activists at best establish political structures that normally prevent illegitimate coercion; we liberals establish political structures that capture our essential intuition that illegitimate coercion is impermissible and thereby prevent *all* such coercion." But liberals cannot say this. The best they can do is to propose legal hurdles that a majority of citizens would have to overcome before mistreating some minority. But even the Bill of Rights can be minimized by statute and court interpretation, and even Germany's entrenched rights can be overcome by a majority in other ways. Political action of the civic activist sort can always trump—even in liberal democracies—any liberal absolutes. In the political realm, absolutes act only as hurdles, and these hurdles can block genuine discourse as people rest their cases on their rights and not on shared goods. While liberals try fruitlessly to eliminate illegitimate coercion—and resign themselves to the fact that they can at best minimize it—civic activists realize that the minimization of illegitimate coercion is the best we can achieve, and we achieve it by the best means—that is, by maximizing political participation. Consequently, a civic activist state would not try to make rights unwaivable but, in the interest of a full participation, would make them defeasible. Thus, in a community where all religious organizations and atheists are secure because their institutions have survived a certain number of years, there would be no nondefeasible right to church and state separation. A new religion or form of atheism, as well as a new political jurisdiction, might, for a limited time, be allowed to exercise this right as it is exercised today; but no member of one of the established religions or forms of atheism would have retained the right. It would have been waived by relevant forms of due process.

Put in its strongest form, our claim is that the liberal picture of a person alone reflecting on his or her experience and the best models of human life handed down to him or her and then altering a practice or choosing a life option is a picture of social and political breakdown. For some unfortunate reason, this person has been excluded from discussion. He or she has been shipwrecked on an island, so to speak. Clarity and resolutions (though not liberal judgments) come through ongoing discussions that transform us and in the process make us amenable to various resolutions. This is our alternative picture, but in presenting it we have not yet dealt with what is most powerful in the liberal examples.

Most liberals agree that tolerance arose as the solution to religious persecution in Europe,[18] and most liberals still see tolerance as a ground for protecting rights. We continue to need liberalism, they say, because our culture continues to be persecutory. Contrary to the civic activist picture, liberals ask, "Does not our culture refuse to enter into discussion with gays and certain other minorities in roughly the same way it refused discussion with religious sects in the past?" Isn't the gay person, like the recusant priest of old, a paradigmatic case of someone who makes decisions in a closeted condition? Civic activists could answer that in the case of both religious minorities and gays, our society has *not* worked well. We might also add that the list of people mistreated in this way is not short. In the United States it includes women, African Americans, Native Americans, and a host of others. In Europe, Jews would hold a prominent place on the list. But while we must learn from our mistakes, it would be self-defeating to build a political culture on the assumption that we normally act at our worst. It would be equally self-defeating to hold as the chief theoretical justification of our democracy that it prevents us from acting at our worst. (That is in large part what Dworkin's envy test[19] and Rawls's more famous original position under the veil of ignorance are supposed to do.)

Our democracy works, when it works, by articulating goods, even ones that have been ignored or repressed. The case of gays is exemplary. The elimination of antigay statutes and the institution of gay rights do not result from the fact that more and more people are realizing that sexual practices per se are a matter about which justice requires us to be neutral. We are not at all neutral about incest or bestiality. It is not, in other words, that we have agreed that reasonable people cannot come to agreement over the matter of sexual orientation and yet a viable, indeed endorsable, public order must be maintained. Instead what has happened is that more and more gays are coming out of the closet, describing their experiences, and forcing recognition of the fact that they are already at the table while closeted and ought to be openly at the table where important discussions occur. Discovering that a good friend, a trusted colleague, or a family member is gay brings about the necessary change more surely than any argument about abstract rights. Indeed, the backlash statutes are the ones justified by such abstract reasoning insofar as they charge reverse discrimi-nation. Where gay rights are maintained, however, we do not just grant that gays ought simply to be left alone. After the surprise wears off about how pervasive this sexual orientation is and how we have mistreated gays, all but the most doctrinaire of us go about supporting the welfare of gay goods in the same positive way that we support the goods of others identified with groups to which we do not belong. We are saying, in short, that the picture that best describes how religious minorities and gays become valued members of the community with their own goods supported along with the goods of others is the civic activist picture.

A second exemplary case will bring out additional evidence for the case that civic activism focuses on what, in fact, governs a decent, if not just, society. Jews in the United States have enjoyed various rights to tolerance for a long time now. But, like some other minorities, they have in the past been prevented from living wherever they wanted, being offered certain jobs, joining certain clubs, feeling secure in their neighborhoods, and so forth. Indeed, like homophobia, anti-Semitism still makes the lives of some in the United States difficult.

Much of this anti-Semitism, however, has been overcome in just the way that we have described for homophobia. It happened because people met Jews at work, at school association meetings, and in their neighbor-hoods. But in the case of the Jews, it also happened because of imaginative works. It has happened, that is, not because of some stunning electoral or judicial victories, but because Jewish writers such as Saul Bellow, Bernard Malamud, Norman Mailer, Isaac Bashevis Singer, and Philip Roth have taken a leading role in public discourse, speaking as citizens struggling to understand what it is that their country cares about. Thus most college-educated U.S. citizens in the 1960s and 1970s found themselves reading novels by Jews describing their experience of coming to terms with their society. These books recorded well-articulated voices that spoke of concerns easily identified by most U.S. citizens. The tales were about the unsophistication of immigrant parents, about being mistrusted or mistreated because of one's background, about balancing ethnic identity and the desire to be part of the larger society. These concerns were raised in ways that spoke directly to the American sense that the country offered to every new citizen a fresh start and an open space for inventing oneself. All U.S. citizens feel, as these Jewish writers described, the stress of such a notion on the bonds of community, and these writers spoke in ways that illuminated these stresses. So far as anyone in the United States undertook to make sense of these concerns, he or she was also articulating Jewish concerns. Consequently, people found themselves supporting Jewish goods if they wanted to clarify certain more general U.S. goods. This is the subtle way in which we come to share in helping in the work of articulating the goods of others who are speaking.

From this first form of support followed a second way of supporting the goods of Jews. As people became more accustomed to Jewish concerns, they found their own ways to extend practices of good neighborliness to their Jewish neighbors. And insofar as non-Jews already helped their neighbors with their neighbors' projects, so they now found themselves able to help Jewish neighbors. Through these practices, Jews were drawn into communities and into national discussions. Abstract tolerance alone, we argue, would not have brought Jews into the mainstream to this extent, because abstract tolerance can be filled with hatred. Only the familiarity that comes from working closely together and listening to the other's intimate voice in its most expressive form can yield the kind of mutual understanding and acceptance that is necessary for creating a polity.

One might think that the history of African Americans provides a clear case of the victory of liberal principle. After all, it is true that war, constitutional amendment, legislative changes, and signal court cases marked stages of progress in the treatment of African Americans. But viewing the record in this way ignores the important achievements of African-American writers such as Richard Wright, James Baldwin, Gloria Naylor, and Alice Walker who have given voice to an African-American identity. We would argue that this literary identity building is as much responsible for the changed condition of African-American lives as the

Voting Rights Act or any similar legislation. The difference between civic activists and liberals is that we see the development of an identity as responsible for making legislative and court victories actually work, whereas liberals see legislative and judicial victories as the ground for the development of an identity. For them, modern identity formation requires freedom for reflective self-formation. We doubt that such reflective self-formation takes place except in rare circumstances. Normally, detached reflection is parasitical on social involvement, and identities formed through this shared public and political involvement guarantee freedom.

We need to stress that we are not advocating civic activism because its practices are already running political operations and failure to join up means a loss of effectiveness. Rather, we claim that people who grow up in the West sense that their lives are going better when they understand themselves through participation with other people than when they are making judgments in ultimately private individual spaces. We also claim that we have a neater, more intuitively clear, picture of how humans work than liberals have. For liberals, there is the moment of inculcation, of cultural shaping, and then a second moment of reflection and judging. Our picture says that cultural shaping simply continues and expands. Not only does one receive more shaping from one's interactions with others, but one increasingly takes a role in shaping others oneself by virtue of the concerns one brings forth for discussion. The liberal account of reflective judgment is not empty. Sometimes breakdowns in our participatory practices do occur. A lesbian brought up in a fundamentalist religious community might have had no one to talk to about the unusual attractions she has felt. After a few such experiences, she may have to make a judgment alone. But more likely she will remain in a state of confusion until she can find a community in which she can talk through these experiences. These cases are lamentable, and ways should be found to avoid them, but we should not build a politics or model democratic practice on the basis of the environment people find themselves in when breakdowns in participatory practices occur. This would be like modeling our pollution policy on a situation in which someone has "blown the whistle," so that our policy simply encourages more and more whistle blowing. Of course, we want to protect and enable whistle blowers, but we need to remember that our main goal is the positive production and perpetuation of an affordable, clean environment.

In our view, liberalism promotes an aloof resignation by setting up an expectation that the course of one's life is ultimately determined in private judgments. But a judgment made in private reflection is a judgment that one is not ready to follow. Such a judgment grows out of dispassionate ratiocination—the weighing and sifting of ideas and potential consequences. It may tell one that one should change one's heart, but a reflective judgment does not amount to a change of heart. A separate act of heroic will is then required before one can act. A resolution that emerges through group action, conversely, is precisely one that has emerged because one's practices have readied one for it. Liberal life is ultimately made desperately voluntarist by the necessity of taking actions for which one—if one follows the liberal model—has not yet developed skills. Fortunately almost no one acts according to the liberal model. Few responsible people now decide to have a baby without talking to friends, physicians, parents, and partners. And few decide to write a novel without first developing a sensitivity to what a novel is, practicing imaginative writing on a smaller scale, and so on. Those who do decide to have a baby without lots of talking or who write a novel without developing skills and sensitivities are precisely like the lesbian who openly reveals her sexual identity in the fundamentalist community in which she was raised. She may succeed in pulling her life together or fail; the community may adjust or it may fail to. Whatever happens, the woman and the people around her will have less of a sense of how they cultivate their community or their lives and more of a sense of life as a series of unexpected and severe challenges.[20] Such a series of unexpected challenges leaves one resigned to a necessary heroism that breaks with the past and is therefore condemned to an ahistorical meaninglessness. In short, liberalism breeds ahistorical resignation. In civic activism, people participate in producing history.

Liberalism has a famous answer to this sort of challenge. It is the activity of participating in the "public sphere." We take this form of participation to be positively dangerous. We turn now to the public sphere and then to our account of the virtuous citizen in a democracy.

2. Democracy as Civil Society: The Merits and Dangers of the Public Sphere[21]

We sketch briefly an important account endorsed by liberals of one of the principal forms of democratic activity—namely, Jürgen Habermas's discussion of the public sphere. This shows in greater detail the connection between liberal freedom and democratic practices; it also presents us with a foil against which we can elaborate our own understanding of the paradigmatic form of democratic practice, which differs radically from that suggested by the public sphere.

The eighteenth century saw the development of an autonomous public with its own "opinion." Through the circulation of newspapers, reviews, and books among the educated classes and scattered, small-scale, face-to-face exchanges in salons, coffee houses, and (in some cases) political assemblies, there emerged a sense of the nation, or its literate segment, and of an opinion that deserved to be called "public." Public opinion in this sense is not just the sum of our private individual opinions, even where we spontaneously agree. It is something that has been elaborated in debate and discussion and is recognized by us all as something we hold in common. This element of common recognition is what makes it public in the strong sense.

The public sphere is a locus in which rational views are elaborated that should guide government. This comes to be seen as an essential feature of a free society. As Burke puts it, "in a free country, every man thinks he has a concern in all public matters." This is, moreover, different from the ancient polis or republic because the modern public sphere is self-consciously separate from power. It is supposed to be listened to by power, but it is not itself an exercise of power. This extrapolitical status is not just defined negatively, as a lack of power, but is also seen positively: exactly because public opinion is not an exercise of power, it can be ideally disengaged from partisan spirit and thus rational. In other words, with the modern public sphere comes the idea that political power must be supervised and checked by something outside it.

It is not difficult to see how the public sphere can be understood to embody and contribute to the goods of both negative and positive freedoms. As an institution that not only operates (and is seen to operate) outside of power but also operates as a *check* on power, the public sphere has been important to the limitation of state power and hence to the maintenance of negative freedom. For those who emphasize this form of freedom, the public sphere is ideally constituted by media that claim total political neutrality. But the public sphere does not simply play a limiting, whistle-blowing role. It can also serve or disserve, raise or lower, facilitate or hamper the common debate and exchange that is an intrinsic part of conscious, informed collective decision. The public sphere can thus also make an important contribution to positive freedom, for this requires that the rules and decisions that govern us be determined by the people. That means that (1) the mass of the people ought to have some say in what these are going to be and not just be told what they are; (2) this say should be genuinely theirs and not manipulated by propaganda; and (3) it ought to some extent to reflect their considered opinions and aspirations. A healthy public sphere contributes to positive freedom on all three fronts.

The public sphere effectively constituted large classes of citizens *as* citizens. It made them understand that they could be involved in the design of their public lives by engaging other citizens in discussions about the issues of the day. People came to see themselves as citizens not because they were working to get some individual advantage in the design of the state, not because they were voting or requesting elected representatives to vote in a certain way on a certain issue, and not because they were caught up in the general will of some movement, but because in engaging others in discourse, even argumentative discourse, they were contributing their knowledge to shaping a consensus that would eventually influence the elected representatives.

In spite of this constitution of citizens as citizens, however, we do not think that participation in the public sphere, even a revitalized public sphere, should be considered—as Habermas seems to suggest—the paradigmatic form of democratic participation. This is not to dismiss the importance of the public sphere as a bulwark of freedom, negative and positive, but rather to suggest that other forms of participation provide a superior paradigm of democratic citizen virtue. We shall come to see that the dispassionate freedom from power, which is constitutive of the public sphere, blocks the exercise of skills for genuine political action.

There is comfort and safety in the idea that the public sphere lies outside of power. If all the public can do is observe and reflect, one can be secure and at the same time have opinions on everything. If there is no possibility of decision and action, one can look at things from all sides and always find some new perspective from which to put everything into question again. But with everything up for endless critical commentary, the possibility for commitment is undermined. The public sphere becomes a kind of idle talk in which one merely passes the word along. Thus what seems a virtue to detached Enlightenment reason looks like a disastrous drawback to those who understand human activity as requiring commitment and practical rationality.[22]

Furthermore, the public sphere promotes anonymous, ubiquitous commentators who deliberately detach themselves from the local practices—the context and tacit understanding—out of which specific issues grow. Since the conclusions such abstract reasoning reaches are not grounded in the local practices, its solutions are also abstract. They would presumably not enlist the commitment of the people involved and therefore not work even if acted on.

The most serious weakness of the public sphere is its contribution to the loss of practical expertise. What is lost in disengaged discussion is precisely the conditions for acquiring the expertise that is required in dealing skillfully with specific situations. Only by learning to distinguish a variety of situations and how to act appropriately in each can one acquire expertise. This learning in turn requires interpreting the situation as being of a sort that requires a certain action, taking that action, and learning from one's success or failure. There is no way to become an expert without making commitments and thereby experiencing both failure and success.

Without rootedness in particular problems and without the expertise acquired by risking action from a particular perspective and learning from one's successes and failures, the public sphere is reduced to anonymous callers on talk shows, all of whom have opinions on everything and are only too eager to respond to the equally deracinated opinions of other anonymous amateurs. The authorities who appear on more serious media events, such as the United States's *NewsHour with Jim Lehrer*, also speak in the role of professional commentators, heroes of the public sphere, who have a view on every issue but do not have to take a genuine stand on those issues and therefore lack the passionate perspective that alone can lead to risk of serious error and therefore also to wisdom. Listening to such commentators, who take up at least half the time on erudite talk shows, is like listening to articulate chess kibitzers, who have an opinion on every move, and an array of principles to invoke, but who have not committed themselves to the stress and risks of tournament chess and so have no expertise. Since chess masters, like all experts, do not act on principle but have learned from experience to respond appropriately to each specific type of situation, there is no point in debating the quality of a chess move by debating the principles that supposedly support or refute it (except to heighten abstract, public excitement).

Moreover, if one is interested in wisdom, little is to be gained by making the genuine experts enter the public sphere by requiring them to assert the principles on which they allegedly base their actions. And this is what takes up the other half of the time in public-sphere commentary. To ask experts for such principles is to ask for rationalizations that, if implemented, would not result in expert performance.[23] Managers, legislators, and others who are not cut off from power and must therefore make decisions cannot simply rely on their learned wisdom to answer the questions of commentators. Under the pressure of such questions, they tend to look for principles that dictate what they have done and then use these principles to justify whatever stand they have taken. But expertise consists precisely in responding to the particular situation without the aid of principles and rules. What articulate experts more genuinely do, in fact, when defending their recommendations for action before other experts is to come up with interpretive narratives that allow the other experts to see the situation as the expert sees it. This phenomenon, of course, ought to give rise to an ideal of democratic discussion different from that of general, disinterested, rational commentary. For the public sphere to make a serious contribution to genuine participation, then, one would have to tie it back to precisely what it resists: power, partisanship, and local issues.

3. Free Associations: How Citizens Can Change Their Society's Practices

In our opinion, the fundamental act of citizenship in a civic democracy is to form an association in order to advocate a particular change. The virtue of a citizen, as opposed to a subject or any other kind of member of a state, is that a citizen exercises the skill involved in changing what fellow citizens do by changing the way society understands and treats certain phenomena. We call the exercise of this skill *interpretive speaking*. Before we proceed to a general description of this activity, we consider an exemplary case.

Constituting an Organization That Produces Clarity

We take as our exemplary political action group Mothers Against Drunk Driving (MADD). We choose this group not because we agree with its cause and seek passage of the legislation it promotes but because we respect its origin and the methods (so far as we know them) that it employs.[24] MADD started as a group of women who had each experienced the death or maiming of a loved one at the hands of a drunken driver. They discovered that they shared a common experience of extraordinary pain and that they could articulate this pain more clearly by speaking to each other about it. They knew the experience directly, not abstractly, and they had the intuition that this experience was one that, if properly described, would awaken the moral imagination of their fellow citizens to a consensus that (1) certain habits ought to change and (2) the state ought to take a lead in changing these habits by altering the law. As their goals, they proposed an increase in the penalties levied against those who kill or maim while driving under the influence of alcohol and a decrease in the minimum blood level of alcohol that counts as driving under the influence.

Rather than discuss the precise legislative proposals the association generated, however, we consider the mood and actions that led to them. Examining the mood in which MADD saw what practices mattered, and the interpretive speaking with which it responded, will show us that MADD did more than change the laws. The example clarifies the skill of citizen virtue.

Uncovering a Disharmony

When a child is killed by a drunken driver, its mother feels the same sense of injustice as she would if the child had been murdered by a robber. The killer drives to a bar knowing that he is going to drink and knowing that he is going to have to drive home. He bears the child no malice but knows that drinking will impair his driving. He knowingly drinks; he knowingly drives. Yet when he kills, the event is often treated more or less like an accident. In going over and over the similar events they had experienced, the group of mothers who founded MADD began to see that there was an inconsistency in the law, not an incontinence in their overburdened hearts. Their mood became not just grief but bitterness that their society should protect such killers and condone such irresponsible behavior. In this mood, the practices that perpetuate such behavior obtruded as out of tune with practices that promoted socially responsible behavior.

What made the loss bitter was the strength of the social tolerance for the drunken driver. He (and it usually was a he) was often seen as an upstanding member of the community who had just had one drink too many. That behavior, of course, was bad, but what sense would it make to punish a productive member of the community who was engaging in a communally recognized recreation and was simply unlucky? In response to this complacency, the mothers felt not grief alone but a grief mixed with the outrage that comes from seeing and feeling an injustice that is not recognized by the community. This was their motivating mood. And it is our contention that all genuine political action associations are motivated by a similar sense of disparity—not necessarily grief mixed with this kind of outrage but distress mixed with the sense that something important is not receiving recognition by the community.

Before the intervention of MADD on the American scene, drinking was a way of glamorizing oneself as hard-working and successful. One needed to drink in order to wind down from the fast pace of one's important actions. One had a couple drinks at the bar before hitting the freeway or at a cocktail party before going to dinner. This was just obviously the right thing to do; there had to be a calming-down period where normal responsibilities were relaxed. If one worked intensely, one drank intensely. Even the puritan work ethic (so much a part of virtuous American life) seemed to stand behind such social drinking; one needed to earn the right to drink, and then one drank with the self-satisfaction of a man exhibiting his personal salvation.

MADD drew our attention to these background sensibilities and others like them that supported our practices with regard to drinking. Another way to put this is to say that MADD drew our attention to our style of social life so far as drinking was concerned. It was the style of earning rights of relaxation.

Discovering the Disharmony in Multiple Disclosive Spaces

MADD not only called our attention to this style, it made us sensitive to how we drank, and it did this in order to show how our practices worked against themselves. We might have earned the right to a drink or several drinks and the social dissipation that goes with them, but we had not earned the right to drive irresponsibly and kill or maim those whom we did not happen to see while driving drunk. Members of MADD focused on the sense of responsibility and the need for relief from responsibility to show us that our relief was unjustified in our own terms—that is, in terms of our own feelings and sentiments. MADD laid bare the astonishing, often counterintuitive, news that we had to be responsible for our own releases from responsibility.

MADD thus brought us in touch with a problem that is always implicit when we take pride in intense responsibility but nevertheless seek moments of release from responsibility. We must eventually come to terms with the need to take responsibility even for those moments of release. Drinkers must appoint designated drivers at the very least. What MADD showed was that drinking behavior had to change. Drinking could no longer be a matter of "I've worked hard, so I have earned the right to drink hard in the company of those who are like me." Rather, the practice of taking responsibility that lay behind earning a right to drinking had to be transformed into a practice that dominates the style of life that includes drinking. People had to see themselves as responsible for the design of every aspect of their lives and had to see that responsibility running through everything they did.

So now we work responsibly, eat responsibly, engage in sex responsibly, and drink responsibly—all for the sake of making the most out of our lives. Here, however, *responsibly* does not mean moderately or in conformity with some physician's rule but rather as someone who has become expert at enhancing the joys of life while minimizing the pains. The point, again, is not that MADD actually invented or brought into prominence all the new practices just described. Rather, MADD was foremost in focusing us on acting in a responsible style (as opposed to all the alternative styles that we might have adopted in light of what we have learned about work, cholesterol, sexually transmitted diseases, drinking, and so on). And it is in terms of this new style that the laws advocated by MADD make the most sense.

Cross-Appropriating

MADD as a political action group that spoke to various citizens as citizens did not just speak to citizens in the context of urging them to agitate for the change of a particular law. It urged them to put a high priority on acting differently in order to alter society's style for dealing with drinking. Consequently, MADD members talked to physicians, lawyers, educators, executives, and so on. Their mood told them how to approach each group. The embittered grief that led them to see the disharmony between the practices that society took for granted, and the nature of their loss also enabled them to see how different groups of citizens in different subworlds were taking for granted some subset of practices that contributed to condoning drunken driving. The medical community, for example, seemed to take for granted that a few drinks each day was not a crucial danger to health, while some members of that community had already begun to discover that drinking hard liquor daily was itself a health hazard. Thus the mothers' mood made them sensitive to whatever communities and whichever constituents of these communities were useful to them, and it also enabled them to approach these communities with the relevant variations of their story. The mothers did not feel that doing so compromised their deepest feelings; rather, these feelings opened them to the plurality of subworlds that could contribute to their cause and to some of whose concerns they could contribute.

In each case, MADD members found ways to make these groups sensitive to the practice of full responsibility. Indeed, the success of the group lay in its ability to show other groups the advantage of incorporating the practice of full responsibility into their practices. In our introduction and first chapter, we called this activity cross-appropriating. It occurs when people from one world generate a practice and give it to people in another world who can receive and use it but who would not have generated it on their own. The MADD members showed physicians that it made sense for them to train their patients to have full responsibility because patients who drank responsibly would suffer fewer health problems. Such patients were less likely to be involved in automobile accidents, which would save physicians from engaging in depressing, futile attempts to put them back together in operating rooms. The mothers could entice tort lawyers to take up the practice because full responsibility revealed a whole area of liability that was not before visible. Business executives could appreciate having employees who drank responsibly, since it meant fewer employees with morning hangovers, fewer absences in general, and a more productive attitude toward work. The hard-drinking, hard-working ethic did not generate as much productivity as a work-responsibly ethic.

Proposing a Social Change

As MADD drew members of various groups to take on various versions of the practice of full responsibility, the practice gathered greater strength in society. As it took off, people came to associate it less and less with MADD's cross-appropriating activities. People joined health clubs, developed a taste for mineral water, and gave up smoking for reasons that were often not entirely clear to them. Or, rather, where the reasons were clear, they had been clear for a long time and only then seemed persuasive because people were adopting the style of full responsibility. People who engaged in these individual practices were bringing the practice of full responsibility into more and more domains of their lives. This helped MADD members change the law, but more important, people changed their practices because it just seemed no longer as sensible to drink hard liquor or drink very much at all. One worked out, drank a light beer, and saw drunks as unpleasant and irresponsible.

Cross-appropriating allowed MADD, we believe, to become a leader in changing the style of their national culture, much as an entrepreneur could change a style by introducing a new product. What we emphasize here, however, is not the change of style but the means by which practices were changed. While entrepreneurs change practices by means of some product, new practice, or service that people find attractive and must adjust their practices to use, MADD members spoke interpretively to lead people to take up new practices. In this case, they spoke interpretively in a society that had a dominant style, and they caused various subworlds to make changes. When enough changes are made in subworlds, there is a change in the general style of the nation. What is interesting here is that the politics of citizen action need not be limited to subworlds all held together within a single disclosive space with a single style. Insofar as citizens' action groups work by cross-appropriating, they may offer practices to groups with which they share no general style. We develop this possibility in the last section of this chapter.

Developing Relations with Legal Specialists

Finally, the changes that MADD proposed had to be refined as it sought to lead more and more citizens to see how well its legislative proposals concerning definitions of and penalties for drunk driving answered their intuitions that something had to be done. This required the development of a second set of skills. These skills enabled MADD members to determine sensible, enforceable changes in laws. Here they worked not only with citizens as citizens, but with legislative staffers, lawyers, and enforcement officials—those who have experience in handling the law in legislative, administrative, executive, and judicial arenas.

We can now summarize the features of the skill MADD members were using to produce political change. We note that the skill involved in seeing that a personal tragedy has a political significance is precisely the skill of being sensitive to a disharmony, but it is not the sort of disharmony in the relationship of central to marginal practices that we described in discussing entrepreneurial skill. Rather, the disharmony arises from a disparity in the central practices themselves. The political skill consists in (1) constituting an association, (2) discovering a disharmony as a disparity worthy of investigation, (3) determining that the practice that the disparity reveals permeates many domains of life, (4) cross-appropriating practices with people in other disclosive spaces so that they become sensitive to the problem and respond to it in their own domain, (5) proposing a social change in the light of what one is seeing anew, and (6) talking with people who are specialists in making legal changes.

4. Differences between Citizen Virtue and Entrepreneurship

The entrepreneur reconfigures the practices of a culture by marketing a product that requires new practices. The virtuous citizen does something similar in seeking the passage of a new law. The emphasis of the virtuous citizen's activity is not, however, on the new law but on the talking that produces cross-appropriation of practices in order to change the background. Both the entrepreneur and the virtuous citizen, then, create social change, and our next step must be to clarify the differences between their changes.

The MADD members' mood of embittered grief made a disparity in the practices for acting responsibly—a disparity revealed by the acceptance of drunken driving—show up as significant. Their grief also showed that the taken-for-granted social practices perpetuated a wrong and therefore seemed to be something about which all citizens ought to be concerned. Thus their bitterness enabled MADD members to see that their experience did not speak to them only as mothers who had loved ones who were maimed or killed by drunken drivers. It did not even speak to them as mothers. Rather, they saw that their experience spoke to them *as citizens*. That is to say, they saw that if they described what had happened to them from the appropriate perspective, their fellow citizens would react by saying that something ought to be done—that the laws ought to be changed. And these parents then determined that they would risk time, money, and their sense of worthiness as citizens in order to pursue elaborations of their stories to bring about a political change.

Here it is worth reiterating that their very entry into the political process presupposed that their experience spoke to them as citizens and therefore would speak to other citizens as citizens. Their action was not based on personal desires plus the cynical belief that they could use their story to produce enough money to leverage some politicians to vote as they wanted them to on this matter. They did not have the sense that they were in the business of achieving what they wanted through contributing to electoral campaigns. Nor did they involve themselves with the interests of drinkers or argue with drinkers in an attempt to change their behavior. Rather, they were in the business of achieving their goals by appealing to their fellow citizens' concerns about responsibility.

In so appealing they gained experience in speaking to other citizens. This made them more sensitive to who they were as citizens and to the sense of the political world that other citizens shared with them. These mothers turned advocates developed a new kind of expertise. They became experts at understanding the consciences of their fellow citizens. They also developed accessory skills—how to raise funds, produce pamphlets, organize offices, become fiduciaries in handling contributions, plan rallies, and handle all the other activities involved in taking political action on a large scale.

One might wonder, though, why these parents became involved in anything more than finding a way to tell their stories so that they appealed to their fellow citizens as citizens. After all, is not this the true measure of their initial privilege? They had the good fortune (from the state's perspective) or bad fortune (from their personal perspectives) to have had an experience that revealed a weakness in the way the state treated people. Why not leave it to experts to make the necessary adjustments? But if they did this—that is, if they just told their stories to create a need for change— they would not be appealing to their fellow citizens as citizens or as fellow participants in the running of a state. They would be appealing to them as an audience for touching stories or as commentators in the public sphere, whose assent to certain claims they were seeking. Only if the mothers told their stories in a setting where they were taking a stand could the stories become a ground for joining the group or opposing the group—that is, for *acting* on its basis. No comfortable, intellectual middle ground would exist. Only when they told the story in a setting where an action must follow did they appeal to their fellow citizens *as* citizens, as participants in civic life.

5. The Rewards of Civic Action

Two questions remain to be addressed before we can contrast the virtuous citizen and the entrepreneur clearly. First, we need to explain why these mothers should have cared so much about being citizens. Was all the painful effort worth the laws they succeeded in getting passed? And, second, we need to ask, if they had failed to change the laws, would their actions have been meaningless? Answering these questions will enable us to understand the weakness of less exemplary political action groups that fragment politics and to distinguish them from the kind of political participation that the MADD members display. It will also support our civic activist claim that the goods of achieving clarity and serenity in one's life through discussion are the basis of political associations.

It might seem that a description of citizen virtue is complete when it shows the grounds and skills needed by citizens to take action in order to change laws or regulations and thereby make a community better. But such an understanding of citizen virtue makes it into a terribly unpleasant duty. Not only must one deal with one's own distress, but one must also change laws so that others will not have to feel a similar distress. True, success in changing the government in marginal ways often brings some rewards. But one cannot help but think of Dr. Johnson's quip about such successes. He said that he was twice ruined by litigation. "Once I sued and lost," he said, "the other time, I won." The real costs of litigation, like the costs of political action, are so high that any winnings usually fail to cover them. Dr. Johnson was presumably thinking of the costs of time and money, but his point would be even stronger if emotional costs were included in the calculation. For anyone committed to cultivating responsible behavior, political action that could return only rewards of changed legislation or successful litigation would make no sense. If citizen virtue is to make sense *and* be understood as grounded in particular concrete experiences, it cannot be exhausted in making certain regulatory changes or obtaining favorable court rulings. The activity that we call citizen virtue must also speak directly to the motivating distresses that would make people commit themselves to bringing about, for example, a new form of responsibility.

But how can this be? Political action of the sort that MADD engaged in could not stop with changing government regulations. It also had to change a style of drinking and the background practices expressed by that style, for only by making that kind of change (supported and enforced, of course, by changes in government regulation) could the mothers distance themselves from their own tragic experience, compounded of loss and rage. That is, by changing the style of drinking practices, they also changed the practices with which they responded to drinking, and in so doing they distanced themselves from the bitterness that had been part of the pain of losing their sons or daughters. After the change in style of many disclosive spaces, it was as though their bitterness had occurred in another world.

Any implausibility in this suggestion can be removed by considering another example. Since the advent of feminism, many women have come to find married life difficult or even unbearable. It is not that they now see their husbands and children as oppressive but that they feel they cannot have full lives caring for houses, husbands, and children. Many women, moreover, express a sense that they have awakened from a powerful self- or social deception. "How," they ask, "could I have been so hoodwinked into thinking that housekeeping and caretaking would be satisfying for most of my adult lifetime?" "I married too young," such women say, or "I didn't know myself when I married." The formulations are numerous, but they all articulate the same experience. These women cannot make sense of what they were thinking and feeling when they married—that is, they cannot retrieve the feelings they had in such a way as to see that they could have made sense.

If we attend to cultural practices and the styles that they express, we can see what has happened. When these women married and became housewives, they entered a world that offered room for them to express themselves. Mothers regularly met for coffee after their children went off to school to compare notes on how their families were doing. They belonged to charitable organizations that did important community work. They supported their husbands' careers by giving cocktail parties and so forth. And they compared ideas with other women, their friends and colleagues, who were in similar positions.

But the world changed. Housekeeping and caretaking came to seem an unfulfilling practice. Conversational openness among housewives came to be seen as mere gossip. The role of housewife did not permit women to express themselves—as producers of wealth, as fully sexual beings, or even as beings capable of the full range of feelings (such as rage) that their husbands and children could express. So new practices developed for women that tended to marginalize the already subordinate housewife style and its practices. Women who had entered marriages as housewives did so to gain certain identities. But when, for whatever reasons, those identities became marginalized, marriage began to feel like a trap in which women came to feel empty. And from this position, living in a world where some women had developed assertive, full-throated styles of acting, they could not retrieve a sense of how they had felt before. The coordination of practices into a world that would have made sense of the old feelings was no longer there. Consequently, these women could not feel a full sense of themselves as housewives filling one satisfying role among others; they could only feel repugnance at their narrow fate.

This example has been developed at length because we assume that many readers will recognize it. In this case, it is precisely because the style of practices according to which people have lived their lives has changed that those people no longer have any ground for making sense of their past feelings. With this example in mind, we can better understand the claim made earlier about MADD and citizen virtue. We claimed that it would be sufficient for citizen virtue to answer to its motivations if it changed the style of the practices of the community. Only when the style or coordination of practices is changed can citizens' action relieve the distress that compelled action in the first place. Once the change occurs, the particular quality of the distress seems to be part of a distant world, and the distress therefore is only partially retrievable. Changing a style as part of a political action, then, is the way a citizen as citizen responds to those distressing experiences where part of the distress comes from a disharmony between action and belief in a community. Whether the laws are changed or not is only incidental. Indeed, if the laws were changed without a change in style, MADD's legal achievement would only continue to remind the mothers of their grief as people resisted or ridiculed the unpleasant new laws.

6. Interpretive Speaking

MADD members moved people to see things in many different and new ways that led to a change of style; they did not speak to persuade others to take particular actions such as voting for candidate X. Because such groups change the coordination of background practices and not just regulations, we call their transformative kind of speaking *interpretive* and not *persuasive*. We call speaking interpretive when it allows some practice, thing, or identity to appear as worthy of consideration by a mixed community—that is, a community composed of a wider range of interests than those of a group of professionals or technicians.

Interpretive speaking consists in (1) articulating an experience that does not fit comfortably with the normal, commonsense descriptions of life in the polity, (2) uncovering the grounds of this unusual experience (in the MADD case, these were practices of something we might think of as full responsibility, the kind parents have for their children), and then (3) offering some description of the relation of these marginal practices to the dominant practices. Clearly, such a description amounts to advocacy of some sort—that is, an assertion that the marginal practices and the experiences they produce ought either to remain marginal or to become dominant. But the real work of interpretive speaking comes in making people sensitive to the experiences and the practices behind them. That additional sensitivity will be incorporated into the lives of citizens in the measure that the marginal practice is useful in their lives.

We assert that interpretive speaking is the highest form of political discourse because only interpretive speaking forces people to (1) remain true to the concrete experience of their subworlds, (2) acknowledge and respect the different experiences in other subworlds, and (3) seek opportunities for cross-appropriating practices from other subworlds. In other words, interpretive speaking emphasizes expertise, recognition of difference, and collaboration. Other modes of speaking, which we discuss shortly, fail in these terms, and they fail largely because they give too important a place to detached reflection.

In the MADD example, we see no important place for detached reflection and strategies based on it. Rather, we suppose an organization like MADD starting when two or more mothers, whose children have been killed, start talking about their grief and their sense that they have been wronged. At some point in the conversation, one suggests that they involve more people like themselves in this conversation. They then exercise skills that they have learned for putting on meetings, forming clubs, and so forth to enlarge the conversation. They meet. One set of conversational possibilities leads to another. The term *responsibility* or some other like it begins to take on new meaning. Someone says that she thinks that the way they are talking about responsibility and grief reminds her of what is being said in some other professional organization; and then someone else chimes in with the idea of presenting ideas about responsibility before that other organization. Joint meetings are set up, and MADD is off and running. There is no moment when the mothers need to stand back and form a strategy based on their needs, desires, and the objective situation of the political world. In their coping, the mothers make feelings, hopes, desires, cares, appointments, and so forth explicit, but this is all done in order to work out what the immediate situation calls for. One can be sensitive to situations only if one remains skillfully coping in them. One can even propose changes to the law in this way, by saying, "Would proposing such and such a legislative change make clear what we are all feeling and thinking about?" Such a way of proceeding is quite different from standing back and asking about an idealization of justice: "Do we see that justice would be served if the law regarding this class of activities were changed in the following way?" The first question is involved, the second detached, though the proposed law may be identical in the two cases. This is a specific case of the priority of involved over detached coping that we discussed in chapter 1.

What about the various forms of persuasive discourse? Other forms of speech certainly have a place in the polity, but we argue that the polity ought to be structured in such a way as to discourage forms of discourse that are most distant from interpretive speaking. When an issue goes to such a broad community that few can have the experiences to which a citizens' action group points, then discourse must be, at least at first, what we call principled speaking. Instead of relying on the description of a common experience, this kind of speaking depends on general principles that have been abstracted from the way of life of the community as a whole. Political discourse of this sort argues that one claim or position fits better with these abstracted principles than another claim or position. Or this kind of discourse argues that a particular abstract principle must be added or subtracted based on its coherence with other principles such as justice. It is on this level that most academic political discourse takes place, and we see it as a falling off from interpretive speaking by virtue of its appeal to peoples' abstract principles rather than to their expertise. It is the kind of talk that pervades the public sphere. This is to say that on a divisive issue such as abortion, those who have undergone abortions or have been partners with those who have undergone abortions, physicians, pastors, judges, and others who have dealt with the various effects of the availability or unavailability of abortion, and others with concrete experiences should be attended to in the formulation of laws rather than those whose principles lead directly to accepting or condemning abortion.

When principled political discourse fails, its place is taken by a wide range of political speech that we can characterize as expedient. Expedient speaking includes negotiation, horse trading, and manipulation. Many different kinds of discourse fall into this category. The appeals made here are to the benefit of particular interests independently of how they are related to the claim being advocated. The typical form of such speaking is, "If you vote with me on X, I will vote with you on Y." But such speaking can also be a matter of coming together over what each side can "live with." And it can fall as low as threats such as "If you don't support us on this, we will do everything we can do to destroy you personally and politically."

All these forms of political discourse exist in every polity. We propose that the polity should be structured so as to encourage interpretive speaking as much as possible and to discourage in increasing degrees the other forms of political discourse. Restructuring government so that local levels have more authority and money, we think, would tend to give people with concrete experience a larger voice. Encouraging interpretive speaking should not be difficult once people see that changing the background practices to correct a disharmony in a meaningful, historical way (not by invasion) is the most effective and least divisive way of achieving their ends. Political action groups are effective precisely because, by changing the meaning of people's lives, they do an end run around normal, principled, and expedient political speaking.

7. In Defense of the Free Association

No doubt some will feel that the whole argument so far has been motivated by an idealistic or naive account of one particular political action group and its operations. To this charge we answer that we acknowledge that many political action groups lose their grounding and become corrupt. We believe that this generally happens because there is so little understanding of disclosive skills, interpretive speaking, and the other history-making practices. We therefore began our account with a fairly clear and pure case, but the case is not unique. Environmental associations and neighborhood groups have produced initiatives to change city charters, laws, and practices in communities throughout the

United States. Political action groups that work by reinterpreting relevant practices and not by acting as bullies are not the rarity that those who dislike political action groups would make them out to be.

An important distinction needs to be made here. Many dislike political action groups because they identify such groups as making political changes they simply do not endorse. One could hate democracies for the same reason, and we believe such narrow consequentialism leads to no examination of the political, just a veiled statement of partisan preference. We are interested instead in how political action groups promote their causes and in whether there is a general tendency in them toward either principled or expedient discourse.

Three main charges are made against political action groups. The first is that they tend to fragment the political process—that the people who join them are caught up in the single issue for which the group stands and do not pay equal attention to all the other issues that vex their communities. Consequently, in the world of political hard ball, they will scratch the back of whoever scratches theirs. This means that they are willing to damage the general good for the sake of advancing their own concerns. A second charge is that political action groups tend to form a bevy of elite lobbies to whom legislators pay disproportionate attention. This leads to legislation that might satisfy these elites but is not in the interest of the nation as a whole. A third charge is that successful political action groups become so powerful that they spend their time fighting each other. This leads to short-term coalitions based on mere expediency. When this happens, they tear apart the national communal identity, so that the nation seems to be nothing more than a contingently established container of conflicting interests. And since these groups do not find much solidarity with each other, they produce a general gridlock where most legislative proposals are concerned. If these charges were accurate, political action groups would end up producing widespread dissatisfaction with all political activities.

Notice, though, that these breakdowns in political action, as we conceive it, take place for contingent reasons of expediency, not because of anything implicit in the workings of political action groups. Rather, if a political action group starts from an experience that has political implications, the driving force behind the group requires it to show how this experience is linked to the national interest. Therefore, as the group develops, it must create an ever more refined sense of how its interest converges with the national interest and practices. When such groups resist simple expediency, they help focus the questions, concerns, and tendencies that constitute the national interest rather than fragment it. And only if they help in this way will they effect sufficient change in the background practices to change their worlds.

Consequently, when political action groups are pushed to act according to sheer expediency, they act against their own best interest—indeed, against their own driving force, which is to resolve disharmonies in ways that remove the distress of their members. Once a political action group acts for the sake of sheer expediency to make a political change, it will no longer be in the business of changing practices by making more and more subworlds resonate with its core experience. Changing the culture's practices by cross-appropriation will have been given up for the sake of influencing someone in a way that is only indirectly related to the core experience. The group may achieve the desired political result, but the new law or new regulation will seem oppressive to those who suffer under it and unclear to those who accept it but who have not developed a new style of life to go along with it.

This is what has happened in many large Western civil democracies. The laws seem to be expedient policy decisions made to please some political action group or other and are thus cut off from any grounding experience that has been made clear to the majority of citizens. This is to say that Western democracies have lost the sense of the passage of a law as an event that shows us what we are becoming. And since this is the case, those who joined the successful political action group in the first place will not have dealt with the mood of distress that first got them going. They will not have changed the styles of their communities and so will still feel their distress as plainly as ever. We can hear this when activists who seem to have received what they wanted are still obviously unsatisfied and complain about the dilution of their proposals by the courts.[25]

The fact that the distress remains gives us exactly the clue we need to solve the problem. If with the changes in regulation the distress still remains, others ought to be sensitive to it. Even if the source of the distress is partially relieved by political measures already, others should form groups. The more that people who have the skills to form political action groups do form those groups, the better, because certain groups will be likely to distinguish themselves by not giving in to expediency. In Germany the Greens have resigned elected positions on city councils because they have found the pressures to cave in to expedient solutions too strong. And with more groups, people who want their distress relieved will be likely to jump from the group that offers the expedient solution to the group that offers real healing and real change. Moreover, the more groups, the more choices legislators will be have among them for campaign contributions and the like. They will not need to support the group that offers the expedient contribution, so they will be in a position to take contributions from groups with whose core experiences they resonate—that is, with whom it makes sense to cross-appropriate practices.

In short, we argue that political action groups harm the quality of political life only when they fall away from the practices that sustain them. If this is true, then strengthening these sustaining practices should produce more than enough valuable new political action groups to make up for the distortions produced by the decadent ones.

With a genuine choice, citizens will join groups that best offer the possibility of the kind of historical change, not regulative change, they need. Citizens in a democracy want to change their lives, not a regulation here and there. Thus more action groups and a wider dissemination of disclosive skills should end up correcting the problems produced by desperate expediency. The only thing, we claim, that would prevent a sufficiently representative variety of groups from forming would be a misallocation of disclosive skills. That, indeed, may be the severest problem in our democracies. Wealthy children are taught skills of historical disclosing, while the rest are left to learn such skills according to happenstance. That problem must be solved by a redistribution of opportunities to acquire disclosive skills and thus of the skills themselves.

8. Customary and Detached Political Activity

We now return to the questions that opened this chapter: How do virtuous citizens depend on what we consider to be customary citizen behavior, and how can we distinguish this behavior from its detached form, which inhibits citizen virtue?

In our discussion of the development of theories of democratic action, we claimed that the public sphere gave us a seductive description of genuine citizen action. We claimed that the description was deficient, however, because it constituted citizen action as a detached, riskless commenting on matters in which the citizens have no direct involvement and hence no expertise. Our account of virtuous citizen action in political action groups remedies these deficiencies. We now want to examine the nature of a good citizen's citizenship when he or she is not participating in a political action group. We want to see what structures of public life *enable* participation in such groups. We call such public life and the structures that support it *customary democracy*, and we will contrast the good citizens of customary democracies with the good citizens of the public sphere.

The public sphere, as we have noted, effectively constitutes large classes of citizens *as* citizens. It makes them believe that they can be involved in the design of their public lives only by engaging other citizens in discussions about the issues of the day. People come to see themselves as citizens not because they work to gain some individual advantage in the design of the state, not because they vote or request elected representatives to vote in a certain way on a certain issue, and not because they are caught up in the general will of some movement, but because, in engaging others in persuasive discourse, they contribute their knowledge to shaping consensus that eventually influences the elected representatives. A citizen comes to be understood as one who debates issues with others in such a way as to shape the eventual resolution of the debate in the legislature, courts, or executive departments of state. A good citizen is defined as someone obliged to offer his or her views. Unfortunately, the public sphere has developed in a way that turns most political talk into deracinated commentary, but it also has had another effect. In creating citizens, the public sphere creates human configurations whose actions and discourse extends into political action groups and also comes to inhabit the customary practices for dealing with people. One acts as a citizen not just in debating principles in coffee houses and salons, not just in the pages of newspapers and on talk shows, but also in conversations with friends, relatives, and neighbors.

Fortunately, these conversations require a different dynamic that is not easily overridden by that of the public sphere. Talking with friends, relatives, and neighbors includes within it a kind of reticence that is foreign to the public sphere's mode's of speaking. In a situation where one is always dwelling with friends, relatives, and neighbors, one is already familiar with their views and tendencies of thought and action. And in such cases not speaking is as much of a way of dealing with these tendencies as speaking. Spouses do not say everything to each other that they think could serve for general family improvement, only those things that are likely to make a real difference in the way their lives are conducted. So while one effect of the public sphere is to produce citizens like Edmund Burke's stable boy, who could comment on every public issue that came before Parliament, sensitivity to talking, independent of the public sphere, also produces citizens who understand that they ought to speak only when they base their speaking on their firsthand knowledge of practices at stake in the issue at hand. Moreover, implicit in this form of talking is the trust that others will not talk every time they have an opinion but only when they have expertise. It may seem that we are simply describing normal talking here, and we would like to think so. But the democratic political structures appropriate to this model of citizen speech are quite different from those required by the public sphere.

The structures necessary to support a public sphere are a popularly elected and powerful legislative body *and* a powerful and effective media and salon culture. The job of citizens when the public sphere dominates political action is to argue so as to achieve a consensus on the terms of discussion of the public issues. Since legislators are elected and must answer to the articulated concerns of the public, they must reach decisions that are intelligible in terms of the public debate. For this reason, citizen action in the public sphere becomes an intellectual's game. In speaking to the press and speaking in salons, one must speak to those who do not have hands-on knowledge about each issue. Consequently, one must speak in terms of general principles. Indeed, getting the precise general principles and general terms in which the debate is to be mounted is the point of public sphere activity. Legislators must also become like intellectuals, for once the debates and the terms of the debate are presented to them by the media, they must then make actual decisions and defend them in terms that the media can understand and report on. Legislators must defend their actions using arguments that are responsive to the facts, to the general principles they and their constituents hold, and to ways of reasoning from facts and general principles that make sense to their constituents.

The form of citizenship that includes reticence and practicality, however, needs different structures. This form of citizenship requires a popularly elected and powerful legislative body but not such a powerful press. For public life does not amount to making arguments that are reported in the press and that shape debate. Rather, when a disharmony occurs in the activities of the state, citizens, in our model of customary citizenship, either remain reticent because they see that they have no concrete experiences that illuminate the problem or visit their elected representatives. Such visits make sense only if there is a basic trust that citizens will visit elected representatives only when they have something concrete to say. Moreover, the talk of the customary citizen will not be the principled talk of the intellectual in the public sphere. It will be much more pragmatic. Citizens will suggest that the legislator look at the problem on the basis of this or that practice with which the citizen is quite familiar. Citizens will be talking in terms of their expertise, whether they are university professors who have expertise in the foreign cultures that are doing business with their state or farmers or small-store owners speaking about concrete problems that need legislative solutions. Since citizens will be asking legislators to look at particular problems on the basis of particular practices, the legislative solutions suggested will be fairly narrow and not based on broad general principles. Such a way of proceeding assumes that legislators are not intellectuals but are elected because they represent the general ordering of goods or values of their district and *because they have the skill of being receptive* to the suggestions of their constituents. This is to say that if a constituent asks the legislator to look at the matter from a certain perspective based on a specific practice, the legislator will be sensitive enough to practices and different ways of looking at things to be able to do so.

What we have just described is precisely what happens between legislators and those of their constituents whom they have learned to trust as *reticent citizens*, who speak on the basis of expertise that comes with concrete experience. The problem is that such constituents tend today to be limited to the legislator's friends. Indeed, customary democracy shows more of the trust characteristic of friendship than does the public–sphere democracy with which many of us are more familiar. This is why those familiar with the public sphere forms of political participation are often suspicious of what is going on in the democratic activity of private meetings. It may even look to them like special pleading and corruption.

Just as our rationalist practices encourage entrepreneurs to think that they would be better able to cope if they could make their skills explicit as sets of rules, so reticent citizens will feel that they could better serve their country if they could *explain* clearly why they think their representatives should vote a certain way, rather than merely insisting that if the representatives shared their hands-on experience, they would see things their way. In our rationalizing world, appealing to ineffable, intuitive wisdom seems like special pleading or a kind of demagoguery. Reticent citizens thus feel compelled to discover and announce the beliefs and principles that justify their recommendations. Everyone understands that only a recommended action that can be seen to follow from critically tested principles can be rationally accepted or rejected. If they succumb to this temptation, customary citizens lose touch with their expertise and become detached contributors to public debate.

Our description of the public sphere already shows us what normally happens when political action becomes detached from the background practices of reticent, trustful talking. With this detachment, customary reticent citizens become intellectual citizens—citizens who have an opinion on every matter. Such citizens do not elect legislators or leaders who have the same ordering of goods or values that they have and who are ready to listen. Rather, they elect people who have similar intellectual habits, who give voice to similar general propositions. When people vote and act politically in terms of ideas instead of practices, political life becomes much more embattled. Ideas, like money in detached business actions, do not readily restrict themselves to particular situations where they make the most sense. One may have practices for dealing with farmers that are different from practices for dealing with small shop owners that differ again from practices for handling newspaper owners. But as soon as these practices are thematized in terms of ideas, the ideas must be shown to be consistent and grounded in larger general ideas. If this is not the case, someone, it is claimed, will be getting special treatment. Ordering principles will be developed, and much political debate will turn on the ordering principle or political ideology to be instituted rather than on the practices that actually determine how people live.

Worse, instead of becoming an intellectual citizen, one may cease to be a citizen at all in any interesting way. Instead, one becomes an individual optimizer of desires who sees the political system as a massive game—like the market system—for attaining one's ends. A description of this form of life would mirror what we said about detachment from market-economy practices. Instead of gaming economic practices, such a person would game political practices.

Finally, the balancing of ideological dispute in various kinds of agreement comes to be a matter for theory. Political scientists and philosophers seek to define the conditions under which political disputes (modeled on ideological disputes) can be said to be resolved democratically. Here ideal speech communities or conditional ignorance are theorized to ensure the rationality needed for democratic or just agreement. Other theorists determine the conditions under which agreement can be said to be reached freely. We hear then about the marketplace of ideas. In all these cases, the theorists start by looking at political action that has become detached from customary practices for citizens' talking. The effect is that the ways of reaching agreement they prescribe make citizen action groups and active participation that is practical rather than ideational look inferior to ideological disputes. Indeed, they come to appear as antirational attempts to change people's minds and are therefore discouraged. We have tried to show, however, that democracy makes better sense in the hands of those sensitive to concrete anomalies, those who take risks, cross-appropriate, and change the cultural practices that determine our form of public association.

9. The Politics of Cross-Appropriation on an International Scale

So far we have examined how political action groups and interpretive speaking work within a national culture. But since cross-appropriation, as we have described it, does not require a large disclosive space with a single style, cross-appropriation politics has the advantage of working where there are many local worlds (or nations) related to each other in ad hoc ways. If national cultures are becoming fragmented so that they act like a mosaic of different local worlds, international relations are already in this condition, and certain groups, commonly called *new social movements*, are already engaging in the politics of cross-appropriation on this international level. The feminist movement is one; the environmental movement is another. To illustrate international citizen virtue, we focus on a small group within the environmental movement.

Although we may think that we can characterize the one thing that the environmental movement is about—for instance, saving the planet's biosphere—even the meaning of "saving the biosphere" divides many in the movement. Should environmentalists preserve the biosphere in its current state? Should they return the biosphere to some better state? Or should they simply try to decide what the nature of the biosphere is, develop a list of what harms it, and then reduce those practices? We can see further division over the *nature* of the biosphere. Is it like an animal or a plant or a mechanism? More divisions could grow up just in determining what counts as the biosphere. The kinds of differences around the sorts of actions needed to save the biosphere are even more diverse, ranging from attacking those who damage the biosphere to practicing passive resistance, funding ecology clubs, purchasing as much of the surface of the planet as possible, and supporting scientific enterprises for cleaning up the planet.

In the environmental movement these divisions are not merely theoretical. For each of the divisions we have mentioned, there is a corresponding association that defines itself in terms of that division. And there are many more, each different from the ones we have mentioned. There are hunters' groups interested in conserving their hunting grounds and aboriginal groups interested in conserving not only their hunting grounds but also their sacred lands. From this we can see that it would be impossible to come up with a single, interesting, substantial claim that one could say united all members of the environmental movement.

So in what sense can we say that this movement has unity? First, each group is related to other groups by specific principles and practices that they share. The principles and practices a group shares with scientists, however, may be widely different from the principles and practices it shares with hunters' groups. Second, the way in which each group interprets its own interest is modified by the activities of all these other groups. So, for instance, if more groups like Greenpeace and Tree Spikers proliferate, other less interventionist groups would attract support by bringing out their less interventionist character.

To see a social movement in action, we look at the case of Chico Mendes. Mendes, the founder of one of the many groups devoted to saving the rainforest, started out as a small subsistence rubber tapper. As cattle ranchers took control of larger and larger swaths of land, he realized that he and his way of life would soon disappear. Out of a simple desire to preserve his way of life, Mendes organized his fellow rubber tappers into the Rubber Tappers' Union. Mendes started out being interested only in ways of improving the lives of the rubber tappers by setting up cooperatives to sell their products and preserving the rainforest as their resource. However, he soon formed alliances with others whom he could help and who could help him. These alliances were not merely expedient. Each group learned from the others, broadened its perspective, and changed its strategies and style.

The best example is the interaction between Mendes, representing those who were trying to keep the forest as a means of earning a livelihood, and the environmental groups, interested either in preserving the rainforest to save species or in protecting it to save the planet from global warming. The coalitions Mendes formed were international, and each group cross-appropriated to itself some practice or understanding from the others. The Washington environmental lobbies, for instance, discovered they had people, not just birds and trees, to fight for in their rainforest programs. The environmentalists in Brazil saw that if the rubber tappers' cooperatives could be made to work, they could provide an alternative to the old-fashioned large-capital enterprises that alone seemed able to tame the Amazon. As one reporter said:

[The rubber tappers] recognized that common ground was shared by the big Washington environmental lobbies, budding environmental organizations in Brazil, the trade union movement in the Amazon, and development agencies such as Oxfam: they all wanted to preserve the Amazon in a sustainable way for the people who lived there.[26]

Mendes saw that if the rural unionists broadened their goals to include the fight for the environment, the movement could gain enormous strength, but the cross-appropriating of these diverse movements was no easy task. Andrew Revkin reports:

No one thought it would be easy to sustain this new bond between the rural unionists and the environmentalists. After all, the environmental organizations outside Brazil would have to acknowledge that people lived in the pristine forests. And the hard-line labor groups in Brazil would have to recognize that environmental questions were not just superficial issues for the idle middle class; Brazilian labor unions and political parties had usually spurned environmental causes for that very reason.[27]

Indeed, the styles and concerns of the various groups that Mendes cross-appropriated together could hardly have been more diverse:

The struggle of the tappers had always been cast as one of justice and free labor and land rights. . . . [Now] Mendes understood that the environment itself—the extraordinary biological splendor of the Amazon—could help them win support and save their way of life. He recognized the possibility that with the environmental issue on their side, the rubber tappers might well be able to have a voice in the national debate over the Amazon.[28]

Many rubber tappers saw such a union as merely expedient:

One of the more politically minded tappers, Osmarino Rodrigues, initially saw the environmental issue as a bit bourgeois, something of luxury. Even after he became convinced that this strategy would help the tappers, his persistent impression was that the alliance "joined . . . the useful and the pleasant."[29]

But Mendes's approach was not merely expedient. He "was not just quick at absorbing the new environmental approach, but quick at making it a fundamental part of his mental and emotional framework. Mendes equated ecology with his life-long love for the forests in which he had grown up; he was inherently an environmentalist."[30] As he showed visitors through the forest, he "stopped every few minutes to pick up some nut or fruit or scrap of wood and explain what it was used for."[31]

"Although the tappers continued to voice their old calls for social justice, workers' rights, and agrarian reform—standard issues of the political left—at the urging of Chico Mendes . . . they modified their message in a subtle but important way. For the first time, they made a simple call for the preservation of Amazonia—not only for the sake of its peoples, but for its own sake as well."[32] The new manifesto of the rubber tappers—"We demand to be recognized as [the] genuine defenders of the forest"—revealed that something had really been cross-appropriated. Mendes started stressing that the future of the rainforest did not have to be bound to rubber. "One goal of the movement thus became the promotion of research into other forest products, ranging from oils and nuts to crops such as cocoa, which grows naturally in the shade of the canopy."[33] Mendes then proposed that the tappers call for a special system of agrarian reform to be established for the Amazon basin that would create areas reserved for "extractive" activities such as rubber and nut harvesting.

After interacting with Mendes, the Washington environmentalists also understood their work in a new way:

Here was a movement by a productively employed local population that had a vested interest in keeping the rainforests as they were. The existence of Chico Mendes and his tappers' union meant that Brazil could no longer make nationalistic claims that the fight to save the Amazon was merely a case of foreign ecologists meddling in Brazilian affairs.[34]

When the struggle was seen in this new light, the Amazon Indians could also join the movement. The Union of the Indigenous Nations talked of the alliance of the forest people and backed the idea of declaring the rainforest an extractive reserve. They pointed out that Indians extract fourteen or fifteen native products. In a meeting that Mendes planned, two hundred rubber tappers and Indians convened in Rio Branco to celebrate formally the Alliance of the Peoples of the Forest. As Mendes recounts the story in a documentary film:

People became amazed at the time, saying, "Indians and rubber tappers together? Didn't you fight before? Weren't you enemies?" . . . And we responded, "We understand today that our fight is the same one. The struggle of the Indian should be the same as that of the rubber tappers. . . . We should be together today to fight to defend our Amazonia."[35]

This new alliance presented the first prospect of an end to a century of animosity and violence between the two groups.

At this point the Brazilian government became interested:

One study showed that a rubber tapper family—in areas where the tappers were free of rent and other obligations to the rubber bosses— earned more than $1,250 in cash in an average year from the sale of rubber and nuts, and that did not include the value they gleaned from the forest by hunting, raising manioc and other crops, gathering fruits and building materials, and the like. The total income was estimated at $2,400, more than double what a family in the slums of Rio Branco scraped together. And the quality of life among free tappers was uniformly considered far superior to the life of those who moved into town. If research were undertaken to boost the rubber harvest and develop markets for other tropical products, the extractive reserve could prove to be a positive component in the Brazilian economy.[36]

In England, whose industrial cities and deforested hills seemed to have little in common with the green wilderness of the Amazon, the link was labor:

To the English, Mendes was the incarnation of a typical British trade union leader of the 1920s, when the unions were first fighting for power. As [one leader] put it, "Chico was the person—there always was somebody—who cemented the brothers together. . . . If you'd said he was a rubber tapper that didn't matter." The Guardian, the Observer, and other papers were quick to pick up on the story.[37]

The rubber tappers not only resonated with labor; they also related themselves to business. The rainforest came to be regarded as a source of goods that could be marketed worldwide:

Entrepreneurs . . . were lured to the Amazon, hoping to develop everything from body oils to pharmaceuticals based on products taken from the rainforest in ecologically sound ways. Ben & Jerry's Homemade, Inc., introduced Rainforest Crunch, an ice cream containing Brazil nuts harvested by Acre's rubber tappers.[38]

So long as tappers asked the developed world to subsidize the rainforest, they were seen as blackmailers. But when they sought from the developed world low-interest loans to sustain their work collecting rubber, nuts, and other valuable commodities, they could be seen to be acting as businessmen.

Chico Mendes, unfortunately, was murdered shortly after he formed an association that was developing these practices, but it is important for us to see how Mendes developed relations among the various groups with which he was associated. Starting in one group, Mendes tried to bring out the problems that were causing its failure. At the same time, he paid close attention to what was happening in other groups that had similar interests to his own. The Rubber Tappers' Union formed coalitions with groups fighting for social justice such as Oxfam and the Pastoral Land Commission; groups opposed to environmental destruction such as the Institute for Economic Botany and the Environmental Defense Fund; the Indians, as represented by the Union of Indigenous Nations; workers' groups such as the Brazilian Trade Union Congress and the Landless Workers Union; and political parties such as the Brazilian Socialist Party and the Green Party. Among the environmentalists Mendes found practices that he could, with a little adaptation, bring into his own group. From the workers' unions he learned how to organize the rubber tappers to sell their products as a union and not one by one, and so to engage in international trade. These were practices and concerns that his own native group of subsistence farmers could absorb but not ones they could have generated out of their own concerns.

The Chico Mendes story shows cross-appropriating in a particularly illuminating light. The rubber tappers could receive environmentally sound practices from environmental groups, practices of treating the rainforest as a cultural space from aboriginal groups, political tactics from the labor unions, and so on, while these other groups each cross-appropriated to themselves different practices from the rubber tappers. The U.S. environmental groups cross-appropriated to their interest in saving the rainforest an interest in saving rainforest ways of life. This cross-appropriating generated the notion of an extractive reserve rather than a simple conservation zone or simple agricultural zone. But more important, Chico Mendes's politics did not respect normal political borders. Other groups engaged in extractive agriculture could link up with the various associations the rubber tappers linked themselves with. And there need not be one government managing all rainforests or even all extractive resources for Mendes's tactics to work. In this way, we may see a new model for international politics. No longer would international politics be the preserve of state-to-state negotiation conducted by diplomats. It would be closer to the kinds of business negotiations international traders and merchants have conducted for centuries. Interest groups of various kinds could form coalitions with related interest groups based in other countries for the sake of acquiring practices, entrée, money, and know-how.

This allows us to make sense of the paradoxical notion of an international "citizen" virtue. Normally we would say that since there is no international state, there is no way to extend the rights and responsibilities of citizenship beyond the nation state. But with the development of social movements that cross borders, one becomes a virtuous international citizen by holding on to a disharmony and cross-appropriating various practices with as many local associations as possible, until the background practices of all relevant places are changed. In creating these cross-appropriations, the same ability is required as was required for producing resonance in a national culture. In cross-appropriating, one must express concerns with which one has experience in a way that touches the concrete experiences of others.

We can see then that post–Cold War global politics need not involve all the apparatus of huge sovereign state diplomacy. If democratic politics thrives on the citizen virtue of political action groups, then international political action groups may well produce a more activist and democratic world order, without the burden of new world bureaucracies.

4

Solidarity: The Ground of Meaningful Community

Solidarity, as we define it, is a sense of ultimate responsibility to the most encompassing disclosive space that makes the activities of the entrepreneur, the virtuous citizen, and others matter most. For most people in the contemporary West, the most encompassing such space is the nation or national culture. We begin this chapter by presenting and criticizing the Romantic philosophical view that, until recently, determined our understanding of the nature and importance of national culture as the basis of solidarity. We then develop a two-stage alternative account of responsibility to one's community. We start by introducing two sets of distinctions necessary for unclouding contemporary debate: (1) the distinction between a collection of goods or values and the ranking of those goods or values and (2) the distinction between two sorts of patriotic feelings, one that relates us *each* to others in our nation and another that intensifies our everyday sense of *us* as sharing together in activities that have a national consequence. With these distinctions in hand, we can see how shared activities constitute a *"we."*

The discussion then turns from the conditions necessary for solidarity to ways of cultivating and maintaining it. We start with a description of Martin Luther King Jr. as a paradigm of how a culture figure can bring our understanding of ourselves as a "we" to public attention by retrieving a good that the nation has lost sight of. We next argue that, when we lose the culture figure's skill of solidarity cultivation, we either come to think of our ultimate concerns in terms of a detached, objective, theoretical account of values or we care only for successful coping. The first possibility leads to endless divisiveness; the second heals divisiveness at the cost of losing anything shared that is worth dying for. Finally, we discuss how, in the absence of culture figures, solidarity may be preserved by public institutions such as courts of law and universities.

1. The Modern Concept of Solidarity

In writing about entrepreneurship and citizen virtue, we have taken for granted that these activities take place within a cultural or national disclosive space that gives them their meaning. We approach the subject of solidarity from the point of view of the nation because we have observed that many people still are willing to die for their nation who are not willing to die for their community or for social movements of which they have become members. This current social fact may change. Indeed, by our account, if civil democracies are going to preserve citizen virtue, they will have to structure themselves in ways that more closely approximate the structure of social movements such as feminism or environmentalism. But that would not matter for the substance of our claim, which is that the best life is lived when the association whose recognition matters most is also an association for which one would be willing to die. Thus what we say in this chapter fits, *mutatis mutandis*, with new social structures as well as with the current national structures.

The modern understanding of national solidarity was articulated late in the eighteenth century by the German philosopher Johann Gottfried Herder,[1] who argued that nations develop an identity very much like the personal identity most of us experience as individual human beings. Herder noted that each nation has specific interrelated fundamental concerns that it cares about, specific talents (related to its concerns) that it develops, specific related habitual feelings and moods, and a rich web of practices for preserving and perpetuating all of the above. We exemplify our continuing underlying acceptance of Herder's thesis when we casually think of "the Japanese" as hard-working perfectionists or "the French" as food-loving sensualists. We may feel uncomfortable with Herder's thesis on the grounds that it can lead to the sort of national stereotyping that can foster racist thinking. Yet we note that different peoples do have different practices and that these practices imply different ways of dealing with things, other people, and themselves. We see these differences manifested in aptitudes, manners, and moral outlooks. Of course, we necessarily characterize these differences from our own perspectives, which are given by *our* practices, aptitudes, manners, and moral outlooks, and so it is likely that our descriptions of others miss important aspects of their national ways of life. Still, this disability suggests not that there are no general differences but only that our resources for characterizing them are limited.

If we put aside our scruples about identifying the differences between cultures, we can see that Herder's thesis offers a powerful explanation of national solidarity. Solidarity amounts to a version of self-love, the love most of us feel toward ourselves. This is a love bred of familiarity with our specific way of coping with things and our developed expertise in dealing with the world, others, and ourselves. National self-love is the same. That is why it is so often expressed in stories that tell of military, artistic, moral, political, or even technological success. Such stories tend to show a people endowed with a single national character typified by the protagonist. This national character might focus on cleverness, persistence, warmth, a sense of duty, or any number of other virtues.

2. Values, Goods, and Concerns: From the Inculcation of Shared Concerns to the Recognition of Concerns as Shared

Many philosophical confusions arise from what are, in fact, three distinct approaches to developing an account of what makes actions worth doing and things worth respecting.

Until recently, philosophers have been concerned to distinguish subjective preferences (which Nietzsche called *posited values*) from goods that are more binding on us. Those who argue for binding goods tend to give two different reasons for why they are binding. First, these goods simply show up as aspects of things from the first-person perspective. Thus, because we have practices for acting courageously or magnanimously, certain situations have the look and feel of requiring or obliging us to act heroically or generously. Since all action and valuing takes place from the first-person point of view, these goods are, for all relevant intents or purposes, simply objectively present. Our virtuous practices give us *access* to such goods. The assumption here is that if someone did not recognize the good straightaway, sharing the practices by which it is accessed and then pointing it out would be enough to give that person the good. We consider Charles Taylor the major proponent of this position.

Another line of thinking allows that we experience certain goods as simply binding on us, but that only third-person reflection can tell us whether they really are binding. Such reflection gives us a kind of access that will test and warrant what we have found in the first-person attitude. If critical reflection shows that the good is binding, then the good is indeed objective. Jürgen Habermas defends this view.

From our point of view, these distinctions miss what is important. We are interested in the nature of the goods or values that, taken together, form the basis of national solidarity. It seems obvious to us that these are cases both of posited values and of objective goods. Caring about endangered species, for example, is a posited value in the West. Many countries have passed legislation on the basis of this value, but few (if any) people see whales, for instance, as soliciting protection. Conversely, we believe that any culture of human beings who are skillful and who live in a non-Edenic environment will be competent, even if they currently have no practices for gaining access to this good—that is, even if they never notice that situations call for competence and that they are responding competently. As soon as we show them this good, they will recognize that it binds them.

The goods and values that form the basis of national solidarity, however, have a different hold on us. They are transformed in our recognizing that we care for them in their interrelatedness as the goods and values that make us who we are. We distinguish such goods and values by calling them *concerns*. Concerns are constituted in our daily practices as the basis of our identity as members of a community. As such they are posited, but, as we are inculcated into them, we come to see situations as requiring action according to them. Concerns, then, bridge the two traditional distinctions.

In order to speak in a way that engages the claims of those who have written before us on solidarity, we will, in the appropriate contexts, speak of goods and values in the way that these terms have been used elsewhere. But it is neither goods nor values, as normally understood, that we are willing to die for as the "we" of a community perpetuating its identity. It is, rather, concerns, as we have defined them, that are what the community identifies itself as caring about.

How do we come to feel that we are promoting and perpetuating a shared identity (that is, living in solidarity) with our fellow citizens in the first place? Here personal accounts vary, of course, but we believe that there is a common structure to such accounts. We are obviously not born acknowledging a certain set of concerns and not others. Nor are we born with the practices that support particular concerns. The early years of our lives are spent being *inculcated* into the concerns of our nation. Along with the concerns being inculcated, we are frequently also taught the name of the concern supported by the practices we are being shaped to conform to. Thus, for instance, in many cultures children not only are negatively sanctioned when they grab toys away from others but also are told that they must share and even that it is important that all share equally. This concern is called *fairness*. Notice that we claim that children learn *the name of* the concern but not that they know the concern *as* a concern. What is the difference? When children are learning the virtues practiced in their nation and the names of the concerns supported by these virtues, they do not *experience* the practices as their culture's own in distinction from those of other cultures. They simply learn that they should develop virtues such as sharing and treating people fairly, and they assume that everyone everywhere either follows or ought to follow the same practices.

Children may learn that there are other cultures where different concerns are cultivated, but they will see these other cultures either as inferior or as wonders that need not be taken seriously. Even in cases where children grow up biculturally, they do not experience themselves as engaged in learning the practices of two different worlds. Rather, they see themselves in one world learning about what is done in different situations, roughly on a par with learning what can be said at the family dinner table as opposed what can be said when guests are present at a celebratory feast. They do not see themselves in two different worlds because they do not have selves that are fixed enough in each national culture to make moving from culture to culture feel like moving from one personal identity to another. Because people start out being inculcated into a nation's social practices, they do not recognize at first that national or cultural goods and values are national or cultural.

In the West, the recognition of goods and values *as* national or cultural concerns generally occurs when men and women are in their twenties. We find ourselves both fully socialized into the practices that support our nation's set of concerns and living in practices that support some concern or concerns that are not in that set. This can happen in many ways. We can travel abroad, experience coping in a foreign culture, and thereby recognize that coping in our native culture is different from coping in other cultures. Or we can discover that we were brought up in practices that give us concerns that are peculiar to our local community or to the culture that our family came from but that do not number among the concerns of the nation. We then discover that we have two ways of coping—one appropriate to being at home and the other appropriate to being a citizen of the nation. The realization also can occur through literary experience. We can so steep ourselves in reading the literature of another nation that we develop a sense of the way life is felt in that nation. The possible experiences are manifold, but the structure of these experiences is the same. We dwell in practices that promote goods and values other than those that support our identity as citizens, and because of this contrast, we come to see that we also live in a way that supports particular concerns that our nation recognizes as its own.

A sense of relief usually accompanies this experience because, under conditions in which we once saw ourselves as perpetuating certain goods, we have been slowly learning to care for new goods or to treat new goods as though they were part of our identity, and this has brought about a sense of confusion. Some of these new goods may have fit uncomfortably or not at all with our older concerns. When, however, we see what is going on, that we are a member of X and not Y, then the confusion evaporates and we can finally see what large portions of our life have been about. This will give most people a new way of cherishing what they have already cared about.

A contrast case can help bring out the generally positive nature of this experience. After World War II, many Germans in their late teens went through de-Nazification programs in which they were made aware of practices that had formed their identity as Germans under the Nazi regime. Many of them came to experience strong feelings of self-hate because their sense of national identity had been focused on aspects of their early training that they were now being taught to abhor. In contrast, under normal conditions in which there is continuous historical development, people experience a pleasant sense of recognition when they realize that they are engaged in the preservation and perpetuation of certain nationally specific concerns, such as the concern that life should be lived as an experiment. They experience this recognition as pleasant not because their lives have necessarily been generally happy but because they now see that their most fulfilling moments have occurred when they were in tune with and thereby perpetuating such national concerns.

Three important things happen in this experience that allow us to appreciate the goods and values of our culture *as* cultural or national identity-based concerns. First, we see that the goods and values that distinguish our identity as our own exist only to the extent that certain practices support them. Second, insofar as we take up these practices, we see that we are already in the business of preserving and perpetuating these concerns. Third, we experience a sense of pleasure at being a member of the community that cares about and perpetuates these concerns. It is at that point that we can share an identity with our fellow citizens as fellow preservers and perpetuators.

3. In Defense of Dying for One's National Identity

Why have people, at least until very recently, found themselves willing to die for their nation's concerns? Why have people traditionally been able to assume that others in their nation felt the same way? Like family and personal commitments, one's national identity is crucially important. A concern that we have perpetuated or preserved with our own sweat in the fellowship of others says who we are and what we are made of, and therefore losing such a concern, even if it did not mean losing one's life, would nonetheless mean losing one's identity. Thus, according to our account, one fights and dies for the sake of the integrity of this cultural identity that one has perpetuated, that supports one's personal identity, and that would itself die without our work toward preservation and perpetuation. Devotion to this identity that shows how one is connected with one's fellows is the kind of love that has, until recent times, been called *national solidarity*.

To see that most still respond to the call of a national identity or of some communal identity that is like national identity, we begin by considering our connection to people who risk their lives for us.[2] How are they and the risks they undertake related to us? Police officers, firefighters, and others are expected to risk their lives in the name of their professional identities even when their nation as a whole is not being threatened. Why are people willing to die in the performance of professional duties? One explanation might be the existence of some special talent. If this were the case, we could admire the willingness of people to risk their lives in the same way that we admire the genius or the saint—people with a special talent that we do not oblige ourselves to have. We claim, however, that if certain occupations necessary for preserving our way of life required people who were as different from us as athletic, scientific, and religious prodigies, we could not comfortably count on the services of those people. Because they were so different from us, we could only try to *predict* when they would be willing to risk themselves to help us and when not. We would find ourselves relying on contractual relations to provide assurance of appropriate responses (much as in the case of professional athletes). If our contracts included stipulations of their being willing to risk their lives for us, then we would have a contractual claim to expect this; what we want to emphasize, though, is that no sense of solidarity would give those of us outside the ranks of the specially talented group a warrant to expect members of the group to take risks.

When we examine our attitude toward these risk-taking professions, however, we find our sense of them does not support the model of special talents and necessary contracts. When police officers, firefighters, physicians, nurses, lifeguards, and others risk their lives, we find that we admire them in a way different from the way we admire prodigies and saints. We do not find ourselves filled with awe at their achievements. Instead, our admiration takes the form of hoping that we would do what they have done if we were in the same situation. They have risked their lives, that is, for concerns that we recognize as ours too, even if the day-to-day conditions of our lives do not include such a risk.

If we grant that certain fellow citizens in their everyday lives must be willing to die for concerns that we all share, then we must ask, What keeps those citizens from feeling that they have been cheated by those who lead relatively risk-free daily lives? In order to see why they do not feel cheated, we note three aspects of present-day Western societies. First, our way of dividing up social roles seems to be based largely on maximizing skillfulness. A high respect for competence is one of the concerns most people in the West share. Second, by being willing to die for the shared collection of concerns that constitute one's identity, we mean that one is willing to give one's all. In the cases we have cited, this means being willing to give one's life; but there could certainly be cases in which dying would be easier than continuing to shoulder societal burdens, and in those cases solidarity would require going on, not dying. Third, for certain people, acts of physical courage come more easily than, for example, acts of psychological persistence. A firefighter may very well find it easier to run into a raging fire to save a child than to spend years in a laboratory investigating the nature of a disease that kills children or in library archives researching the history of childhood in our society.

If we accept these observations, we can see why firefighters do not feel that they have been cheated. We will claim that each role in our society requires the exercise of some virtue that we all admire because it supports one or more concern that is part of our society's shared collection of concerns. In the case of the firefighter, the virtue is physical courage; in the case of the researcher, the virtue is intellectual persistence.[3]

Our second point follows from this claim. Giving one's all will look different when different virtues are involved, and in a society with solidarity, all members will understand and appreciate these differences. We would all hope to act as they do were we to find ourselves in the shoes of the firefighter *or* the researcher; we feel camaraderie with them because we understand the concerns they perpetuate. We are all, in short, citizen-firefighters and citizen-researchers.[4] And, on that ground, we expect our counterparts to exercise the virtues appropriate to their identities in a way that entails making appropriate sacrifices when necessary. We have this expectation in the name of the collection of concerns that we all perpetuate as ours.[5]

If people were willing to die for their identities but the nation was not the institution through which they expressed such a commitment, problematic social situations would arise. Consider a society in which social inculcation is done by families, villages, churches, trade unions, professions, political parties, and other associations that do not possess a monopoly on the use of force. Association with these groups gives people the identities that they are willing to die to preserve. Members of these organizations do not walk around with chips on their shoulders seeking fights to prove the strength of their convictions. But the ordering of concerns into which people have been inculcated and the practices that support these concerns provide them with identities that enable them to make sense of the world and to find their actions mattering to such an extent that they would be willing to sacrifice their lives for the sake of preserving the associations that have given them these identities. If the state were not such an association, then the loyalty citizens had for it would be no more than the loyalty a consumer would have for a store. In this case, people would not defend the state unless they each saw good reasons to do so.

Even in this type of society, threats to one's nation—a totalitarian regime determined to control the world, for example—would require one to fight even to the point of death. A citizen in such a state would nevertheless always prefer to have someone else risk his or her life to save the state. And every reasonable citizen would know that every other reasonable citizen had reached this conclusion. Indeed, given that there would be strong loyalties to families, villages, trade unions, professions, and parties, one wonders if it would be possible to escape the consequences of this corrosive thought in daily life. Could a professor trained at university A, from political party B, village C, and family D engage with trust a lawyer trained at university W, from political party X, village Y, and family Z? Given the lawyer's loyalties to W, X, Y, and Z and her merely rational commitment to the state and thereby to her fellow citizen, the professor would constantly have to wonder whether she might at some time decide that it was better for her essentially foreign client to suffer than to suffer herself. And what goes for lawyers would go for police officers, physicians, plumbers, and so on. There are only two ways out of this situation. One is to inculcate everyone not to love any of the concerns of their way of life. The other is to trust that the ultimate commitment of our fellow citizens is to a collection of concerns that we all share. This is, in fact, the way most people in the West have been raised. Our daily relations with our fellow citizens are mediated through our shared commitment to the nation (even if there are almost inevitably occasions when we are forced to wonder about the selfishness of a particular lawyer, police officer, physician, or plumber).

What would the police force and military of our hypothetical society be like? We assert that a trust based on a commitment to shared concerns among police partners and soldiers must be absolute in order to be effective. If people's loyalty were to some institution other than the state, we expect one of two situations to hold: (1) professional and partner commitments might frequently trump the choice to abide by the national law (who would turn in the partner one trusted with one's life on account of a little corruption?) or (2) members of the police or the military would not be willing to die for the association or their comrades unless rational analysis indicated that this was in their own interest. In the latter case, morale in these organizations would be extremely low. In societies where the shared concerns of the nation remain more important than those of the profession, in contrast, commitment to professional concerns will not generally raise fears that military and police units might become either renegades or incompetent. In such societies, professional associations will usually develop the high levels of trust that are necessary for competence.

So we claim, as another way of seeing the importance of solidarity, that we expect that those institutions that give us the identity that matters most to us should also be the institutions that have ultimate power over life and death. If this were not the case, our commitments would become vexed in one of two ways. We could be faced with matters for which we would be willing to risk our lives but find that our state had no powerful institution through which we could express this willingness. Or we might find ourselves called on to risk our lives for matters that had little to do with our identity. It is obvious that the nation-state meshes well with this way of stating our basic intuition because the nation-state has ultimate police power and is bounded by a national culture one is willing to die for.[6]

4. Saving Herder's Intuitions: The Search for the Highest Good or Value[7]

So far we have tried to collect the intuitions that support an account of solidarity roughly like Herder's. Two series of events, however, have caused leaders and thinkers to distrust Herder's approach. First, two world wars and innumerable conflicts based on racial, religious, and national hatreds have made national self-love appear to be something that is at heart violent and primitive, bred merely by familiarity and not by reason. Many would even argue, on the basis of this recent history, that it is a proclivity that ought to be resisted by human beings.

Second, given the flow of people and information across national borders that characterizes our age, it has become increasingly difficult to argue that the large, postindustrial, liberal democracies are each consti-tuted by one people with one national character. Individual nations no longer seem to have a single, interrelated set of fundamental concerns. Indeed, it is often impossible for the people of a modern nation to agree on a central national narrative or even a single set of narratives. At academic institutions in the United States, from the major universities down to the primary grades, this debate takes the form of "canon wars." Citizens can no longer agree about the works of art that express fairly and accurately what the national culture is about. All seem problematically exclusionary. Some people feel that this situation of disagreement is desirable, for in such a situation it is impossible to generate any national form of self-love. Those who embrace a politics of difference celebrate this state of affairs and try to teach us to embrace it. But most of us cannot see how to embrace what seems to be an endless jarring of concerns and feelings, where in principle not even a stable background exists on which to have disagreements that matter.

Those who cannot embrace proliferating differences hold that some sort of love or other wide-ranging feeling (whether national or not) is still needed if we are to continue to care for our political and economic institutions. Otherwise, we would simply seek individual security and articulation, while remaining apathetic about the larger economic and political contexts in which we live. For reasons we have advanced in the previous two chapters, a shared love of difference alone is not likely to overcome this individualism because designing lives that make people feel competent and satisfied will sometimes require changes in *shared* practices that unite us. Think of MADD. If the institutions that incarnate our shared social practices had ceased to matter and therefore to be open to meaningful change, the founders of MADD would have had no field for expressing their sense of the error of those practices.

Sociologist Robert Bellah claims that to a large degree people in the postindustrial democracies have in fact sunk to a state of selfishness and apathy. Bellah calls for the revival of old commitments that will make public institutions matter again. Those who, like Bellah, seek such a reinvigoration have adopted several approaches, looking either for a highest good that all can agree on or for some procedure that everyone does or ought to follow. Both of these approaches work out of the dimension of thinking opened up by Herder.

The first approach, which is closest to Herder, is to find one substantive good that all people in a multicultural, democratic state can affirm and therefore share. The idea is that all institutions should be passionately affirmed or rejected in the name of this agreed-upon good. Bellah and the pragmatist philosopher Richard Rorty are exemplary here. Rorty holds that everyone living in multicultural, liberal democracies would agree that humiliation is an evil and that kindness is therefore the shared highest good: "The liberal ironist just wants our *chances of being kind*, of avoiding the humiliation of others, to be expanded. . . . She thinks that recognition of a common susceptibility to humiliation is the *only* social bond that is needed."[8] Rorty thinks that all can agree in affirming passionately that the pain of humiliation ought to be wiped out.

In a similar vein, Bellah and his coauthors note that all people in modern, multicultural, liberal democracies find themselves having to engage—whether they like it or not—in relations of trust with many others, such as physicians, auto mechanics, and teachers. Moreover, those others must trust the people who are requesting their services: "Viability depends, far more that it did in the past, upon the mutual trust and goodwill of all citizens."[9] Bellah hopes to resuscitate a passion for caring about public life by reminding citizens of this trust and goodwill. Yet Bellah is clear that "the impulse toward larger meaning, thankfulness, and celebration has to have an institutional form, like all the other central organizing tendencies in our lives, so that we do not dissipate it in purely private sentiment."[10] Trust and goodwill, however, are too insubstantial to be the basis of shared celebration. They constitute a feeling that many people happen to share, but this feeling that we trust those with whom we deal in our ongoing coping does not enable us to ground the sort of communal identity on which solidarity is based. No one could say, "We are who we are because we trust those we deal with."[11]

Kindness and trust may well be, by default, the highest common good left in multicultural societies. But this leads to a serious problem. Such shared goods, which draw on no special virtues and narratives that give a group its identity, are too thin to form the basis of an identity that citizens might find it meaningful to live for and therefore be willing to die for. These goods are so universalistic in character that one could hardly even build a shared identity as the people that cares most about them. To those, like Rorty, who advocate a politics of difference, this looks like an advantage, since, if people cannot form an identity that can be sacrificed for such a thin and deracinated good, they will surely not be willing to kill for it. We doubt, however, that a group that shares only such attenuated goods is a meaningful community at all.

Some contemporary thinkers who have given up looking for substantial goods have taken a second course. They recognize that certain feelings of attachment develop around any engagement that produces success and enables people to experience expertise. Having noted this, such thinkers as John Dewey and Benjamin Barber claim that there are specific *processes* that people living in democracies engage in—such as acting in a community with equal respect for the actions of each member, advocating proposals though reasoned discourse, and making agendas—to which people commit themselves. Barber writes:

The agenda of a community tells a community where and what it is. It defines that community's mutualism and the limits of mutualism, and draws up plans for pasts to be institutionalized or overcome and for futures to be avoided or achieved. . . . Strong democratic talk places its agenda at the center rather than at the beginning of its politics. It subjects every pressing issue to continuous examination and possible reformulation. Its agenda *is*, before anything else, its agenda.[12]

Here again, however, we would argue that a procedure engaged in for its own sake, even a successful one, seems too empty for anyone to live or die for.

Yet another approach is to claim that there is some formal procedural principle to which all members of the human community already owe allegiance. Thus Habermas claims that all members of a linguistic community share an implicit commitment to help bring about an ideal speech situation in which everyone has an opportunity to express his or her views freely, and in which the resulting agreement takes account only of the validity of arguments and not the power of those propounding them. Solidarity would then be based on a shared respect for these universal requirements and a dedication to putting them into practice. Thus Habermas sees solidarity as growing out of "the realization that each person must take responsibility for the other because as consociates all must have an interest in the integrity of their shared life context in the same way."[13] Such procedural proposals are like the thin substantive proposals; neither the thin substantive good nor the process-engendered feeling would be naturally restricted to one state or one national people. The shared good of the integrity of the speech community or of making an agenda seems, however, too abstract and programmatic to support a solidarity capable of demanding sacrifices from a community's members.

All these thinkers want to find a single, unifying, highest good that grounds solidarity in any democratic state. To the extent that they are looking for a highest unifying good, they are thinking out of the dimension opened by Herder. But once a nation becomes multicultural, taking up Herder leads to an insoluble dilemma. On the one hand, if one tries to find and conserve a shared highest good as the source of solidarity, one finds only universalistic goods like kindness or trust or respect for the procedures of rational debate. On the other hand, if one proposes some substantive highest good particularistic enough to ground a meaningful community, like being chosen by a particular god, such a good will divide rather than unite a multicultural, pluralistic democracy. (Think of the politics of identity as it is being played out in Canada.)

This dilemma suggests that the thinkers we have discussed implicitly accept the piece of Herder they should have rejected—that national solidarity requires a strong national identity based on shared adherence to a single highest good—while rejecting what Herder got right—that solidarity must be based on a sense of meaningful community strong enough that people are willing to set aside their private interests and even their lives to preserve it. Our approach to solidarity, in contrast, moves away from Herder's notion that national identity is based on a commitment to a single highest value and emphasizes his intuition that genuine solidarity involves a commitment one is willing to risk one's all for.[14]

How can multicultural nations both preserve concerns that are substantive enough to be worth dying for and give up the traditional account of Herder-like cultural identity? The answer is actually quite simple. In multicultural, civil democracies in the West, citizens agree on the substantive concerns of a nation. Vàclav Havel lists these concerns as "respect for the uniqueness and the freedom of each human being, the principles of a democratic and pluralistic political system, a market economy and a civic society with the rule of law."[15] One might add to this list equality of opportunity and the possibility of self-transformation. In pluralistic states citizens may not agree on which of these concerns is the most important, but we contend that the *ordering of the concerns* is a matter for *politics*, while *holding a shared set of concerns as one's own* is a matter for *solidarity*.[16]

Having a common style or a shared world can be roughly described in abstract terms as having a set of concerns in common. We can see the connection between a shared style and concerns if we imagine a simple case. People living in a culture that has an aggressive, "cowboy" style will share such concerns as individualism, decisiveness, and nonchalance. Different groups in a cowboy culture could order these concerns differently, which would produce different inflections of the style. Members of the culture might prefer one inflection over another, but they would all share the same collection of concerns. Thus sharing a style amounts to having a set of concerns in common and ordering them in various ways subject to some shared restrictions. For instance, in a cowboy culture no one could treat love of one's horse as the top concern.

We claim that solidarity is founded on familiarity with, and competence in, practices that support shared concerns but that these concerns need not be ranked as to importance and that therefore people do not need to share love of a single, highest concern. Our thesis is that solidarity in a multicultural society lies not in a passive experience of a common, unifying good but in the active cultivation of a set of shared, roughly ordered concerns and that this cultivation produces a "we" identity. We turn now to showing how such a claim makes sense of life in multicultural societies.

5. Solidarity in a Pluralistic Society: A Shared Collection (Not a Shared Ordering) of Concerns

Caring for the collection of concerns that one's nation sees as valuable is different from political activity (though the two tend not to be distinguished). Political activity amounts to advocating for one or another ordering of the nation's concerns.[17] Think of the debates surrounding abortion in the United States. Those who believe that women ought to be able to have abortions claim that women have the right to control what happens to their bodies. Those who argue that women should not be allowed to have abortions claim that innocent human lives must always be preserved. Such debates concern ordering: prochoice people think that choice is the higher of the two concerns.; prolife people think that life is the higher. Nevertheless, all but a radical extreme think that both concerns are among those that U.S. citizens live for. Both prolife and prochoice advocates can honor the sanctity of both human life and freedom of choice.[18] And although it may seem that the dispute is over the technical matter of when a human life begins, in cases of rape and incest we find that many who believe that human life begins at conception would agree that the mother should be free to choose whether her body nurtures the fetus. Likewise, if it were somehow demonstrated that human life really does begin in some deep sense at conception, then prochoice advocates might well split over whether the good of the sanctity of human life could give the fetus the right to inhabit the mother's body against her will. Both life and choice, then, are goods, and much of the debate is over the ordering of these goods.

Once we understand the distinction between appreciating a collection[19] of concerns and ordering those concerns, we see how people with very different political positions can coexist. Conservatives generally think that a government's first task is to provide for a stable free market that guarantees opportunities, while for liberals government's first task is to provide social welfare. But both conservatives and liberals think that their country's products are improved by competition, and both feel that people should be prevented from falling into such impoverishment that they cannot hope to live a life that accords with the concerns of the nation. Thus, both feel that the market and the prevention of suffering are goods, and both understand that all citizens in their nation share these concerns.

When we think in this way, the distinction between appreciating concerns and ordering concerns seems quite natural. Yet it is seldom made. We need only look at the problems the United States has had with various cultural groups that have sought special rights for actions in their own communities to see how quickly it can be lost.[20] Recently, for example, U.S. courts addressed the issue of peyote use in traditional Native American ceremonies. In arguing the issue, both sides focused on the relative importance of ecstatic religious experience (even when drug-induced) and of fully lucid and responsible public behavior. As most U.S. citizens would expect, lucid and responsible public behavior trumped ecstatic religious experience, even though religious experience is generally protected. We believe that the courts would have done a better job if questions had focused on whether the Native Americans shared the collection of concerns that most U.S. citizens share and added no concerns that most citizens detest but only ordered them differently. Then the courts would have found that both groups feel that ecstatic religious experience *and* lucid and responsible public behavior are goods. On the matter of peyote use, the courts would probably have found that the laws of both groups indicate that both detest its purely recreational use and that the practice of religious peyote use is neither detested nor favored (that is, there are no laws specifically prohibiting religious forms of peyote use). Such a finding would have left the Native Americans in solidarity with the concerns of the United States, and therefore, under our analysis, they should have been granted the cultural right to continue the religious practices within the bounds of their own communities.

Basing legal decisions on the ordering of concerns rather than the collection of concerns is not a matter of political orientation. Lest it be thought that only right-leaning courts focus on ordering, consider another example from a more liberal court. In the early 1970s the Amish sought exemption from mandatory public high school education. Unlike the Native Americans, the Amish won their case. The court reasoned that the ordering of concerns among the Amish was precisely the ideal that most Americans sought but could not obtain. The Amish had an extensive program of education by doing, which was at the heart of the best of U.S. thinking about education. Thus, instead of asking whether the collection of Amish concerns included all the dominant culture's important concerns and none that the dominant culture detested—that is, instead of asking whether the Amish could live in solidarity with the dominant culture while disagreeing over local political matters such as the importance of the concern for mandatory attendance at accredited schools—the court asked whether there was basic political agreement concerning the ordering of concerns, and in this case found that there was.

If, *on matters of cultural rights,* the courts asked whether U.S. citizens could remain in solidarity with subordinate cultural groups, many cases would not seem to vex reasoning as both the Amish and Native American cases do. To see this we look at a case where the concerns of a subordinate culture were *not* concerns that U.S. citizens could live with in solidarity.[21] Several years ago, two parents in a tight-knit community murdered their daughter for continuing to date an outsider whom they had forbidden her to see. The parents claimed that their action was justified according to their community's understanding of honor. Assuming for argument's sake that the community did share this sense of honor, the problem here is not just that this community has a higher concern for honor and a lower concern for the preservation of life than most other Americans. Rather, the community's sense of honor is constellated with other concerns that U.S. citizens detest, such as nonjudicial or quasi-judicial killings. For this reason, U.S. citizens could in no way feel solidarity with the collection of concerns the defendants' community supposedly shared. Following our reasoning with our distinctions, then, the law ought not to allow any group such a cultural right.

Once we attend to sets of shared concerns rather than to their ordering, we can distinguish among national democracies. For example, most U.S. citizens who spend time in Western Europe report that they find European education systems overly regimented and express astonishment at the scarcity of older reentry students. Two U.S. citizens probably will agree on this even though one is for national school testing in the United States and the other is against it, or one is for school vouchers and the other opposes them. What leads political opponents to agree on their assessment of European systems is that most U.S. citizens share a concern for starting life over, for transforming oneself, at any point. A school tracking and testing system that determines one's career path early on, with very little opportunity for changing or beginning anew, does not seem to most U.S. citizens desirable, regardless of how efficient it is. Indeed, blocking self-transformation probably is seen as detestable. Political fights over the precise importance of this concern could be ferocious, but almost all would agree that it is among the concerns U.S. citizens hold dear.

A clear example of activities that cultivate the recognition of concerns as distinct from the ordering of concerns can be found in the new social movements such as feminism and environmentalism.[22] These movements are constituted of many subgroups. As we saw at the end of chapter 3, each of these subgroups advocates a certain ordering of the concerns of the movement, but each sees itself in coalition with the other subgroups. Insofar as members of these subgroups see themselves as feminists or environmentalists, they can say that they recognize and share a number of concerns in common. Thus feminists highly regard both descriptions of shared experiences and critical examinations that show how experience is almost always constructed by oppressive structures. But younger feminists tend to see the second concern as almost always higher, while older feminists see just the reverse. Because both groups share both concerns, however, they work together easily in coalition. The coalition structure of these social movements reveals the difference between recognition and ordering: when subgroups form coalitions, they are recognizing shared concerns; when subgroups articulate their own concerns, they rank them.

6. How Feeling Promotes Solidarity

We feel solidarity with our fellow citizens when we recognize that we have *already* been engaged in preserving and perpetuating certain concerns. That is, we recognize that when we act according to practices that produce our culture with its particular identity and produce ourselves as citizens with identities appropriate to our culture, we all are engaged in the activity together. The *together* here means that we do this as a "we."

To understand solidarity it is important to see that we may experience most feelings, including adoring our nation's collection of concerns, in two different ways, each of which produces its own brand of political and cultural action. The way of understanding feelings most common today is to think of them as private experiences. Thus we may experience excitement, joy, elation, sadness, sorrow, love, love of country, and love of our fellow humans as private feelings burning in our hearts. When we speak of such feelings, we say that they are subjective, meaning that each person experiences them inwardly. In this regard they are like pain. One may feel them in the absence of other people feeling them. One may also hide what one is feeling. Such feelings are part of what constitutes our difference from others. Claims of this sort make most sense in a world where we understand ourselves in Cartesian ways.

By the time of the Romantics and later, our feelings came to be understood as what is most important about us (because they have their source in what is natural to us or because they are what is most individual about us or because they are the part of ourselves that we can develop most and best). This is how we, today, ordinarily understand feelings. But we need not experience our feelings *strictly* privately. Many people experience heightened feelings together. And they may even be moved to valiant actions on the basis of those feelings. So what becomes important in such cases is the power of the feelings to move us to action. Under this intersubjective understanding of feelings, one cultivates solidarity by cultivating activities in which people are led to feel the same patriotic feeling strongly. Politics, culture, and solidarity become aestheticized or sentimentalized. An example of this is the 1969 Woodstock rock festival. There musicians sought to generate in masses of people a feeling of liberation from restrictive and authoritarian social practices. Pleasures were to become open to all, freely possessed, and freely acknowledged, not shamefully had in dark, private places. These feelings were produced by mass gathering, fervid songs, and high-tech equipment that expanded people's sight and hearing and made them feel more powerful and free than they ordinarily were. Public rallies and events frequently produce emotional peaks that overwhelm us with their power. We seek them again and again and often act on the basis of these feelings.

When it is effective, this kind of solidarity motivates us to extraordinary actions that cut us off from our everyday lives and casts public life as something removed from ordinary life. For this reason it cuts us off as well from the kind of citizen virtue appropriate to civic democracies. We are thinking, of course, of the virtue that comes from attending to everyday life. In contrast, athletes sometimes jump up and down out of sheer joy at a success or punch an opponent in response to a failure. Many of us have engaged in similar activity. Our point is that such activity is not central to the kind of solidarity we want to emphasize. We argue for a solidarity that enables people to maintain a sense of an extraordinary "we" within everyday activity.

In focusing attention away from momentary feelings, we are not proposing a new stoicism in the name of solidarity. Heightened feelings often make an important contribution to perpetuating and cultivating solidarity in ordinary life. They highlight the concerns that guide the actions of a "we." When a region's sports team wins a world championship, people in the region express their joy by celebratory activity such as dancing in the streets, honking car horns, hugging neighbors, setting off firecrackers, throwing parties, and holding impromptu parades. More important, so far as solidarity is concerned, as people settle back into their workaday lives, they may find that their concerns have shifted and are now guided by greater thankfulness and responsibility, highlighted by their joy the night before. This changes the way they behave, at least for a while. People are more courteous, give more money to civic foundations, and take part with more good will in neighborhood associations. Because they feel in general that the region is doing something that makes a difference in the world, formerly annoying events, such as fundraisers, now look like opportunities to express thanks and take responsibility.

A heightened feeling of joy experienced by a "we" can thus highlight a change in the concerns of the "we," but it can also highlight concerns that were ignored for a time and are now being reactivated. Some travelers to foreign countries discover positive reflections of their own country that make them feel a sense of pride in the achievements of their fellow citizens. (This could be as simple as the fact that people in the foreign country appreciate and rely on the products of one's own country.) In most cases this sort of pride and sense of connectedness is temporary, but it can reflect a deeper reactivation of concerns. Because such an experience usually invigorates the sense travelers develop of being identified with their own nation, they might find themselves using greater care in acting in arenas that are connected with the welfare of their homeland, such as work, politics, or family. The individual feeling of pride in such cases reconnects and strengthens concerns that may have become attenuated. Before the experience of this pride and connectedness (and even patriotism), travelers may have taken care of work, political responsibilities, and family life as a duty that is part of their sense of self and sense of decency within the community. After the experience, at least temporarily, they take care of business or politics or family because they see these actions as enhancing the life of the nation they care for.

7. How a "We" Is Constituted

We now turn to a feeling of solidarity that is usually passed over. This one inspires us to heightened activity precisely in the name of our ordinary ways of life. It requires us to look at a nonsubjective way of understanding our feelings. Under this view of feelings, we do not merely have what we all know well as subjective feelings; we have concerns. And concerns, as we understand them, are not private and inner. We act on them not because we are motivated by an inner cause but because they call our attention to what we need to do as members of a group engaged in that activity.

Concerns are frequently confused with subjective feelings. But our culture has long been able to distinguish the two, although not with great clarity. We know, for instance, that some people become connoisseurs of falling in love. They savor having the feeling of infatuation in a heightened way and consequently fall in love again and again, ending romantic relationships for the sake of beginning new ones. They act out of love for the feeling of infatuation. Love of such a feeling is quite different from having one's actions guided by love. In the second case, one feels love for someone as focusing what matters during the day. A telephone call to find out how the day is progressing will be routinely appropriate. Trying to reschedule meetings so that lunch time can be shared, planning an evening's activity, and so on, appear to be actions that matter year after year when one has the concern of love. Once we see this distinction in the case of love, we can see a general distinction between self-regarding *feelings* and action-regarding *concerns*.

Active solidarity, experienced when a group shares the same concerns, occurs most strikingly when we engage with others in actions in which we must appeal to our fellows as citizens. Preparing for a case at law is an example. Acting as a member of a political action group or working on a political campaign is another. We have the same concerns regarding things and people when we all see the same details, steer a course toward the same end, and judge new ideas as relevant or irrelevant in the same light. All these actions constitute people working together as a "we"—as people who have the same concerns and so see events as having the same import. They have developed a disclosive space in terms of which they are defining themselves. All this makes for an occasion in which solidarity is shared among a group of people. But in such cases solidarity is not yet being cultivated. Shared concerns are, no doubt, the basis of what matters, but that we share them as a "we" is not being attended to and shaped. To cultivate this solidarity, we must somehow call attention to the fact that we all share in the same concerns.

How are we to do this? As moderns, our first impulse is to find a way for each person to recognize that he or she is individually sharing in the concerns that guide the action. But how can we do this without appealing to each individual as an individual? How can we draw people as a "we" to attend to their shared concerns? To see the answer, we have to turn our attention to events that are typically supposed to cultivate solidarity. When the president speaks to all citizens about something they take seriously, the speech works if the president is guided by the sense of the ways of thinking that articulate or manifest the shared concern that citizens need to focus on a shared national task. If the speech works, citizens begin to share the concern. But how does a citizen come to recognize that he or she is sharing the national concern with others? Here the manner of staging the event can play a key role. While listening to the speech, a citizen will note the setting, the pomp and circumstance, the festive sense that daily chores have been put aside for the sake of this moment. All of these details make us see that we are engaged with our fellow citizens in something important. Each of us recognizes as we move in and out of absorption in the president's words that something special is happening and that we are part of it. Many Christians have the same sort of feeling at Christmas or Easter services when the church is specially decorated, the choir is accompanied by extra musicians, and the vestments are of special hues, so that even when one drifts from the content of what is being said, one's senses are stimulated in a way that reminds one of the specialness of the event. Indeed, many Christians go to church on holidays just for the special thrill festive decorations give. Many citizens go out of their way to attend political ceremonies for much the same reason. We argue that these seeming instances of solidarity fail because people recognize that they are engaged in sharing only when they temporarily disengage from the actual act of sharing and notice the splendor and the responses of others to it.

We need a way in which we can recognize that we are all absorbed in acting out of a shared concern. It may seem that recognition must be a private experience that would necessarily undo absorption in the public activity, whereas absorption in the shared action would undo recognition.

To see how an involved recognition that we are acting as a "we" can occur nonetheless, consider how in many small Texan towns, the high school football team articulates meaningful aspects of the community's life. The community is responsible for producing well-coached and healthy athletes, but citizens also see the ethical strength of the town reflected in whether the athletes know how to play hard, to be unyielding, and to show cleverness, intelligence, skill, and strength under stress. A town whose team regularly does this is understood to be more in touch with these virtues and generally with what it means to be a Texan than a town whose team does not reveal these virtues. In the weekly contests, the town's whole way of local life undergoes a test, and town residents must conform themselves—indeed cannot help but conform themselves—to the results of the test. It determines who they are.

If what is at stake in such an athletic contest is not just a style of play with which one identifies personally but rather one's identity as a citizen, then one is absorbed in actions that are defining one's identity as a "we" anew. If the outcome of the event determines *what sort of people we are*, then being involved in the concern is part of the feeling and part of the event as a whole. Our excitement is not a private feeling that just happens to be shared by our fellow citizens. Our concern about the athletes' activities also makes us appear to ourselves as significant because *our* activities and who we are are at stake. Our concerns draw us not only to see an activity but also to see ourselves as a "we" because the activity transforms us.

People who live in countries whose leaders have been assassinated generally have the experience of attending to such news as a concerned "we." At such times, we are not personally involved as with the success or failure of a sports team, but we all share that the events are determining who we are. We focus on such questions as, Who will take charge? What will happen to the assassin? Who were we that such a thing could happen? We also have such a sense of sharing our shared involvement when our country is at war. We see that each scrap of food or metal that we save, each extra hour we put in at work, and any extra care we take in training our children to decency helps the war effort by making the country morally, financially, and militarily strong. Under such circumstances, all such acts aid in determining who we as a nation are.

How, then, is the recognition of shared activity *as* shared normally cultivated? We can try to answer this question by looking at the national commemorative-celebratory holidays, which are traditionally understood to cultivate solidarity. By and large, however, in most modern civic democracies these holidays are treated as vacation days. When serious commemorative activity does take place, it is at the level of the family or the extended family or a local group. Graves of those who died in defense of the country may be visited; veterans may come together for a commemorative dinner; a legislator may speak at a local memorial meeting. As far as solidarity is concerned, however, these events remain at the level of the staged displays described earlier.

These events could become the national events they pretend to be only if they involved a national *renewal*—an *assimilation* or *rededication* of some familiar concern—if, for instance, on the day celebrating a nation's founding or its independence, the nation's leader explained in what new direction he or she was taking the nation and showed citizens how that course was based on some experience familiar to the nation. If such a speech genuinely called people back to a concern they had forgotten or drew on one they had ignored, then people would become engaged not only in the shared concerns that produced the speech and made its points matter, but, insofar as their identity was being changed or reinvigorated, they would feel themselves as a "we" in their absorption in the concerns expressed in the speech. They would not merely feel in a special way that elevated them above their quotidian concerns and caused them to notice that others felt the same way. When genuine history is being made or when a people rededicate themselves to the historical mission in which they see themselves engaged, the average everyday is both conserved and redesigned. This enlivening of the average everyday so that our daily actions are part of a certain kind of historical redefinition of who we are is solidarity cultivation. We turn next to a paradigmatic case of this process.

8. The Cultivation of Solidarity by a Culture Figure

In other times, poets have articulated the meaning of a culture's practices, sharpened its concerns, and thereby transformed the shared "we." Today, our articulating culture figures—people who do the job of cultivating solidarity—include movie makers such as John Ford and Frank Capra, folk singers such as Woodie Guthrie and Bob Dylan, political leaders[23] such as Charles de Gaulle, Lech Walesa, and Winston Churchill, and even philosophers such as Jürgen Habermas, Charles Taylor, and John Dewey.

Martin Luther King Jr. is exemplary in this regard as a culture figure who brought the U.S. way of seeing people as equals to new life for his fellow citizens.[24] Some might say that King's contribution was to make white Americans realize that they ought to see people of color as well as fellow whites as equals and that the rest of King's acts and speeches—his concern for love, for example—was extraneous. But in seeing matters this way, they miss precisely what made King so different from other civil rights leaders and so important to his fellow citizens. True, he may have had the effect of making U.S. whites see people of color as equals, but why he was able to do this and how he had this effect are the crucial questions we must answer if we are to understand how culture figures cultivate solidarity.

In the 1950s—when the United States had developed a strong international presence, when a cadre of highly talented scientists seemed to reflect the nation's wisdom, and when U.S. business practices were being imitated widely—many U.S. citizens felt that equality under the law was a simple reality and that it could be left to judges to work out the technical aspects of that equality. King thought that the National Association for the Advancement of Colored People itself suffered from such an ethos. Thus King found himself in an environment in which the concern for equality that was part of U.S. practice was being ignored and even occluded as other, elitist, nonegalitarian ways of dealing with people (according to I.Q., for example) were becoming prominent.

King was deeply sensitive to this problem of technocratic antiegalitarianism. He was first of all an African American who had experienced the effects of racial inequality and could therefore speak with authority of deep injustices in American life. As a member of the middle class, he could have followed the tradition of successful African-American pastors such as his father and helped his parishioners improve their economic as well as spiritual conditions. But Martin Luther King Jr. was also a Boston University–trained theologian, strongly influenced by both Reinhold Niebuhr's criticism of Social-Gospel optimism and Brightman's Personalism, which focuses on a passionate, personal God. His studies enabled him to see the American way of dealing with equality differently from his contemporaries. The principle of equality was not just legal dogma in the United States; it expressed the early colonists' sense of the infinite worth of every soul and the practice of agape love that ought to obtain if individuals appreciated the souls of other individuals. For King, the retreat from equality was not merely a legal problem that had been with the

United States from its constitution but was a falling away from a concern that was a fundamental part of U.S. culture and national life—namely, a sense of being chosen and consequent spiritual equality that had been part of American self-understanding from the time of the Pilgrims.

King could have become merely another public-sphere critic of the way Americans had fallen away from how they once understood themselves—how they were becoming unworthy of their institutions. Indeed, before he became engaged in his first important civil rights action—the Montgomery bus boycott—King was seeking to leave his position as a successful preacher and enter a more intellectual world as a dean and professor of religion and philosophy. But both because he was intellectually engaged in the problems of his culture and because he lived those problems in their cruelest form, becoming a culture critic would not have fully and honestly articulated the influences on his life. Becoming a culture critic would have taken up his historical understanding of what was wrong with American life only intellectually. To be true to how he was being touched by this problem, he had to respond in terms of his whole life. And here we can begin to see how vexed King was. While his drive toward middle-class stability and success pushed him toward the academic life, as a next step up in prestige after having proved himself a successful preacher, he was at the same time becoming drawn into public service through the activities of a local chapter of the NAACP. These tensions among the academic study of theology, middle-class success, and the bitter conditions of African Americans have been interpreted as accounting for his late arrival at the planning meeting for the Montgomery bus boycott as well as for his eloquent speech and his victory in the election for president of the association that managed the boycott. King could win this crucial position among his factious African-American colleagues just as he could win the hearts of many whites because he revealed himself as someone who openly struggled with the same concerns they had or aspired to have. As an intellectual, he sought genuine clarity; as a member of the middle class, he sought success in his career and family; and as a victim of segregation, he sought social action to correct the wrong. As his career and thinking progressed, he came to see that an integrity that eased these tensions could be reached only by developing an understanding of self and society based on agape.

What was true of King as a representative of various cultural tensions is generally true of culture articulators. The culture articulator must be open to acknowledging all the determining influences on his or her life in their historical character *and* must respond to them in like currency. This response—in its honesty, historicity, and fullness—focuses attention on and articulates a defining concern as something that people ought to live clearly and coherently but instead live in an occluded or dispersed form. Unlike the entrepreneur, who reconfigures a domain of practices by remaining true to the anomaly that he or she uncovers in his or her activities, an articulator tries to respond adequately to the culturally central influences in his or her life. If there is a disharmony, he or she tries to embody it to discover the hidden concern that reveals the disharmony as such. Martin Luther King Jr. attempted to embody our occluded concern for equality, the originating source that makes it sensible, and his current condition as an African American.

King, then, is an exemplary articulator because his actions reminded Americans of a concern that was an essential part of their past and thus of their identity. The fact that it was a central part of their past marks him as someone who was engaged in articulative retrieval and not primarily reconfiguration or cross-appropriation.[25] He took an understanding of the American past that made sense of why the nation's founders cared so much about equality, and he revealed its critical power for showing the inadequacies in the current sense of equality. By being open to the determining influences in his life and answering them in kind, he found a way to act that gave a coherent shape to the tensions he was experiencing. His activity did not draw to the center something that had been only marginal but rather recovered something central from dispersal. In making such a recovery, many solidarity figures have compromised themselves and their actions by finding a group to blame for the dispersion of important concerns. In such cases, blaming the group tends to become more important than retrieving the lost concern. Culture figures who are misled in this way inspire a solidarity of resentment. King avoided this pitfall. Consequently, by recalling U.S. citizens to the defining concern of agape and rededicating them to it without blaming anyone for its loss, Martin Luther King Jr. created a shared "we" concerned with righting the wrong of racism.

King also engaged in political actions. He claimed that the religious concern for equality trumped every other concern that led to racial inequality. For King, therefore, retrieving agape equality meant that all African Americans should be treated as morally equal to other Americans, despite local traditions or national concerns that suggested otherwise. Many resisted the political consequences of King's religious/moral concerns, but all U.S. citizens can celebrate King for retrieving the American concern for equality. This is how cultivation of solidarity works in multicultural nations. Concerns are drawn to our attention out of their hiddenness in our lives, and they are called to our attention as important, not as top concerns in a particular order.[26] Calling them to our attention transforms us in a way that affects our everyday transactions. Consequently, engaging in and acknowledging such a transformation allows us to deal with ourselves as a "we" while we engage in our normal practices.

9. Value Wars or Adaptive Coping

We have describd how culture figures cultivate solidarity by retrieving concerns that have been dispersed. But culture figures are rare. What happens to a nation when there are no such figures to rededicate a sense of "we"? In the United States two opposed tendencies have become prominent—an appeal to objective goods or values and a rejection of shared values in the name of mere success in coping.

We consider first the tendency to dogmatic objectification, using the example of marital fidelity. The exemplary practice is that spouses vow to be faithful to each other in their hearts and in their actions. This means that they share no romantic/erotic intimacy with others *and* that they live a life that reveals the meaning of such vows. Mutual trust and closeness pervades everything they do. But what happens if disease or other tragic circumstance strikes? A husband is in a coma. A wife is captured by enemy troops and is reported missing and probably dead. The anguished spouse receives intimate comfort from someone else while still attempting to honor the marriage by talking to the children about the return of their parent, by working with physicians or diplomats to save the spouse, by maintaining relationships with the spouse's relatives, and so forth. According to our view, these actions count as perpetuating fidelity because the practices that constitute fidelity include all the actions we have noted and are not limited to sexual ones. For us marginal cases where all but one or two of the practices that constitute fidelity are observed—even if the most perspicuous one of sexual fidelity is not—could count as perpetuating fidelity. For us, then, a value admits of degrees. At some point, of course, we would say that marital fidelity is no longer being perpetuated.

But precisely where this point lies remains subject to interpretation. We believe however, that, in any functional community, the divergence over where fidelity ends will be slight. Indeed, even in a community where there is a great deal of divorce litigation, few cases will be about what counts as a ground for divorce.

The notion that a value like marital fidelity can be practiced in incompatible ways seems to be nonsense to people who think that fidelity is an objective standard rather than a changing and flexible norm preserved by a community. Those critics find it contradictory to say that one remains faithful to one's spouse either by making love to him or her exclusively or, in certain circumstances, by caring for the children while having sex with someone else. One account of fidelity must surely be wrong. No matter how much sympathy the objectivist critic may feel for the spouse who cares for the children in the absence of the other spouse, the critic holds that a technical breach in fidelity has occurred and the spouse has degraded the marriage. Indeed, making such objectivist assessments themselves can come to be regarded as a virtue.

Defenders of objectified values look very different in different societies or different contexts. They might defend a canon of great books as teaching the values that the nation stands for in the form in which these values have been manifested by the tradition, allowing substitutions only with scrupulous care and even expressing fear that substitutions might damage the nation's moral health. They might call for guarding the country's borders against immigrants who bring with them alternative ways of living. They might argue for at least outward religious conformity.

Like objectivist critics, moral theorists understand what we call concerns, which are always in need of cultivation and preservation, as objective and hence independent of our nurturing. Moral theories such as those propounded by egalitarians, utilitarians, libertarians, Marxists, and even some communitarians form the last step in detaching concerns from historical practices. Like game theories of the market economy and liberal political theories of difference adjudication, moral theories ask us to see the basic structure of human relations as fixed and encourage us to engage in the practice of deriving a rational—that is, consistent and universal—set of criteria that any just society must meet. Such theories seek either proximately or ultimately to account for all structural moral innovations that have occurred as revealing principles of the theories that were already operating but not yet discovered. And since these theories are constituted of principles and not practices, they do not lead us to refocus our societies around the perpetuation of concerns that we must bring out ever more clearly. Another way to put this point is to note that articulators of cultural practices sense that the practices and concerns they articulate could, under certain conditions, become irrelevant. Moral systematizers such as egalitarians or utilitarians try to find social principles that become irrelevant only if human beings become extinct. Moral systematizers leave out of their account, then, the relevant kind of activity that we claim brings out the best in human life: solidarity cultivation.

Both objectivist critics and moral theorists focus our attention on standards or procedures that are supposed to be universal and withdraw our attention from our customary life and the anomalies we encounter within it. We are consequently drawn to abstract reasoning, applying objective standards to particular situations or developing and adapting ourselves to universal procedures. Since these activities are not tied to the way of life we share in our communities, they involve us not in practices that we share but in building autonomous moral principles or institutions. When we make our values or institutions autonomous, we lose the concrete way of experiencing concerns that holds us together. Hence, when these values or institutions are called on to resolve rifts in the community, they can only provide abstract solutions in the name of a technical sounding value or principled form of justice. At best, such a solution can stop the two sides of a rift from pulling apart, but a nation full of such rifts is ripe for the forgetting of difference that drives what we call skill-based solidarity. Hence, societies that try to order themselves on moral theories end up with the nihilism of skill-based solidarity and forgetfulness.

The idea of skill-based solidarity, which is indebted to some aspects of the work of Friedrich Nietzsche and Maurice Merleau-Ponty, holds that Westerners are at their best when they cope effectively in a domain according to the terms of success in that domain. Nations and communities are functioning well when equilibrium exists among all the domains in which people cope, such that coping in the various domains is either supported or, at least, not interfered with by coping in other domains.[27] Thus both the feeling of solidarity and the event of solidarity occur when people freely cope in a way that enables them to sharpen and refine their characteristic skills. Forgetting in such circumstances amounts to forgetting how things and people looked when one acted in a way that produced "bad results"—that is, results that did not accord with success in one's domain or that threw the community out of its equilibrium among domains of activity. Such forgetting is just a part of skillful coping at its best. For instance, picture walking into a restaurant and being surprised that it looks much larger on the inside than it does on the outside. As soon as one realizes that the walls are covered with mirrors, the restaurant no longer seems big. One loses the ability to or forgets how to see the restaurant as big. (One may not forget that one saw things as odd, and one may see things this way on another occasion, but one cannot generally make oneself see things as one did in the first place.) This sort of forgetting amounts to consolidating skillful learning.[28]

Any form of life that perversely holds on to ways of feeling about and looking at things in the way they appeared before it found a way to cope more effectively with these things would, from the point of view of a purely skillful form of life, seem nonadaptive.[29] It is our contention that Westerners are precisely such a "maladapted" form of life. We cling to ways of doing things that promote and perpetuate the concerns that constitute our cultural identities even when we are shown more effective ways of coping. We do not abandon our old ways in the face of a new way of doing things unless the new way supports our concerns. For this reason, in the absence of a major nonhistorical transformation, people in the United States could probably never adopt an educational system that tracks students early and with little flexibility, even if it were shown beyond doubt that the European tracking method was the most efficient and effective way to educate the greatest number of citizens. The skillful coping of people in the West is directed not only toward effectiveness but also toward producing enduring identities that people regard as worthy.

We agree that people sometimes operate according to the pure coping view, and we do not deny that there is reason to think that people operate this way more and more. We discussed in the introduction how people are becoming nonhistorical, and we shall return to these matters. For now we argue that solidarity is not a form of forgetting by giving a picture of the form of life in which solidarity and forgetting are the same. That form of life is obviously (we think) not ours.

Such a form of life tries to maintain an equilibrium among the different kinds of skillful coping going on in society so that they support or at least do not interfere with each other. We can have a glimpse of how such an equilibrium among forms of skillful coping works if we think of the relations among teenagers. When a group of teenagers wants to buy a new CD, the one with the car (with the driving skills and capacity) will be most important until they arrive at the store; then the one with the money (with the purchasing skills and capacity) will lead; and then when they want to play the CD, the one with the CD player (with CD playing skills and capacity) will be on top. At each step, the teenagers coordinate themselves to emphasize whatever relevant skills (or possessions) they have, such as chatting pleasantly, carrying stuff, reading maps, tuning the car radio, making wisecracks, scouting out things that could be done for free. Consequently, they develop those other skills as well. If at one point in this process the one with purchasing skills sees the situation in such a way that it looks as though she should lead at some point other than purchasing, a breakdown will occur. Since all members of the group are interested in optimizing their skillful performance, the problem will soon be identified, and the rightful leader (given the particular situation) put in place.

People who live their whole lives in this constant regestalting or improvising mode understand themselves only in terms of situationally differential relations of power.[30] They have no stable identities to which they are committed. Solidarity amounts to sharing the same contingently formed equilibrium; forgetting is the mechanism that prevents people from becoming attached to particular social identities.

Given the example we have used, it should be fairly clear that we do not think that this Nietzschean view characterizes the way people in the West generally live today. People in the West do still die for their identities; they still make commitments that define them and their actions. And they still feel that when they engage in defining identities, they are living life at its best. Therefore, we still depend on culture figures to make us sensitive to ourselves as a "we." But culture figures are not always present. What can we do in their absence? Must we drift between fights over objective values and universal theories, on the one hand, or pure coping, on the other?

10. How Solidarity Is Preserved in Institutions

When no leader is cultivating solidarity among a people through historical rededication, solidarity can be maintained by cultural institutions. Solidarity is strong when the institutions are public and participated in widely; it is weak when the institutions are informal. We make this last distinction because the current problems with solidarity in the West can be traced largely to public institutions that no longer consistently perpetuate a sense of solidarity. Our institutions generally maintain solidarity only through the efforts of committed and talented officials, who are rare. Two institutions, however—the courts, and colleges and universities—gather enough of these officials so that they can work to cultivate solidarity regularly.

The Courts

Our first example of a public institution that maintains solidarity in the absence of a culture figure is a nation's common law courts. (The courts of a nation that uses civil law would probably work as well to promote solidarity, with some minor adjustments for the different understanding of authority in the law.) Some people feel that court decisions have effect only because they are backed by the police force of the state. Others think that judges are little more than experts applying a body of rules that most of us do not know well enough to apply. When the rules are not clear, the judge renders a decision that best fits with the body of rules as a whole or with what the lawmaking body seemed to intend. All these gray-area decisions are guided, people tend to think, by the judge's politics. Indeed, most of us assume that the judge was appointed or elected on the basis of politics. There is much in the U.S. court system to support such a view. When courts work *in this way*, they do not produce a "we." Sometimes they do produce solidarity, and we now describe how this happens.

When the courts work well, judges understand themselves not as technicians but as part of a tradition that has been articulated by culture figures of the past and by their own professional figures. In the United States, many judges see their work in terms that have been articulated for them by Oliver Wendell Holmes, John Chipman Grey, Felix Frankfurter, and Earl Warren. They understand themselves as perpetuating a tradition with its own interpretation of the law, so that the law becomes a historical enterprise of a historical people. These judges think of themselves not as applying rules but as focusing the concerns of their historical practice in a way that makes them relevant to the case at hand.

When they hear a case, those judges who maintain solidarity do not simply try to determine who obeyed the law most precisely according to their own standards of what amounts to obeying the law. Rather, they listen to both sides and decide which admired cultural practices make the clearest sense of the actions of both the plaintiff and the defendant. Judges don't look at an action here and a response to it there. They determine the concern that each action articulates and then how the law has understood that concern over the law's own history. Each case, then, is seen in terms of the traditions the plaintiff and defendant are developing. This is just the first step of their thinking and their writing. Second, judges must determine whether the plaintiff and defendant are repeating the activities of a tradition with little change or whether they are innovating. If they are innovating, judges must describe the innovation. They must see the marginal practice that is being made central, the neighboring practice that is being adopted, or the native practice that is being retrieved or gathered. This is a judge's responsibility in hearing and articulating the case.

When such judges make a decision, they seldom simply uncover facts. Rather, they determine under what circumstances one social concern is subordinate to another social concern. They see plaintiff and defendant as acting on the grounds of different social concerns, and their job is to determine which concern takes precedence in the current context and why. To figure out the why, judges must show how the body of law has dealt with these concerns and shaped our sense of their relation to each other.

Consider a simple nuisance case. A plaintiff complains that his neighbor has been playing loud music that interferes with the quiet enjoyment of his property. The defendant answers that as a property owner herself, she ought to be free to do what she wants with *her* property. In the common law tradition, these two positions on property rights go back to the time of Henry VIII. The judge must look at how the law has developed regarding the shared concerns for using property for quiet enjoyment and for enabling the owner to express herself. The judge will note, for instance, that if the defendant is making the disturbance as part of productive labor, the law will give her greater latitude; but if the disturbing activity is simply recreational, the law will give the defendant less latitude. The law has for a long time interpreted the concern of absolute ownership—of doing what one wants with one's land—as giving a person the power to innovate in producing a public identity but not in producing private pleasures. The history of nuisance disputes gives many other hints to a judge about which side should be favored under what conditions. And it is in the context of being sensitive to these hints and how they have shaped the present that the judge makes a decision. A judge who looks only to the most recent "relevant" decision in a superior court will not produce solidarity.

The judge's real work, however, is to justify decisions. The judge's job is to show that the decision is right and to convince both parties that their claims have been seen in the best light and thoroughly understood, and that the decision is based on the way they both live their lives insofar as they are members of the historical community in which the decision is made. To do this, the judge must show how the law has come to understand the various details of the case *and* that it makes sense for the law to continue its historical understanding today. In other words, the judge must articulate a principle for adjudicating between the two concerns that is already dispersed among previous decisions. In making a ruling, the judge builds on the great articulations produced by earlier culture figures who have influenced the way the law works.[31]

If the judge performs well, the plaintiff, defendant, and those who have witnessed the trial come to see that they have taken part in a tradition, raised important issues in the tradition, and caused the tradition to be established anew. They feel that they have made history and have taken part in explicating the practices out of which they both live and are constituted as legal persons. They therefore feel a sense of solidarity with their fellow citizens.

In perpetuating solidarity, the judge must have an explicit sense of history and a developed historical sensibility. It is, we argue, the judge's job to put people back in touch with the concerns supported by their practices and not just to settle disputes. The judge puts people in touch with their concerns by understanding the history of those concerns and how culture figures such as Henry VIII have transformed them. The judge explains to us how our simple everyday practices came to be worthy of us, who brought them into that sense of worthiness, and how they did so. Making people see that their own actions are making history is the job of anyone who produces a sense of solidarity.

Colleges and Universities

The second institution that can—and we think should—promote national and cultural solidarity is higher education in the humanities. Unlike the present confused condition of the humanities in the United States, from the early seventeenth century through the mid-nineteenth century, colleges (there were no research universities) were understood to be responsible for transmitting the cultural heritage of the West by teaching Greek and Latin, Christian theology, and moral philosophy.[32] The Romantic notion that the quality of a nation's literature determined its greatness and justified its law and international standing became current shortly after the U.S. Civil War at the time when research universities were being founded.[33] On the basis of arguments that the national literature articulated the concerns of a nation's social and political institutions, the study of English literature triumphed over Greek and Latin in the United States. This nineteenth-century cultural nationalism led to the expansion of the research university as well as to the establishment of departments of French, German, Spanish, Slavic, and so forth in the colleges.[34]

Today, several views of the role of the humanities fight for our loyalties. One faction argues that institutionalizing a humanities curriculum on the basis of works that articulate the main concerns of a national culture is a political act that privileges a set of concerns primarily because they are the concerns of people who are more politically influential than others within the culture.[35] Another faction argues that education makes people more intellectually competent and that intellectual excellence (the highest standard of competence) should therefore be the measure by which students, teachers, and the content of instruction are judged. We should teach then only those works that excel in intellectual merit.[36] Another faction appreciates the claims of excellence but asserts that in a diverse, let alone a multicultural, society, no consensus can be achieved either on the domains in which excellence is to be judged or on what counts as excellence in each domain. This leaves us in the position Alasdair MacIntyre has well described: "[W]ithin each partisan camp there has emerged a[n] . . . agreement as to what weight is to be assigned to different types of reason within different types of context, but there is no general academic consensus on this within whole disciplines, let alone between disciplines."[37]

So within each partisan camp in the humanities (MacIntyre thinks that there are three main ones), questions about what ought to be taught and how it should be taught can be raised and debated to produce increased clarity. But those who believe in the religious grounds of human understanding (Thomists, Augustinians, and some neo-Hegelians and neo-Aristotelians), those who believe in the unity of human reason and practices along with the commensurability of the world to that reason and practice (neorationalists), and those who believe in multiple worlds or perspectives (neo-Nietzscheans) might well be able to understand enough of the others' views to deem them ordered enough to count as marginally reasonable but not enough to find their claims or arguments persuasive.[38] Indeed, debates and discussions among partisans of different general views tend to leave the various participants amazed that the others could believe something so counterintuitive. At their best, such discussions lead participants to try to imagine why people would see things in such unusual ways. But more often, participants simply hear each others' conclusions as *reductios* that ought to be understood to show that the whole general view that produced such a conclusion is incoherent.

Though they differ over the causes, most writers on the state of higher education in the United States concur with MacIntyre's description of strong partisan camps, each with its own ways of reasoning about and understanding how human beings make things intelligible and all living within a disordered realm of intellectual and practical considerations (usually called the deliberations of the university). This realm, unlike that of the camps, identifies concerns and practices in such a way that we cannot recognize the ultimate worthiness of any of the concerns and practices. This realm of dim confusion, which the university constitutes, is lamented by virtually all who write about higher education. Gerald Graff and Alasdair MacIntyre both argue that it should be transformed into a realm of debate. Graff would have religious thinkers, neorationalists, and neo-Nietzscheans more or less constantly debating one another by offering jointly taught courses and by also offering separate courses taught by members of the different camps but linked together by common discussion sections where the instructors discuss and debate.[39] Graff's intent is for the confused realm of dim agreement to become the lucid space of shared debate. One could think of Graff's program as turning a bunch of street fighters who attack each other at night into prize fighters who engage each other under spotlights, in rings, with referees and managers, and before the combined gaze of the national culture. He wants the intellectual warfare of the universities to become like the intercity rivalries among Texas high schools that we have already described. MacIntyre has a similar solution in which academics develop their own modes of inquiry, debate with others engaged in other modes of inquiry, and join together to organize a university that grants enough space for the different modes of inquiry to develop and that sets up debates among those involved in the different modes of inquiry.

MacIntyre, however, is unsure whether all this can be done in any single university.[40] He proposes that those with different modes of inquiry each develop their own universities and that the universities stage disputations among themselves.[41] Whereas Graff thinks that a democratic national culture can be grounded in such spectacular debates, MacIntyre thinks that the different sides are so divided that agreement on a debate or disputation mechanism and the debates themselves are not enough to ground a culture. MacIntyre's hope is that the disputations will show the general superiority of the mode of inquiry of religious thinkers.[42]

Like Graff and MacIntyre, Charles Taylor wants to transform the dim realm in which cultural perspectives each seek recognition while barely recognizing others; but instead of championing debate or disputation, Taylor calls for a hermeneutic fusing of horizons. Because no genuine conversions or judgments can be made on the basis of principled disputes (as all agree) and because debates cannot promise to open up new ways of seeing things and new problems for people to acknowledge (which Graff and MacIntyre think can come out of disputes), Taylor claims that we must learn, much as an anthropologist does, the practices of living that are the ground of the different modes of inquiry. Only after living the different positions from the inside, and hence having a life that contains all the different positions can we make a perspicuous comparison in a vocabulary that is faithful to what each mode of inquiry is trying to say and do.

Unlike those who think there is no common ground, thinkers like Robert Bellah, E. D. Hirsch Jr., John Searle,[43] and bell hooks respond to the realm of dim confusion from different points of view. They all assume, though with different attitudes, that the realm of dim confusion either is implicitly coherent or is connected with one that is. Bellah, for instance, says that he and other academics already have practices for making sense of the various modes of inquiry in our national culture.[44] We need only articulate how we manage to live coherent lives to see the concerns that we care about most.[45] E. D. Hirsch Jr. seems at first to be interested only in protecting a "national vocabulary" that includes shared attitudes (what we would call concerns) and that is ultimately incoherent—a realm, as we say, of dim confusion.[46] But Hirsch thinks that a democracy in which people are self-governing requires more than a shared though incoherent national vocabulary, since incoherence would prevent people from governing themselves on the basis of broad principles everyone understood and cared about. Therefore, Hirsch claims that we in the United States need and have (in addition to our shared national vocabulary) a shared coherent civil religion that tells us which of our concerns are the highest—"tolerance, equality, freedom, patriotism, duty, and cooperation."[47]

Also claiming that the dim confusion is not irresolvable, John Searle argues that once we clarify the presuppositions that underlie our most widely shared ways of understanding and doing things, we will see that our settled ways of doing things do not support the religious and the neo-Nietzschean modes of inquiry at all.[48] Likewise, bell hooks agrees with Searle that the traditional role of the research university has been shaped by the presuppositions of the Western heritage, and she probably would agree that this has been understood as the pursuit of excellence. But hooks sees the presuppositions of our culture of excellence as upholding "white supremacy, imperialism, sexism, and racism."[49] Moreover, she claims that our "culture of domination necessarily promotes addiction to lying and denial."[50] So hooks thinks that we need to criticize our common presuppositions by drawing them out and testing them against the diverse experiences of all members of our culture. It is precisely the criticism of our common presuppositions on which solidarity is built. She writes: "Our solidarity must be affirmed by shared belief in a spirit of intellectual openness that celebrates diversity, welcomes dissent, and rejoices in collective dedication to truth."[51] For hooks, then, education has the job of challenging presuppositions and not of finding out what follows from them. That challenging produces, as she says, "a space of radical openness where I am truly free to choose—able to learn and grow without limits."[52] She is like Bellah, Hirsch, and Searle, then, in thinking that what unites all academics can ground substantive decisions about education, but unlike Bellah, Hirsch, and Searle, she sees this as a danger to be overcome by criticism of the common presuppositions by which we make other people, ourselves, and things intelligible.[53]

Although these views are quite diverse—even contradictory, as in the cases of MacIntyre and Bellah or Searle and hooks—they all assert that antagonism inevitably results from conflicting claims for cultural diversity, on the one hand, and for social unity, on the other. Consequently, they look to education to give stable form to the antagonism and thereby contain it.[54] For Graff and MacIntyre, that antagonism comes to be best contained as a sport or cultural ritual. Taylor describes a process by which the antagonism can ultimately be superseded. Bellah, Hirsch, and Searle claim that a unity behind the antagonism protects us from having to worry that diversity will produce fundamental conflicts. And for hooks, advocating diversity overcomes the dominating tendencies of any social unity in the name of a radical openness. In short, either we accept antagonism between the claims of social diversity and the claims of social unity, or we overcome the antagonism in the name of either unity or radical diversity.

Based on what we have said so far about solidarity, it ought to be clear that we think that this picture of antagonism between the one (social or intellectual unity) and the many (diversity) is entirely wrong. It grows out of the view, which has become embedded in a commonsense metaphysics, that our lives are coherent, that each thing we do fits with other things that we do, that the actions of others fit with our own, and that all these actions add up to an organized world where all nonconfused, serious, legitimate, and sane purposes and actions are interlocking. We treat noninterlocking purposes and actions as negligible, deeply confused, illegal, or insane. On the basis of such experience, we assume that the truths of our life and of the world and their corresponding ways of being are also interlocking and consistent. Thus there is ultimately one genus of truth and one genus of being, even if they are normally encountered in a variety of species, such as, concerning truth, attunement to the cosmos or the correspondence of propositions with states of affairs and, concerning being, the being of humans as opposed to the being of equipment. In recent decades, we have become sensitive to pervasive differences in purpose and action of people of different nationality, race, gender, sexual orientation, class, and religion. Moreover, we have come to note, especially in cases of gender, not only how comprehensive differences in understanding truth and being are but also how we have persistently ignored them.[55]

Such recognitions of difference have led to an internal strain in our commonsense metaphysics. That metaphysics tells us that if we are going to have any sense of being or truth, it must be unified, while our experiences tell us more and more that our grounds for believing in an organized understanding of being and truth are weakening. So there is an incongruity between our commonsense metaphysics and our own experience, which our commonsense metaphysics is supposed to bring into clarity. This puts us out of touch with our own experience, and many turn to the humanities for help. But, as we can see from the sample of writers on education, people looking for help in the humanities have found religious thinkers and neorationalists (MacIntyre and Bellah, on the one hand, and Searle, on the other, with Taylor counting as both religious and neorationalist) telling them that they cannot or should not give up their commonsense metaphysics and that the diversity of experiences will ultimately be resolved in the way confusion is usually resolved. They also find neo-Nietzschean liberation theorists (hooks and Putnam) who say that we need to abandon the order of commonsense metaphysics for the radical freedom of unreined diversity of experience. Nietzsche himself seems to have combined the rationalist and today's neo-Nietzschean tendencies of thought. He argues that we should abandon the will to truth, which is nothing more than a confused will to power, and that a genealogical use of the microtechniques for producing positive historical truth about historical facts (Nietzsche uses these techniques to examine how good, bad, evil, and truth became concerns for our civilization) undermines higher-level claims about the nature of the real and our relationship with it that would ground the microtechniques. Hence, the business of producing truth and a stable understanding of being is shot through with paradox.[56]

Generally, Nietzsche prescribes a redirection of concerns away from truth toward various and inconsistent forms of aestheticized life.[57] These forms of life enable us to reorder the serious concerns of our culture with naive playfulness.[58] Yet despite Nietzsche's sophisticated combination of the rationalist and liberatory tendencies that we find in contemporary thinking, he still leaves us with the choice between despairingly clinging to the contrary-to-experience hope of an ultimately unified understanding of being and truth or the contrary-to-commonsense abandonment of a life organized around consistent actions and purposes. We still have the all or nothing of devotion to an organized truth or a disorganized revolutionary openness.

Only Gerald Graff asks us to change our commonsense metaphysics, but instead of returning us to our experience and articulating that, Graff asks us to take the antagonism between our commonsense view that there has to be one organizing understanding of truth and being and our experience of different senses of truth and being and make that our new common sense. So we exchange an antagonism between ontology and experience for an ontology of antagonism where our experience and common sense are always at odds.[59] Consequently, Graff has not really accepted the experience of difference that is coming to pervade our lives more and more. He has accepted, rather, the contest between that experience and our inherited common sense.

To put this matter in the terms with which we began this chapter, we note that the disputants in the debate over education are still dwelling within the intellectual predispositions of Herder's metaphysical understanding of human beings and culture. They think, like Herder, that clarity requires either an ordered set of reasons, concerns, and so forth or, unlike Herder, that freedom from such an oppressive clarity requires undermining such an ordered set. In Graff's more sophisticated case, there is constant conflict over various orderings of reasons, concerns, and so forth as each tries to displace the other and return to an intellectual and cultural space like the one Herder described. And just as we suggested that national solidarity does not require an ordered set of concerns, but rather a loosely coordinated bundle of concerns, so the educational program that draws our attention to and cultivates that loosely coordinated bundle of concerns need itself be no more ordered. In other words, we propose that we take our experience of differences in understanding and worthiness seriously, not as something to overcome, not as something to see in the light of something else, like Western metaphysics, that has been overcome, and not as a ground of endless contests between those who champion one or another ordered set of arguments and concerns. Our experience—that ordered sets of arguments and concerns are not currently or soon to become dominant—can lead us to better understand our culture. Instead of ordering our inconsistent experiences to make them consistent, we can articulate their genuine differences. Indeed, once we abandon ordering arguments or concerns as giving us either our true identities or our only genuine access to the world, we can begin nurturing our various cultural concerns and their various modes of inquiry. Such nurturing may not give us the intellectual clarity or solidly bounded cultural identity preferred by Herder, but it takes us beyond the dim confusion we currently face at having no predominant form for making things, people, and ourselves intelligible and no ordered set of concerns for giving ourselves a firm cultural identity.

Such a plan for the humanities may seem to ignore all the obvious hard questions. To begin with, no college or university could teach all the texts recommended by the various disputants in the so-called culture wars. Second, how would we determine which mode of inquiry is suitable for teaching any particular text? Or do we advocate that all texts relevant to a national culture's modes of inquiry and identity be taught by each of the culture's modes of inquiry? Third, what evidence do we have that simply articulating the concerns of our culture and the modes by which it enables things, people, and selves to become intelligible would do anything more than reduce the dim confusion and increase the conflicts among concerns and modes of inquiry, which would lead to the proliferation of short-sighted partisans or broad-sighted relativists? To answer these questions, we describe a *general* form for articulating concerns and modes of inquiry.

We propose articulating the national culture's concerns and its modes of making things, people, and selves intelligible and creating courses that determine which practices and other social conditions enable the production of each concern and each mode of inquiry. In today's educational jargon this is called *understanding contexts*. But the proposed form of education would neither glorify nor denigrate beginnings (though surely some beginnings would appear glorious and others shameful). Instead, it would look to our own marginal practices to try to recapture the experience that brought out each concern or mode of inquiry, and it would do so in terms that allowed a student to understand its development. This form of historical analysis is regularly carried out by non-Marxist post-Hegelians, post-Nietzscheans, and post-Heideggerians. But any mode of inquiry that brackets its claim that there is one ordering of concerns and one right way of making things, people, and selves intelligible can be used to articulate our concerns.

For us, however, the clearest model of such articulation is Heidegger's account of the Platonic notion of the idea and other related notions that he sets out in terms of the experience of Greek craftsmanship.[60] These analyses seek to find a way of living that can be made sensible in the present (though it is not a normal way of doing things in the present), that gives people a sense of how things, people, and selves became intelligible, and in particular that provides a sense of how their concerns once seemed a sensible production. Proceeding this way helps us see that in the history of the West things, people, and selves appeared in significantly different ways in different epochs. Hence, the notion that there is any one right ordering of concerns and modes of understanding is bracketed. Moreover, none of these ways of making things intelligible is granted a particular priority at this level of presentation. Concerns today appear in a national culture that emerged from conditions that led people to experience life quite differently from the way we now experience things and people. Consequently, understanding today's concerns requires both attending to marginal aspects of our own life that enable us to make sense of the emergence of these concerns and also attending to how these concerns have been transformed so that they fit with our other concerns.

Once we see that many modes of inquiry are available to articulate a national culture's concerns, we can also allow scholars to choose which concerns to articulate. As long as students understand the contexts for the production of the concerns and explore a number of different contexts of production (minimally more than two), they will learn a way to appreciate and articulate national concerns that does not commit them to only one ordering of those concerns and only one mode of inquiry. Since in articulating a concern we call for understanding the experience that led to its production, we want the concerns taught in terms of the cultural monuments that brought about the shared recognition of the concern by people in the culture.

Finally, once students are taught about the emergence and descent of the various concerns in a national culture's bundle, they still may become historical (and consequently cultural) relativists or crude partisans of one or another epoch's or culture's ordering of concerns and dominant mode of inquiry. Simply teaching students to become articulators of a national culture's values does not show them how such articulation produces solidarity. For this, students have to learn that they actively make the history that produces and reorders both concerns and modes of inquiry. In short, for the maintenance of solidarity in the absence of a culture figure, students will have to learn the skills of history making.

It might seem that maintaining solidarity requires that students be taught precisely those skills that we have identified as the ones that make history—reconfiguration, cross-appropriation, and articulation—but that is not our aim. Others claim that history is made by means of other skills. Derrida claims that deconstruction makes history, although it is history of a new kind. Foucault argues that problematizing makes history. Hegelians argue that fusion of horizons and supersession produces history. What solidarity requires is that students exercise for themselves in a course or set of courses at least one of the various skills for history making advocated by leading thinkers today.

Students who become familiar with the collection of concerns that give their national culture an identity would be drawn to address these concerns in various ways. Only when one understands that one is and must be engaged in active and practical dealing with the concerns of the culture can one cultivate solidarity.

Conclusion

Our goal in this book has been to argue for the importance of history-making skills. We conclude by comparing and contrasting our three paradigmatic history makers—the entrepreneur, the virtuous citizen, and the culture figure—and then showing how each supports the three fundamental ways in which Western nations make history and consequently provide meaningful lives for their citizens. To do this we create a description of modern societies and then use this description to show that historical democratic societies with market economies give us a form of life in which identities matter, as they do in right-wing political configurations, and in which human beings are sensitive to changes in human practices, as they are in radical leftist political configurations.

We have claimed that our three types of history makers manifest three different ways of making historical changes in the style of a disclosive space. We can see that these three modes of innovative activity all have the same structure. The entrepreneur, virtuous citizen, and culture figure find in their lives something disharmonious that common sense overlooks or denies. They then hold on to this disharmony and live with intensity until it reveals how the commonsense way of acting ought to take care of things and how it fails.

In describing our composite entrepreneur, we described how he sought to create a fully developed economic model of his country, in which finances were efficiently allocated to tasks on the basis of a general understanding of economic relations. Instead, he found that he was constantly involved in negotiating arrangements with various ministers, industrialists, members of the press, workers' organizations, and so forth.

These ad hoc negotiations seemed precisely the antithesis of what his country had asked him to do. In describing virtuous citizens, we described how the MADD mothers knew that they ought to believe that the people who had killed or maimed their children were upstanding members of the community who had had accidents, but found themselves feeling that a deep injustice had been committed that had little to do with bad luck. And in describing the culture figure, we described how Martin Luther King Jr. grew up in a culture where rational technocratic solutions were expected to solve even racial problems but found again and again that the way he related himself to people, both racists and others, was not merely rational.

Each of these figures found a disharmony and held on to it long enough to identify the accepted way of acting with which it was in conflict. For the entrepreneur, the established way of acting was to seek a theoretical account of tasks that would lead to identification of the variables that rational planning ought to optimize. For the virtuous citizens, it was an ethos of working hard and then rewarding oneself. For the culture figure, it was the fact that the paradigm in which race relations were supposed to make sense involved only rational technical adjustments to the social space in which people lived—which allowed the existence, for example, of separate but equal institutions for people of different races.

As the source of the disharmony became clearer, each of our history makers became a puzzle solver. What was the importance of ad hoc negotiations for understanding work as a whole? Why did a sense of justice denied keep the mothers from coming to terms with their "bad luck"? What underlying way of relating to other people rendered clever bureaucratic manipulations of social conditions irrelevant and futile? The only effective way to answer questions of this type is to be intensely involved with the practices in which one dwells that produce anomalies. In such a situation, one must carry out the normal operations of life with the kind of captivation one feels when engaged in solving a puzzle. But this is not a specially constructed puzzle; one's own practices for living are themselves the puzzle. One lives to find out what one is implicitly taking as deeply important, without (and this is the hard part) prejudging the issue by adducing established formulations for dealing with life.

We can imagine what our history makers had to ignore. The entrepreneur had to ignore the call to rational planning based on the structure of tasks. The MADD mothers had to resist the social judgment that they were acting like hysterical women who were unable to bring their grieving process to an end. And Martin Luther King Jr. had to overcome the sense that, by not seeking a legal or technocratic solution to race hatred, he was venturing into a territory of irrationalism that could breed still more hatred.

As all stayed with their puzzles and began to see things differently, a marginal practice came to look as though it held more importance in their lives *and the lives of others* than they had initially supposed. The entrepreneur began to see that work could now be understood in terms of speech acts such as requests, promises, stipulations of conditions of satisfaction, and declarations and assessments of completed tasks. The heart of work was not carrying out tasks but designing the nature of the space in which tasks would make sense as worth doing. And, indeed, as more and more of the commodities we purchase are tied to services, we find that we are purchasing relationships with their providers, and we understand more and more that each relationship is unique and must be managed by managing not the tasks involved but the concerns to be addressed by the tasks. The MADD mothers began to see that the responsible stance that mothers have toward their children pervaded their sense of justice, and that such a sense of responsibility profitably fit with the hard-working ethic in subworlds surrounding them. Finally, Martin Luther King Jr. saw that the American ground for how fellow citizens should treat each other was not ultimately rationality but Christian charity of the sort advocated (even if never practiced) by the Puritans, to which King in his new articulation added the dimension of inclusiveness.

Each of these figures came to see that what was at first disturbing to them actually helped them to make sense of how their fellow citizens lived every day. We have already said that entrepreneurs use their anomaly as a basis for reconfiguring some disclosive space. Virtuous citizens use their sense of the disparity between their practices and that of other subworlds to connect with other kinds of people, and then they try to cross-appropriate practices on the basis of the understanding the disparity has revealed. And culture figures act in such a way as to express or articulate the dispersed practice they have found guiding their own actions. But in reconfiguring, cross-appropriating, and articulating, history makers do more than explore the pervasiveness of the new way of doing things that they have uncovered. By making a marginal practice central, adopting a neighboring practice, or focusing a dispersed practice, they disclose that they (and we) are all disclosers. The change they establish changes the way all others in the disclosive space encounter things and people, and everyone in that disclosive space is put in a position of fashioning himself or herself anew. Bringing this about makes the actions of these disclosers historical.

What do we make of the differences among world disclosers? Why, when a marginal practice is being made central, is this most often the job of the entrepreneur who embodies the marginal practice in a new product, service, or business practice? What sort of practice works best by being appropriated by neighboring disclosive spaces? Why do we say that this sort of activity is most often political? And finally, why is it that the focusing of a dispersed practice is most often the job of a culture figure?

We answer these questions in reverse order, moving from the most to the least apparent. A practice that has been dispersed in a disclosive space is one that by definition everyone in the disclosive space already implicitly defines himself or herself in terms of. Martin Luther King Jr.'s famous line about judging a man not by the color of his skin but by the character of his conduct spoke simply to an aspect of the agape U.S. citizens already essentially believed. Attention was thus being drawn to a concern they already accepted. Recognizing this transformed a confused "we" into a more sharply focused "we." But people were not given a new way of seeing work or any similar thing. Nor were they necessarily being called on to reconceive their local orderings of concerns. King called U.S. citizens to recognize how they already acted toward one another—to see that, at their best, they already practiced agape in certain situations. Such an activity is not fundamentally political because it does not *primarily* appeal to people according to their local orderings of concerns and ask them to appropriate a practice that reorders these concerns so that their subworld's form of life is different. Indeed, this is what made King so successful. He was not, in the first place, asking U.S. communities to *reorder their concerns* so that equality looked like a central concern rather than a minor one. He was asking them to *recognize the dispersed concern* of judging people by their character rather than their physical characteristics. This kind of judgment was one that they generally made, at least in judging members of their own races, but nothing in this practice limited it to members of one's own race. Once U.S. citizens understood that this practice was the basis of equality but that they had lost touch with it, it became hard for most U.S. citizens to defend racism.

An articulating activity such as King's does not easily lend itself to embodiment in something that produces a new way of seeing and dealing with things and people. The acts of the culture figure exemplify this practice—as King's peace marches and acts of public disobedience did—and these need to be repeated because people do not immediately grasp what the culture figure is doing. But once they do grasp the point, they need nothing special to keep it alive because they already embody it themselves. The effect is to rededicate the way people see themselves. (Those who continue to resist marginalize themselves and appear less and less to be genuine examples of citizenship.)

Events unfold differently in cases where the disharmony is of the type that MADD uncovered. The mothers found that their concern of full responsibility was supported by some practices and that they could offer their practices to other associations of people in ways (different for each association) that would enable each to handle some of its problems better. Groups such as MADD are trying to convince other subworlds to reorder their concerns. They are not, however, assuming that these subworlds should order their concerns precisely as their group has. Rather, in speaking concretely about their own situation they are trying to connect their concerns to those of their audience and then to build on these connections. This raising of sensitivity to concrete practices is what we have called interpretive speaking, and this activity constitutes political action.

Why could not such a disparate practice as the mothers embodied promote a sense of solidarity? Because the various practices of full responsibility that the mothers had do not exist in many of the nation's subworlds, calling attention to these practices could not produce a new sense of a "we." One might try to understand the mothers as calling attention to the concern of full responsibility, which all related subworlds would share. However, since this concern is not dispersed but is ranked fairly low in the ordering of some subworlds, calling attention to it might make MADD look simply like mothers being motherly. Insofar as this was what they were doing, they would have had little or no effect. What they had to do was to give people in other subworlds a feel for the concern of full responsibility that certain useful practices answer to and show them also why they would want to adopt these practices. For example, they had to make physicians aware of how fully responsible practices of drinking produce healthier patients. They had to show employers how such practices produce more productive employees. The mothers had to make their point differently in each subworld. When they had achieved changes in enough subworlds, they found that they had also changed general background ways of acting.

Why could they not embody such a new way of seeing in a new product or service? And why doesn't the legal change they pursued count as a new product? Our common intuitions ought to show us the answer. The change in law really does not embody the change in practices. The fact that we are all leading more responsible lives may explain the law, but the law does not make us see things in a new way. That has to have happened already for the law to make sense. Someone might suggest that this is a failure of MADD. One might think that the law ought to have worked, or at least could have worked, like the entrepreneur's product. The problem here is that the rare practice the mothers were attuned to was not pervasive enough. Many subworlds could be made better by adopting parent-like practices, but the members of those worlds were not leading lives where adopting such a practice would alone regestalt their whole view of their disclosive spaces. Indeed, our newfound concern for health and the effects of alcohol has been taken up in quite different ways by different people in different disclosive spaces. Some have changed the style of their lives; others have just changed the ordering of some of their concerns.

Entrepreneurial anomalies do not generally lead to this kind of varied behavior. An entrepreneurial possibility occurs when a dominant practice or paradigmatic way of acting seems to govern a large expanse of activities in a disclosive space. But either the dominant practice is not really governing the activities, or it governs them but does not answer many confusions that people have. The entrepreneur who uncovers the disharmony also identifies a marginal practice that will, once taken up, allow people to resolve many confusions in a new way. Unlike the articulator's forgotten practice, the entrepreneur's is not one that tends to call people back to their senses. Nor is it one that many people come to understand in many varied but related ways. Rather, the entrepreneur's attention to a marginal practice looks at first absurd or outrageous. Imagine Gillette trying to tell people that he was working on a disposable razor that would end many of the masculine rituals surrounding shaving and give men a new sense of convenience. The entrepreneur's anomaly speaks, then, for a historical possibility that has not been recognized but that, when it is recognized through a new shared practice, will be recognized by most people in roughly the same way. That is why the entrepreneur must do two things that the culture figure and virtuous citizen need not do. Since the entrepreneur is not simply calling on a practice that people are already familiar with and is not drawing on a practice that will be cross-appropriated in different ways, she must embody the marginal practice in a comprehensible way (so that people begin engaging with it) and with a kind of strangeness (so that people engage with it explicitly). Only in this way will people both overcome their resistance to changing the way they have done things in the past and become attuned to a new style of doing things.

We have now accounted for three different ways of disclosing that one is a discloser—acting as a history maker—in terms of three different kinds of disharmonies. Are there other ways of disclosing that one is a discloser through producing historical change, or have we exhausted the field? Our answer is that these are the only possibilities. We have argued that for a change in cultural practices to be meaningful there must be continuity within the change. The continuity is provided by the fact that change is organized around taking a practice with which people have some familiarity and making it more important. To see why we say we have exhausted the field, we need only ask where rare yet familiar practices could come from. A past practice that was once important could be revived, a neighboring practice with which the society has some familiar-ity could be cross-appropriated, or a practice that has been marginal in the culture and so unexplored could become recognized as important. From where else could a practice come with which we would already have some familiarity? We can imagine practices coming from a distant culture, as, for example, when Western technological practices have been introduced to peoples who had felt no previous Western influence. We believe, however, that the effects of such introductions have always been discontinuities in peoples' histories. We therefore claim to have exhausted the field because we have exhausted the possible sources for noncentral practices with which we are already familiar.

Our threefold analysis of how disclosive practices can be changed leads us to see the worthiness of a democratic nation with a market economy in a new way. If, as we claim, Western human beings at their best are essentially history-making disclosers, and if they make the most of disclosive activity by attending to disharmonies, then a civil democracy with a market economy is the current productive-political formation that most consistently makes possible human being at its best, for it alone allows people to be true to the disharmonies that they experience in their lives. A nation like Singapore, which has a thriving market economy but, in effect, a benevolent dictator in charge of political affairs, is a nation of people who must either ignore certain kinds of anomalies or try to reconfigure practices that should be articulated or cross-appropriated. Likewise, when Sweden had its most socialist political and market structure, anomalies that called for reconfiguration would have been either ignored or, if the democracy was working very well, handled by cross-appropriation. Civil democracies with market economies enable their citizens to hold on to anomalies in the way appropriate to the anomalies. Other political and economic formations do not, and for this reason many chances for historical activity are lost as citizens lose their hold on anomalies suited to a kind of change that is discouraged.

If our study of world-disclosing activity shows why civil democracies with market economies are to be prized above other political and economic configurations so far constructed,[1] it also shows why each of the ways of history-making should be prized.

The cultivation of solidarity, of citizen virtue, and of entrepreneurial product innovation are the activities in which the three basic kinds of world-disclosing take place. A civil democracy with a market economy has three essential interests. First, it has an interest in enabling people to sense that they all share a disclosive space of ultimate consequence in which they live and work. This disclosive space is most often the nation, and for people in a democracy to sense that they all share this space, it must have an identity. Developing that identity is the job of culture figures and the institutions that support them. Second, a civil democracy must occupy itself with the structures of ownership, agreement, and association among its people. Classically, these structures have to do with the way people bind themselves to each other. How are associations structured, and for what purposes are they formed? Also, how are associations related to each other? These questions form the heart of politics and government. This is where cross-appropriation takes place, and we deem this discourse native to politics because it is based on advocating reorderings of concerns through sharing practices in a way that respects subworlds. Third, there is the domain of productivity. Classically, this domain involves producing goods and then holding and transferring them. The law approaches these concerns by thinking about property. Here we suggest that thinking about productivity that does justice to human beings as history makers requires thinking of it in terms of institutionalizing the innovative aspect of entrepreneurial skill.

In each of these domains, there is a normal, nonhistorical, institutional form of disclosive activity that consolidates previous world-disclosing actions. These institutions accustom us to the consequences of the changes in the world wrought by articulating, cross-appropriating, and reconfiguring. We have not discussed all the institutions that consolidate such historical changes, but we have attempted to describe the most illustrative ones. While institutions from the family and the local church to museums, sports teams, and entertainment can consolidate changes in a nation's identity wrought by culture figures, we have singled out the universities and courts as doing this job most clearly. In the domain of politics, various levels of government, particularly regulatory agencies, consolidate changes made in the way various subworlds associate with each other. Finally, as we might expect, customary businesses most illustratively consolidate the changes in the world wrought by entrepreneurs.

Our analysis allows people to diagnose the health of their institutions along two lines of development. One line has to do with whether all necessary institutions are in place for a civil democracy with a market economy to function historically. Leaders should ask the following questions: Does the market have a significantly entrepreneurial business sector? Does the nation have citizen groups involving themselves in legislation and other governmental decision making? Does the nation have institutions like universities and courts articulating the concerns that culture figures have brought out of dispersion? If the answer is no, then some extraordinary measures will have to be taken. Culture leaders will have to initiate the development of such activities by forming exemplary institutions, offering rewards for history-making behavior, and sending citizens abroad to receive training in history-making institutions.

We assume, however, that most of our readers are more interested in a second line of development. The question to ask here is whether normal disclosing activities are receptive to what culture figures, virtuous citizens, and entrepreneurs do, or whether they try to repress their history-making activities. We all know what such repression looks like. Courts and universities can uphold narrow, traditional understandings of a culture's concerns. They can resist the notion that a current culture figure is restoring an old concern that has been dispersed. Universities can attack a culture figure on narrow scholarly grounds, as Martin Luther King Jr. has been attacked. The courts and the universities can argue that the restored concern is not genuine because in the past it did not look precisely the way it looks in its restored form. The same can happen with citizens' political associations. Governments can take recourse in the existence of a silent majority. They can redefine political actions as radical-fringe developments. Most repressive of all, they can respond to citizen action groups with complacency. The members of MADD could have been treated as an association of hysterics when the movement started, and in the same vein, big businesses can easily harass entrepreneurs. They can involve them in endless and expensive litigation, increase the cost of capital, partnerships, or manufacturing, or simply follow up entrepreneurial innovations with cheap imitations. The game-playing techniques for making entrepreneurial activities difficult are endless. Maneuvers such as these will ultimately impair the historical capacities of a nation, and we hope that our analysis provokes concern over the extent to which our history-making capacities are presently being injured.

Businesses need to take the lead from entrepreneurs, governments need to learn from citizen action groups, and courts and universities need to learn the lessons of culture figures. But business, government, and the courts and universities are also the training grounds for entrepreneurs, citizen action groups, and culture figures. If historical figures do not emerge from such institutions, then we have a strong indication that business, government, and the courts and universities have been taken over by the disease of careerism. Customary business, government, courts, and universities should not be seen as the home of professionals—though they need some—so much as the training ground of those who will continue the nation's history. In general, then, the line of development from the customary to the history-making runs in both directions. Customary activities are transformed by the historical ones, and customary activities, customary business, politics, and solidarity preservation serve as the breeding ground for entrepreneurs, virtuous citizens, and culture figures

If leaders find that the customary and history-making institutions are not supporting each other, then they need to consider legal changes and a new form of education dedicated to understanding and producing history-making. We can now sketch what this new institution of higher education might look like.

A higher education devoted to producing entrepreneurs, virtuous citizens, and culture figures should be organized around the nature of disclosing and the spaces in which it occurs. We have described three types of disclosing—historical (or world-disclosing), customary, and theoretical. Each type of disclosing would be the concern of an academic unit, but these would be quite different from today's academic units. Education in each unit would include courses on the ontology of the particular kind of disclosing in addition to courses that apply this ontology. Hence, we call this the *curriculum for disclosing*.

The first set of courses would show how Westerners developed and then concealed an understanding that the human way of being transforms background practices through history-making. In addition to teaching the dominant disclosive practices that have defined different historical epochs in the West, ontological courses also would canvass the various ontological accounts of history-making to provide students with the resources to become involved in history-making themselves and thereby make this defining practice of the West their own. This unit would also include courses in native and foreign (Western and non-Western) literature, history of art, history, and philosophy.

Perpetuating or discontinuing historical practices and institutions can be successful only if students learn that their basic customary skills are already disclosive skills. Students need to study the general constitutive practices that structure all customary disclosing. Courses on communication would provide the ontology for this second academic unit. Communication here refers not to the exchange of information but rather to the coordination of commitments that are already implicitly coordinated by a style.[2] This ontology of communication would structure (and, we believe, ultimately ground) courses in social sciences, law, business, and management.

In the third academic unit, students would study the ontological skills of theory-making that decontextualize everyday phenomena from everyday concerns and then recontextualize them according to the internal structure of a specific domain. This understanding of theory would show why, for instance, *theories* of entrepreneurship, democratic action, and solidarity fail. Decontextualizing phenomena from the world conceals phenomena like anomalies, which exist only in terms of a world. On the positive side, decontextualizing phenomena from the world filters out all that is socially dependent and leaves just those phenomena that can be recontextualized into accounts of the structure and causal properties of nature as it is in itself.[3] Once students have developed this ontological understanding of theory, they would also be taught the skills, procedures, and knowledges of the various natural sciences.

We would now like to summarize as simply as possible our view of entrepreneurship, virtuous citizenship, and the cultivation of solidarity. In a customary situation, a businessperson thinks that her job is to stay ahead of the competition. She therefore tries to maximize output while minimizing input and to outdo competitors in predicting the future. As social and technological change accelerates, this sort of activity becomes increasingly frustrating. As her previously successful coping skills become increasingly disturbed, the businessperson is forced to reflect on what she is doing and to seek a better way of proceeding. She might focus on specific indicators of success and plan strategies for improving those indicators. One strategy might be to devise new ways to game the system, such as creating hedges and trusts. If she finds that this gaming increases her stress but fails to help her outdistance the competition, she may move further toward detachment and rationality. The final stage in this withdrawal from the involved deployment of concrete skills is the attempt to discover and use a generalized theory of business or competition. For a time business schools supplied such game-theoretical models and produced, it is now generally acknowledged, only a further decline in competitiveness.

According to our view, the true entrepreneur is not primarily engaged in competition (although it is, of course, free market competition that makes entrepreneurial activity possible). The true entrepreneur is involved in holding on to an anomaly and producing something that reduces a disharmony by changing the style of a disclosive space. As long as she remains innovative in this way, she will have no competitors. She will instead be engaged in the rewarding and meaningful activity of developing a new enterprise. Her main competition will be not other busineeses but the old style of life she is changing.

Like the normal businessperson, the customary politician is engaged in political debates, telling stories from his experience and that of his constituents to support a particular account of how laws should be changed. This works until there is a disturbance. In contemporary liberal democracies, a major disturbance seems to be the increased power of the media to force politicians to speak not from their local, involved wisdom but in terms of facts and universal principles that they can justify and defend before national audiences. At this ideological level, interests that might have been reconciled locally appear to be irreconcilable. Politicians then see themselves as pursuing the specific interests of the group they represent and devise strategies like expedient coalitions to ensure that the interests of their constituents will triumph. The more idealistic politicians, also under the influence of the Enlightenment faith in rationality, concentrate on attempts to articulate and defend the principles underlying their proposals. The result of their idealism is principled speaking. Success here requires an even more detached and rational political theory that justifies the ideology one is defending.

Meanwhile, the organizers of political action groups are engaged in interpretive speaking and cross-appropriation with other groups in order to change background practices. If they succeed, they will have done an end run around the politicians. Without debating them directly or engaging in detached rationality, they will have achieved their ends and, in the process, have changed the issues and ground rules of the political debate. They will have produced something much more powerful than winning a vote or an election: they will have produced meaningful and nondivisive social change.

Solidarity, too, can be better understood and promoted once one experiences the difference between customary and history-making solidarity cultivation. Customary solidarity, as we have seen, celebrates and perpetuates the bundle of concerns citizens currently identify themselves with. As societies become increasingly multicultural, citizens find it more and more difficult to agree on the composition of this bundle, and this leads to a breakdown of solidarity and to a multiplicity of groups, each speaking for the objectified goods or values that it claims represents the essence of society. As polarization increases, each group defends itself by demonizing the others as dangerous to society's way of life. Finally, each group appeals to moral theory (or revelation) in an attempt to prove that its objectified goods or values are the only necessary or essential ones. The possibility of solidarity cultivation is covered up completely.

While those with objectified values debate which values and practices are the ones that are essential to the national identity, culture figures such as Martin Luther King Jr. act on another level. King did not engage in confrontations over what practices for treating African Americans are most American, nor did he argue the rationality of his cause. Instead, through intensified involvement, he brought to the center of national attention a dispersed concern that almost everyone accepted and thus, in an end run around fanatical defenders of objectified goods or values of all denominations, cultivated solidarity where there had been divisiveness.

In all these areas of life, becoming aware that one is a history-making discloser by developing sensitivity to marginal, neighboring, or dispersed practices not only makes for a meaningful life but also offers a highly effective way of acting in the world. Such effective action is unavailable to those who are satisfied to do the customary thing, who withdraw into detached rationality, or who seek power for its own sake.

We have shown how exploring background practices and transforming them works. We have also shown that such exploration and transformation begins in the most humble of activities. Everyone who engages in productive labor, in conversation, or in community activities has opportunities for changing customary meanings in these areas of life, though many lack the skills to exploit these opportunities. Knowing what kind of beings we are is the first step toward expanding history-making skills and understanding. With this realization, we can pursue new types of education dedicated to focusing our sensitivity to history-making and cultivating the skills we need to be more truly ourselves. Distributive justice and united action must be undertaken not because people are related as bodies, disembodied souls, calculative schemers, or any of the various interpretations of who we are, but because we are related to ourselves and each other as disclosers of the many ways that human beings can be. Only once we see that we are still historical disclosers can we respond fully to the current state of our culture, in which history-making skills are being displaced in the name of practices for constant transformation. If we are at our best in history-making, then we should seek to perpetuate history-making practices in our work, our citizens' associations, our cultural activities, and our everyday life.

A Philosophical Appendix: How We Differ from Relativists and Formalists

Readers familiar with debates within and about poststructuralist, neopragmatist, or existentialist thinking will probably ask whether our accounts of history-making, entrepreneurship, virtuous citizenship, and solidarity cultivation are formalist, relativist, or essentialist.[1] These are somewhat technical philosophical questions. The charge of formalism, as it would commonsensically be applied to our book, implies that the end or telos of being a history maker is, like the end of play, internal to the activity. The critic who makes this charge would claim that our account implies that one ought to be a history maker simply for the sake of being a history maker (or for some good internal to history-making such as changing a culture's background) just as one plays for the sake of playing (or for something internal to playing such as the joy of playing). The critical force of this charge is that, just as play ought to be judged by some external standard that interdicts vicious play, so history-making ought to be judged by an external standard. Charging that our account is relativist implies that it eliminates any ground for claiming that one culture's set of concerns is better than another culture's. Hence, a critic would claim that, by our account, a Hitler who makes history is as good as a Martin Luther King Jr. Finally, claiming that we are essentialists implies that we think that there is a fixed kind called "life at its best." Claims of fixed types in the social world are generally taken to be ethically dangerous because they exclude from serious account those forms of life that are similar to the type but not clearly covered by it.

We believe that our account can easily answer such charges when they are made in a commonsense way. (1) Our answer to the charge of formalism is that history-making strongly supports the institutions of the free market, representative democracy, and national solidarity (or a form of solidarity like national solidarity), which we hold in high regard for many reasons independent of the practice of history-making. (2) As a response to the relativism charge, we maintain that Hitler and similar culture figures are not known for being sensitive to dispersed practices and hence would not be genuine history makers. (3) We claim that what counts as "life at its best" in the West was devised 2500 years ago and may now be undergoing a change. That should be enough to do away with the commonsense charge of essentialism. A philosopher like Jacques Derrida might nevertheless claim that at the most general level of our discourse, we are still trapped within formalism, relativism, or essentialism. Here we answer such philosophical objections. Since they are of a technical order, however, we assume some familiarity with the philosophical contexts in terms of which these questions are raised.

We first take up the issue of whether we are formalists. Instead of assuming that our critic claims that "history-making" is an activity whose telos is internal to it, we adapt the formalist charge to the highest level of our thinking, where we are most susceptible to it. Are we saying that human beings are pervasively skillful and that the goods or the possible teloses of being skillful are all internal to skillful activity?

We have claimed that people in the West feel that they are handling their lives *well* when they are simple skillful practitioners living in the mode of Aristotle's *phronemos* but that they live life *at its best* when they are engaged in practices that change the nature of the disclosive spaces they are in—that is, when they engage in history-making. We think that history-making has been the typical though unthematized way of answering anomalous solicitations in the West since monotheism—either the Greek form of one main god protecting a polis or the Hebraic form of being chosen by a creator God—was developed. There were and are other ways of dealing with disclosive spaces as wholes. Homeric, polytheistic Greeks, for example, thought that one could be overtaken by a number of different whole disclosive spaces during the course of a life. People in such a situation are not history makers so much as receivers. If one day they find themselves driven by Eros, then a whole new disclosive space opens up where everything important makes sense by reference of how it relates to erotic pleasure. Hence, one might leave one's spouse and run off with an attractive foreigner. In such a polytheistic culture, anomalies are seen not as a ground for transforming one's disclosive space but as heralds announcing the opening of a new disclosive space. Even in this case, it is worth noting that in receiving a new world one would receive a new identity or defining project, and this identity would be no weaker than the authority of the world itself. It would grab one totally. Our pack of teenagers who get new gestalts as they forget disequilibriating ways of coping reveal a third way of relating oneself to disclosive spaces as wholes by shifting them, but in this case one would have no stable identity at all.

Each of these ways of being human at its best is a case of skillful comportment that is receptive to new disclosive spaces. To clarify the status of receptivity, which for us is a special kind of ground, and how it is and is not just a formal feature of human activity we must develop a number of distinctions.

First, we must distinguish between the formal aspect of receptivity and receptivity as an ontological good. We start by observing that, for the most part, the actions we perform in dealing with our fellow human beings are skillful actions. We walk, talk, sit, eat, move things, think, organize, write, conduct meetings, drive, direct, and so forth skillfully. We do not do these things, for the most part, by following rules; or if we do, they are rules of thumb that depend on a great deal of skillful activity. One of the chief aspects of skills is that they are receptive. Skillful comportment responds to solicitations in the environment. That receptivity is what makes skillful behavior as nuanced and flexible as it is. Skilled practitioners respond appropriately to small perturbations that rule-followers miss. Skilled teachers, for instance, frequently find themselves bringing out an important new feature of their subject in response to a question. It is only after the fact that deliberative thinking makes clear the importance of what they have done. This skillful *receptivity* to solicitations we take to be *formal*—that is, an aspect internal to skillful comportment that *can* serve as its telos.

There are four other formal aspects of skillful comportment. Second, when dealing with the world skillfully, things *affectively appear* for us depending on the situation in which we are skillfully engaged. Thus, when we are working away on a tough philosophical problem, the offer of a discussion of the problem with a trusted colleague appears affectively to us as a gift, while a phone call from a beloved family member appears with an irritating affect. Third, *disclosing* itself is an aspect of skillful comportment. Disclosing, as we use the term with regard to things, amounts to dealing with something appropriately, where *appropriately* means in terms of a context of things, people, and practices that enable the thing we are dealing with to be treated as the thing it is. Usually the best examples of disclosing come from craftspeople like carpenters who, for instance, deal with a piece of wood by bringing out its aesthetic and structural strengths while minimizing its weaknesses. They do this not simply to be receptive to traits of the wood but to shape it to fit in with communal purposes. It is precisely in that craftlike way that we are constantly shaping our situations; we make a space where we can have a family by attending to our loving feelings, by collecting chairs, artwork, and other equipment suited for use by more than one person, by making commitments in the name of love, and so on. Dealing with things in a way that brings them into tune with our and their context discloses them. Fourth, *gathering* is another aspect of skillful comportment. By gathering, we indicate the tendency for skills to draw related skills into association so that whole skillful domains are established. Thus the skill of hammering draws with it many other skills of working with wood such as sawing, chiseling, and measuring, and these in turn attract others into a domain of related skills that we call carpentry. Fifth, various domains are coordinated in a particular culture at a particular time by a common *style*.

In general, the members of a culture develop a special sensitivity to one or more of the five formal aspects of coping.[2] It thus becomes the good that structures the space or dimension that substantive goods inhabit. We call the disclosive-space-constituting goods *ontological goods*; in this book, we have been describing the situation in the West, where receptivity and style have become dominant ontological goods.

Any particular good such as receptivity can be both an ontological good structuring a whole disclosive space and an ontic concern in the space. Being ontological or ontic are functional and not substantive categories.[3] Thus, we can think of the polytheistic Greeks of the time of Homer as having disclosive spaces structured by the ontological goods of receptivity and affective appearance so that they would be open to receiving new affectively charged disclosive spaces. A disclosive space structured by these ontological goods would, however, be likely to contain such substantive-ontic (nonstructural) goods as openness to new situations and appreciating passions. Our current stage of Western culture, in contrast, while still structured by receptivity to changing styles of practices, seems to be replacing the substantive good of openness with that of controlled flexibility.

Privileging receptive practices, as our culture does, opens us up to receiving different domains of skillful comportment, which we have called different worlds. When style becomes an important secondary feature of skillful comportment, then different worlds come with different styles, and we become a culture that experiences the arrival of new worlds as changes in historical epochs. At our best, we then become sensitive to anomalies that enable us to change the style of our culture. In contrast, the polytheistic Greeks, who, as we have described them, have receptivity and affective appearance as their ontological goods, would respond to anomalous perturbations as calls to enter into different local worlds and would, like Odysseus, move from world to world. Furthermore, if receptivity alone were to structure the disclosive space of a culture, then anomalies would lead to the Nietzschean gestalt shifts we described earlier with our pack of teenagers. Obviously, there may be other configurations of receptivity as the secondary features change. We do not claim that our list of five aspects of skillful comportment is complete.

To see where this analysis has brought us, we need to recall the complaint about formalism. Like the goods of play, ontological goods are internal, and therefore it seems that they ought to be evaluated by exterior standards. We admit that certain aspects of skillful coping, which are obviously internal to it, *can* indeed count as the most important aspects of such coping and can, in principle, count as the telos of skillful coping. Receptivity, for example, *could* be an end of skillful coping.[4] In our history, however, each time receptivity became the highest ontological good, something else—either history-making or exploring other worlds or having intense brief habits—became the telos. Moreover, once an aspect of skillful coping becomes an ontological good, the space and nature of skillful coping change. With this change, the understanding of all other goods changes as well, whether they are internal or external to skillful coping. If the space of skillful coping becomes historical, other goods will be understood in terms of their relation to history-making. If the space of skillful coping becomes one where there are many local worlds, then other goods will be understood insofar as they support this kind of plurality. We see, then, that any external good that someone claims ought to determine how we regard skillful coping would itself receive its precise measure of authority only from the ontological goods that derive from skillful coping.[5]

Suppose we all agree that the dimensions of meaning and of evaluation of worth in the West are structured by receptivity as the primary ontological good and by style as the secondary ontological good. By promoting these ontological goods, are we then left in the position of ontological and ontic relativists? Are we unable to find reasons for promoting one rather than another of the disclosive spaces opened up by certain ontological goods rather than others? And even if we can justify accentuating one order of ontological goods, given that several possible constellations of ontic-substantive concerns could inhabit the disclosive space structured by this ordering of ontological goods, does our position imply a relativistic stance in evaluating the relative worthiness of these different constellations of ontic-substantive concerns?

So far we have simply declared that since roughly Homeric times receptivity has generally been the top ontological good structuring disclosive spaces in what has come to be called the West. Now the question for us is, Do we have any grounds for claiming that receptivity ought normally to be the top ontological good? We answer this question by describing disclosive spaces with other top ontological goods and showing the weaknesses of each. We conclude that, given the general telos of skillful performance, having receptivity as the top ontological good leads to the best state of affairs most of the time.

On the level of skills for dealing with both people and things together, receptivity is a matter of attending to solicitations for action in a way that does not override the nature of what things and people offer these solicitations but rather brings them out most fully. Thus, as hosts we do not respond to each conversational solicitation but only to those that enable us to bring out what is best in our friends, the mood, and the occasion. Even on the micro-level of skillful performance, receptivity will look different in disclosive spaces where receptivity is the top ontological good and those where disclosing, say, is at the top. Thus a skilled *receptive* woodworker might change what she was making altogether in order to bring out a certain texture in the wood. In contrast, a skilled *disclosive* woodworker might adjust to the special texture in the wood by making some small adjustment in the chest she is already fashioning. The difference between the two woodworkers is that the first responds more strongly to anomalies and change than the second.

On the micro-level of skillful performance this difference might seem simply to be a matter of trading openness for efficiency. When one begins to consider whole cultural spaces structured by receptivity on the one hand and disclosiveness on the other, the difference comes to stand out. The receptive culture tends to produce new roles in virtue of its receptivity to unusual human talents. It tends to produce alternative ways of living as different local situations and things are brought out according to their richest intelligibility. The disclosive culture, on the contrary, has a narrower set of more highly inflected roles. Likewise, it tends to have a more unified way of living, where local differences are assimilated to general purposes.

For a stark contrast along these lines, think of Thucydides' opposition of Athens to Sparta. It should be easy for us to see that a receptive culture, like the Athenians', will be more innovative and versatile and therefore more successful overall than a culture, like the Spartans', devoted to tradition and steadfastness.[6] A receptive culture like that of Athens allows for new forms of praxis to come in and branch off from older forms, while also being receptive to the ways in which its widely varied forms of praxis can be coordinated. In contrast, a disclosive culture like Sparta's attempts to maintain the integrity of its basic forms of praxis against solicitations from outside and within and thereby limits solicitations to change so much that it stunts its own internal development.[7]

If what we have said is right, receptivity should be the top ontological good in forms of life where skillful coping is pervasive. But a critic could note that we have merely stated how things look from the perspective of a disclosive space with receptivity as its top good. This is certainly true, but no one could possibly speak from the perspective of a disclosive space without a top ontological good. What we have shown is that once one is in a specific disclosive space, one sees grounds for claiming the superiority of a certain ontological good. We are claiming that our ontology justifies not an objectivist antirelativism but rather a hermeneutic one. What is important is that one cannot sensibly be a relativist on the ontological level.

Disclosive spaces structured by specific ontological goods tend to exclude certain practices and exclude or rank lowly (marginalize) certain substantive-ontic concerns. This is easy to see when we compare the effect of two different ontological goods on the disclosive space for understanding work. Compare, for instance, a disclosive space structured by the concern for the product for the product's sake to one structured by the concern for coordinating relationships. In the second case, meeting normal recognized standards is excluded because the things that the vendor supplies to the purchaser are customized according to particular, not general, conditions of satisfaction, and, consequently, the good of churning out the product is also excluded.

Matters remain much the same when we turn our attention to the five ontological goods of disclosive spaces that privilege some aspects of skillful comportment while marginalizing others. Our receptive, style-oriented, historical way of understanding skillful comportment marginalizes the substantive-ontic concern of flexible changes in identity (now called *morphing*). We do not see ourselves as passing in and out of different worlds where we have different identities. Nor do we, in a Homeric polytheistic mode, find ourselves lovers in a world where everything is erotic, then spouses and parents in a world where everything shows up in terms of domestic stability, and then professors or business consultants in worlds of competitive assessment. Although at some moments of our lives we may find ourselves living in this way, we normally pursue fully integrated experience and one life plan with one stable identity matched to one social security number. When changes do happen, they are ordered by the substantive-ontic concern of integrity. Only when we are born again or undergo a total identity change though the offices of the governmental witness protection program or become reformed alcoholics are we expected to give up our previous identity forever.

If the space of historical receiving marginalizes the substantive-ontic concerns that would enable us to experience multiple worlds (without understanding them to supersede each other), then it excludes both the polytheistic ontic concerns and the postmodernist ontic concern of flexibly seeking equilibria of the Nietzschean kind that we imagined with our pack of teenagers. From within a disclosive space structured according to the ontological goods that produce historical worlds, the restless Nietzschean gestalt-shifting looks like either a case of dysfunction or a lamentable stage of immaturity. Thus, the ontic-substantive concern of seeking flexible equilibria in the name of which gestalt-shifting occurs is excluded. We can therefore say that within the space structured by the ontological goods of receptivity and style, certain ontic-substantive concerns are excluded.

Does this still leave us open to an objectionable ontic relativism? In our endorsement of only those disclosive spaces structured by the ontological good of receptivity, are we not still too permissive regarding ontic-substantive concerns? Are we not obliged to treat receptive Nazis as the ethical equals of receptive liberals?

True, a given disclosive space determined by a particular ontological good is compatible with various incompatible bundles of substantive goods. It is not, however, so easy to adduce dramatic examples of this incompatibility as critics might think. Even if we say that Hitler was articulating the dispersed concerns of the German *Volk* as well as the belief that the German *Volk* would save Europe from its worst tendencies—and it is not unambiguously clear that genocide, expansionism, and German supremacy *were* dispersed *Volk* concerns—it is hard to see how the total technological mobilization of all resources for particular social ends could count as one of the dispersed concerns of the German *Volk*. In contrast to Martin Luther King Jr., Hitler comes out as either a fraud from the start or as a culture figure who turned into a dangerous opportunistic demagogue.

Still, one could imagine a Klu Klux Klan that practiced interpretive speaking on behalf of racist judicial proceedings, including executions, and a Hitler who practiced genocide, expansionism, and the production of German supremacy by *Volk* as opposed to technological means. Since we have attempted in writing this book to use nonfantasy cases as much as space and clarity would allow, we return to the case we cited of the parents who murdered their daughter as relevant in this context. In that case, we assumed that the collection of concerns in the family's tight-knit community and the U.S. collection of concerns both existed within typically Western historical disclosive spaces in which receptivity and style are the true top ontological goods. Yet we claimed that any local community concern that supports parents in killing children who cause shame would be ethically too obnoxious to receive any protection under U.S. law. This is to say that, although the local community and U.S. disclosive spaces are ontologically equal, as people with the U.S. collection of substantive ethical concerns, we judge this local community's concerns to be ethically inferior, indeed criminal. Along the same lines, we would be obliged to act against a receptive Klu Klux Klan or a receptive Hitler. Moreover, if we found them disgusting enough, we might believe that the obnoxiousness of the practice was greater than our concern for national sovereignty. In such a case, international military intervention would be justifiable. It should now be clear that, although ontological goods do not determine substantive-ontic goods uniquely, they do not exclude our taking a moral stand.

In general, the recognition of receptive ontological goods gives us three capacities for dealing with other constellations of substantive-ontic concerns: (1) the capacity to incorporate into our own culture concerns of other cultures that are like ours but ordered in different ways; (2) the capacity to see another culture's concerns as so incompatible with our own that members of that culture must give up certain of those concerns in their dealings with us, even if these concerns are not sufficiently incompatible with our own for us to declare them to be evil; and (3) the capacity to see the concerns of another culture as being so objectionable that we are obliged to change them by whatever means we believe will be effective and in accord with our own concerns. To repeat, although we cannot use ontological goods to justify one final set of ontic concerns and reject all others, we are not committed to moral relativism. We have as much ground for taking a moral stand as any defender of practice-based, substantive ethical judgments.[8]

So far we have argued, first, that the nature of the pervasive skillful coping that human beings engage in entails treating certain formal goods as privileged and that this turns them into ontological goods. Second, these ontological goods are not formal because they are not simply the ends for which skillful coping takes place and because no other goods could have authority over these ontological goods. Third, against charges of relativism, we showed that ontological goods set constraints on the substantive-ontic goods that a people can have. Once receptivity, for example, is a people's ontological good, human beings will have to be sensitive to the sorts of practices that bring things out in the richest (most intelligible) way, and the ontic-substantive good of disclosive craftsmanship could not, as a result, be among the highest ontic-substantive concerns. For instance, a medical practitioner dedicated solely to prolonging life could become quite expert but would show insensitivity rather than receptivity to the human beings she treated. In a receptive culture, being sensitive to what enhances things most richly and intelligibly will come before excellence in producing certain results. Hence, the life-prolonging practice would have little credit in that culture.

If we claim that life is always best when human beings have receptivity as their top ontological good, does this assign an essence to human being? If human being is always at its ontological best when it has receptivity as its primary ontological good, then the background context for making this claim ought to serve as an ultimate context for understanding human beings in any world. To answer this objection we now need to show that receptivity ought not always be the top ontological good and that it can, *for receptive, skill-oriented reasons*, demote itself. It is because of such a possibility that we describe this ontological good as a *gentle* good.[9] In developing this account, we also show how substantive–ontic concerns can take part in the displacement of an ontological good. This suggests that ontological goods do not always hold absolute sway over disclosive spaces.

In order to show that we have not claimed that receptivity should always be the primary ontological good, we provide a case where a receptive, skillful people are led by receptivity and dedication to their substantive-ontic goods to the displacement of receptivity as their primary ontological good. We return to fifth-century Periclean Athens, a culture that has receptivity and style as its primary and secondary ontological goods. Athenians are receptive to their own style and to practices that operate in terms of it as well as to practices that require styles that do not mesh with theirs. Now, suppose the Athenians are again attacked by an effectively governed and militaristic Persia. What happens? By being receptive, Athenians will realize that the Persian way of life has very few substantive-ontic concerns in common with the Athenian way of life, and they will therefore sense that their own substantive–ontic concerns are threatened. As a receptive people they will also become fully engaged in responding to this threat, and they will then become sensitive to practices they can cross-appropriate that would enable them to defeat their enemy. For such practices they will begin to turn more and more to their courageous, militaristic neighbor, Sparta.

Sparta's people live, let us imagine, within a disclosive space whose primary and secondary ontological goods are gathering and disclosing. They are therefore fairly insensitive to anomalies but highly sensitive to uncovering and developing more practices like the ones they already have. They have almost no interest in cross-appropriating or in reconfiguring but are focused almost entirely on articulation. As a people who have disclosing as their other ontological good, they also value skillful excellence at being Spartan. They are thus a people who are always looking for tests of Spartanism. And the best tests they have developed are those involved in military training. Sparta, therefore, produces courageous, disciplined soldiers.

In a drawn-out war with the Persians, we argue that the Athenians will sensitively cross-appropriate more and more military training techniques from Sparta. As they cross-appropriate techniques and Spartan battle strategies, other Spartan ways of being will begin to make sense to them. Receptivity to how these skills will serve Athens will make them all the more attractive. Given the threat to all of Athens' substantive-ontic concerns, receptivity will endorse the introduction of concerns hostile to it, such as not recognizing any difference possessed by another people as worthy and coming to see one's skills as directed not toward bringing things out in their richest beauty but toward using things to bring out one's nonreceptive Athenian nature. (The internment of Japanese by the United States during World War II is an instance of taking on at least one concern hostile to a nation's disclosive space.) Ultimately, given Persian military effectiveness, so many practices will be cross-appropriated from Sparta that the Athenians will begin acting with more sensitivity to gathering and disclosing than to receptivity and style. At that point their ontological goods will have changed—a change brought about by the very nature of receptivity that brought out both the full nature of the threat to Athens and the way in which Spartan practices could help. Thus, the ontological good of receptivity will have produced its own demotion. And if receptivity had not led to less receptive behavior in the face of such a crisis, it would not have been fully receptive.

This example is meant to show that no clear principle can be adduced regarding the working of receptivity. If there were one, then that principle would become the essence of being human. Receptivity, however, only makes human beings sensitive to bringing things and concerns out in their ownmost, richest way and draws people to be fully sensitive to what is being drawn out; when receptivity draws one to sense that the situation requires certain losses of receptivity, that loss then takes place.

The West has been lucky with regard to receptivity. However many times we have lost receptivity and style as our top ontological goods, they have returned. But just as our history-making way of handling our lack of an essence itself became typical at a certain point in time, this form of dealing with ourselves may be in the process of passing away. This book has attempted to make clear the stakes involved in ending history.

Notes

Introduction

1. Although we sometimes refer to *the* market economy and *the* liberal democratic state, these terms are abstractions. Neither market economies nor liberal democracies are natural kinds; they have many forms. We argue for those forms that best support Western culture, and for our purposes, *the West* refers to those cultures that have excelled at the skill of history-making. Thus here the West includes both European and non-European cultures. What decisively marks a culture as Western, as we use the term, is that it is unified by a style or interpretation of what it is about, that that interpretation has undergone transformations, and that the culture's highly valued skills are the ones that produce these transformations, which are also highly valued. Clearly, many cultures, such as South Sea Island cultures and Native American cultures, do not fit this description. But other cultures that have undergone transformations would not fit this description either, since the transformations were not generally valued.

2. Our account of solidarity cultivation draws its inspiration from the traditional monocultural nation-state, but it is developed to include the experience of members of multicultural or polyethnic nation-states. Genuine, heartfelt solidarity can be found in the loose associations that are now called consociational democracies as well as in the traditional nation-state.

3. Alice Echols, *Daring to Be Bad: Radical Feminism in America 1967–1975* (Minneapolis: University of Minnesota Press, 1989), 203. We owe much of our knowledge of the history of the feminist movement to this book and to talking informally with Judith Butler.

4. Ibid., 287–295.

5. See Judith Butler's *Bodies That Matter* (New York: Routledge, 1993), 17–19.

6. The most expressive voices of this new model of woman, which has changed the way we see and deal with women in virtually every prereflective way and has therefore made history, are those of women themselves. This new style can be heard in women's speech even when they speak in the dialect of dispassionate science. Consider the voices of nurses who offer midwifery practices (based on the ethos of caring for vulnerability) to

obstetricians (whose practices are based on the ethos of controlling bodily injury). Modern birthing centers are examles of how effectively these nurses have transferred midwifery practices to physicians and have made joint practice attractive. Such joint practice amounts to ongoing cross-appropriating. Nevertheless, their style of speaking is still that of subversive adaptation. We hear this in their characterization of orthodox medicine as treating "human" concerns as insignificant. Here are their voices:

> Ethical discourse regarding procedural aspects of obstetric care is often limited to rare cases of casuistry or quandary ethics, such as the appropriateness of court-ordered cesareans. . . . Such discussion keeps invisible the rest of the "ethics iceberg"—those elements of cesarean birth and other obstetric interventions that, because they affect so many birthing women, should concern us most but remain unnamed in most medical literature. Those covert issues include not only the excess morbidity and mortality associated with cesarean birth but also the emotional reactions: a sense of powerlessness, insults to self-esteem, depression, anger, long-term grief, repression of some of the experience's negative aspects, and feelings of indifference toward and too much pain to enjoy the baby. If maternal and fetal life outcome is seen as the only issue of import, human concerns of comfort, dignity, and vulnerability are cast as insignificant. [See Lynn McCreery Schimmel, Kathryn A. Lee, Patricia E. Benner, and Leon D. Schimmel, "A Comparison of Outcomes Between Joint and Physician-Only Obstetric Practices," *Birth* 21.4 (1994): 202–203.]

7. Anna D. Wilde, "It's a New Generation of Business Travelers," *New York Times*, November 12, 1995, Sunday ed.: sec. 3, 1, 9.

8. Sherry Turkle, *Life on the Screen: Identity in the Age of the Internet* (New York: Simon & Schuster, 1995), 263–264.

9. Ibid., 180.

10. Ibid., 226.

11. Ibid., 184.

12. Ibid., 185.

13. Ibid., 12.

14. Ibid., 26.

15. Ibid., 192.

16. Ibid., 179–180.

17. In his account of brief habits, Nietzsche describes the life that today we call moving from one hot group to another. Brief habits are neither like long-lasting habits that produce stable identities nor like constant improvisation. For Nietzsche, one of the best forms of life occurs when one is fully committed to acting out of one brief habit until it ceases to be exciting and another takes over. See Friedrich Nietzsche, *The Gay Science*, trans. Walter Kaufmann (New York: Vintage, 1974), §295, pp. 236–237.

Chapter 1

1. In order to have a general term for this capacity of coordinated practices to create an openness wherein things and people can show up, we speak of *disclosure*, and since this

disclosure excludes too, we think of it as opening a space that is bounded by a horizon.

2. On the one hand, style is a broader notion than disclosive space since even an individual will have a style. On the other hand, a disclosive space is a large set of organized practices. The style of a disclosive space is how the disclosive space's practices hang together. Looked at it in this way, style is a narrower notion than disclosive space. Given our interest in how people and things can show up as meaningful, we are concerned only with the style of disclosive spaces. One may live in several different disclosive spaces that offer different variations on the style of one's culture, which is the largest disclosive space people dwell in. And in most cases the style of one of these disclosive spaces dominates one's life.

3. A culture's style is so pervasive as to be invisible, whereas we want to make the "style" of dress we choose highly visible. As soon as the current style of dress begins to be taken for granted and not noticed, the fashion must be changed. Style, as the unnoticed basis of all that we notice, has thus become a term of art for us, and we use the term *fashion* where *style* would be used in its more ordinary sense.

4. To reveal the gist of the way style works, we simplify the specific sociological claims. For some of the precise claims, see W. Caudill and H. Weinstein, "Maternal Care and Infant Behavior in Japan and America," in C. S. Lavatelli and F. Stendler, eds., *Readings in Child Behavior and Development* (New York: Harcourt Brace, 1972), 78ff.

5. It should now be clear that the three history-making skills we wish to describe in detail in the rest of the book operate both on an individual and on a social level to produce *stable* but not *rigid* worlds and identities. They enable individuals and social groups to be open to resources in their practices that show up first as disharmonies but, if skillfully dealt with, can become the source of new disclosive spaces that enable those involved to take better care of their concerns.

6. We should note that our thinking of human beings as practical disclosers descends from Pascal through Kierkegaard, Dostoyevski, Heidegger, Lacan, Derrida, and Irigaray. Of course, apart from the core notion of human beings as engaged in disclosing identities out of the materials given them by their traditions, there are large differences among these thinkers. We should also recognize our debt to a set of thinkers both opposed to us and quite close to us who think that human beings at their core are engaged in practices but that this activity tends to maximize the grip one has on things and the world. The important thinkers here are Nietzsche, Merleau-Ponty, and Foucault. Equally important to us are today's neo-Aristotelians and neo-Hegelians, who would agree with much of our phenomenology except to claim that the identities we believe are *produced* through various appropriations are merely *discovered*. These thinkers include Alasdair MacIntyre and Charles Taylor.

7. The important antecedent here is Nietzsche and his notion of brief habits. See note 17 in the introduction.

Chapter 2

1. Writers such as Henry Mintzburg and Robert Solomon, like us, think that skills are more important than theory when it comes to dealing with the real world. We go beyond these thinkers in that we claim, first, that the skills that form the background for dealing

with people, things, and selves contain an understanding of what it is to be anything at all and that taking up such practices gives one an identity and so gives one's life meaning, and, second, that these skillful practices and the meanings they embody are not homogeneous, that some are central and others are marginal, and that understandings of what it is to be anything at all change when the marginal practices become central. In short, we maintain that the background skills, in the West at least, are historical. The basic difference between us and other researchers, then, is that we examine skills for holding on to anomalies and for getting in tune with the background practices that produce historical shifts in some disclosive space. Further, we claim that entrepreneurs, virtuous citizens, and culture figures have these skills in a preeminent degree.

2. Peter F. Drucker, *Innovation and Entrepreneurship* (New York: Harper & Row, 1985), 26.

3. Ibid., 50.

4. Ibid., 19.

5. Ibid., 22.

6. Ibid., 127–128.

7. Ibid., 111–115.

8. Karl H. Vesper, *New Venture Strategies* (Englewood Cliffs, N.J.: Prentice-Hall, 1980), 25.

9. Ibid.

10. Ibid., 116–145.

11. Ibid., 146.

12. Ibid., 55.

13. Ibid., 139.

14. Ibid., 135.

15. George Gilder, *Recapturing the Spirit of Enterprise* (San Francisco: ICS Press, 1992), 309.

16. Ibid., 194–195.

17. Ibid., 296.

18. Ibid.

19. Ibid.

20. Ibid., 297–298.

21. Ibid., 297.

22. Ibid., 308.

23. Gilder calls these virtues *religious*, but it is hard to deny that humility, giving, and commitment—especially when the commitment is important for attaining an identity— are specifically Christian.

24. To illustrate the nature of genuine entrepreneurial skill and the phases of its application in the development of an entrepreneurial enterprise, we need to describe a

case where the entrepreneurial enterprise is still being developed so that we are not drawn away from our phenomenon by any purely managerial thinking, and we need to work from direct experience of the phenomenon in order not to repeat the lore in the area of entrepreneurship. For these reasons we have drawn on our experience of Fernando Flores's development of workflow software both as observers and as the innovator. But since we are, for this project, interested not in Flores himself but in the phases of development of an entrepreneurial enterprise, we have felt free to supplement our direct experience with the experience Flores has gained as a business process consultant. The result is a composite entrepreneur who, we hope, does justice to the phenomenon of entrepreneurship both in its rich details and in its general features.

25. Our use of the term *anomaly* is inspired by Thomas S. Kuhn's usage in *The Structure of Scientific Revolutions*, 2nd ed. (Chicago: University of Chicago Press, 1970). However, there is a significant difference between his usage and ours. The domain of normal science, as Kuhn describes it, consists of puzzle solving on the basis of the current paradigm for understanding the domain. When a puzzle repeatedly resists explanation, it takes on the status of an anomaly, the explanation of which may require the replacement of the reigning paradigm. By and large, the domains of life that we are discussing in this essay are not like science in that day-to-day activity is not so explicitly a matter of puzzle solving. Indeed, much day-to-day life is not puzzle solving at all. Consequently, the entrepreneurs, virtuous citizens, and culture figures we discuss do not start with a puzzle that they discover resists normal solutions. Rather, they start with a disharmony between their understanding of what they do and what in fact they do. These disharmonies may be ignored (unlike problems in science), but the figures we are interested in do not ignore them. Rather, they embrace them and seek to see how much the disharmony they have found affects life. If the disharmony seems fairly pervasive— that is, if it exists for other people and in more than a few situations—it becomes an anomaly, as we use the term. It is like a scientific anomaly at this point because its identifier looks at situations in which disharmony occurs, senses that the commonsense understanding of what happens in these situations is what gives rise to the disharmony, and sees that normal ways of thinking may have to be revised.

26. Consider the following story about Joseph Liemandt, the founder of Trilogy Development Group. The writer, Josh McHugh, deals easily with the anomaly Liemandt noticed:

> On [Liemandt's part-time and summer jobs during college], he began to notice that when he ordered computer equipment, the shipments often arrived late, or with parts that were missing or incompatible with his computers. Smart technology companies were dumb when it came to selling and delivering products. (*Forbes*, June 3, 1996, p. 122)

But when it comes to describing how Liemandt held onto the anomaly to see what it could yield, all McHugh can muster are the following vague quotations: "'I knew when I got to college I was going to start a software company,' Liemandt says. 'I started doing tons of research. I'd sit in the library going through lists of top 50 software companies'" (ibid.).

27. Managers and employees also can hold on to anomalies and regestalt the smaller disclosive spaces in which they work, but this is not a subject for this book.

28. Michel Foucault used this term in his lecture "*Omnes et Singulatim*: Towards a Criticism of 'Political Reason,'" in Sterling M. McMurrin, ed., *The Tanner Lectures on Human Values*, vol. 2 (Salt Lake City: University of Utah Press, 1981), 225–254.

29. Robert C. Solomon has strong alternative arguments, which we endorse, against the notion that businesses and people engage in productive business activity primarily for profit. See Solomon's *Ethics and Excellence* (New York: Oxford University Press, 1993), 17–18, 34–47. This book comes closest to ours in understanding entrepreneurial and business activity as a skilled activity based on many other skillful practices that remain in the background.

30. Brigitte Berger, ed., *The Culture of Modern Entrepreneurship* (San Francisco: ICS Press, 1991), 31–32.

31. In economics, entrepreneurship is seldom addressed directly. When it is addressed, the essential core texts remain those of Schumpeter and Kirzner. See Joseph A. Schumpeter, *The Theory of Economic Development* (1911; Cambridge, Mass.: Harvard University Press, 1936), and Israel Kirzner, *Competition and Entrepreneurship* (Chicago: University of Chicago Press, 1973). Though we speak of other economists as well, the two most important, following respectively from Schumpeter and Kirzner, are William J. Baumol, *Entrepreneurship, Management, and the Structure of Payoffs* (Cambridge, Mass.: MIT Press, 1993), and Mark Casson, *The Entrepreneur: An Economic Theory* (Totowa, N.J.: Barnes & Noble Books, 1982).

32. Don Lavoie, "The Discovery and Interpretation of Profit Opportunities: Culture and the Kirznerian Entrepreneur," in Berger, ed., *The Culture of Entrepreneurship*, 45.

33. Ibid., 49–50.

34. Casson, *The Entrepreneur*, 120.

35. Lavoie explicitly calls the entrepreneur's activity interpretive. See Lavoie, "The Discovery and Interpretation of Profit Opportunities," 36.

36. It still may well be true, as we suggested in chapter 1, that when families adopt the cellular telephone, the style of their practices becomes inflected in a way that draws it closer to the business style. Hence the nature of facts shifts within the domain of the family.

37. Baumol, *Entrepreneurship*, 19–20.

38. Ibid., 240.

39. See ibid., 15.

40. Kleiner Perkins, a venture capitalist firm in Palo Alto, California, takes such gaming to the extreme of trying to game entrepreneurial activity itself by coming up with ideas for new products, matching innovators with these ideas, and then creating diversified portfolios of such entrepreneurial firms.

41. For additional arguments along these lines, see Solomon, *Ethics and Excellence*, 48–64.

42. We are not going to develop this argument further here, but see Henry Mintzberg, *The Rise and Fall of Strategic Planning* (New York: Free Press, 1994). Other people have seen the failure of rationalistic business schools. Our approach, however, suggests why these schools seek to develop theories and why these same schools inevitably fail to produce entrepreneurs. We are aware that some business schools have focused their programs on a case-study approach. Unfortunately, many of the cases studied are cases of gaming, but in general a case-study approach can be quite useful, especially since businesses must deal with culturally different versions of market economies.

Chapter 3

1. See John Rawls, *Political Liberalism* (New York: Columbia University Press, 1993), 18 n. 20.

2. Rawls thinks that this constrained neutrality follows from the capacity for justice, which presupposes in its reasonableness the recognition that others will not value goods as one does. Dworkin, in contrast, thinks that this neutrality follows from holding a liberal ethics, which requires that a government not provide special extrinsic reasons for developing one skill over another. Justice for Dworkin requires that people be enabled to develop those skills that best fit with their understanding of the world.

3. See Rawls, *Political Liberalism*, 29–35.

4. Will Kymlicka, *Multicultural Citizenship* (Oxford: Clarendon Press, 1995), 81.

5. One thinks of Alasdair MacIntyre, Michael Sandel, and Charles Taylor.

6. One thinks of Kymlicka, *Multicultural Citizenship*, and of Stephen Holmes, *The Anatomy of Antiliberalism* (Cambridge, Mass.: Harvard University Press, 1993).

7. See ibid., 206–210.

8. Kymlicka, *Multicultural Citizenship*, 91, quoting Ronald Dworkin, "Liberal Community," *California Law Review* 77 (1989): 489.

9. Ronald Dworkin, "Foundations of Liberal Equality," in Grethe B. Peterson, ed., *The Tanner Lectures on Human Values* (Salt Lake City: University of Utah Press, 1990), 108.

10. See Rawls, *Political Liberalism*, 207.

11. Certain liberals have taken to heart communitarian charges and have abandoned special Rawlsian or Dworkinian grounds for liberalism. They argue that liberalism is a cultural development with its own goods and kinds of human persons. To put their point in crude communitarian terms, they claim that there is a diverse liberal community (not a society that can include many communal associations) and that this community is the best community to belong to. See William A. Galston, *Liberal Purposes* (Cambridge: Cambridge University Press, 1991), and Brenda Almond, "The Retreat from Liberty," *Critical Review* 8.2 (Spring 1994): 235–246.

12. Dworkin, "Foundations of Liberal Equality," 78.

13. Ibid., 86.

14. J. G. A. Pocock, "Civic Humanism and Its Role in Anglo-American Thought," in his *Politics, Language, and Time* (1971; Chicago: University of Chicago Press, 1989), 86–

87, emphasis ours. See also Pocock's magisterial *The Machiavellian Moment* (Princeton: Princeton University Press, 1975), 506–552.

15. This is Galston's objection (*Liberal Purposes*, 225). Bruce Ackerman would probably share it, since he endorses what he calls *liberal republicanism*—that is, liberalism with its "private citizens" most of the time and republicanism with "public citizens" on grand occasions of constitutional change. See Bruce Ackerman, *We the People: Foundations* (Cambridge, Mass.: Harvard University Press, 1991), 29–32, 230–265.

16. Civic humanists thought it crucial that one discussed or worked through one's important concerns with those on whom one was not dependent. So it seemed that someone in business could never honestly resolve an important concern with his customers, since the customer's desire was always to be taken as authoritative. In our chapter on entrepreneurs we have tried to show that such a notion is simply wrong. Inventing and marketing new products and services are ways to work through concerns. This is not to deny, however, that sometimes dependency forces one to veil one's important concerns. Civic humanist and activist egalitarianism must therefore ensure that people have some institutions where they may articulate their concerns without the worries engendered by such dependency.

17. We may come to know our concerns by inventing some new object for people to use or by inventing some new dance—the expressive options are wide open.

18. See Almond, "The Retreat from Liberty," 236–237.

19. Dworkin, "Foundations of Liberal Equality," 36.

20. It should be no surprise that Dworkin thinks of the ethics we all implicitly share as *challenge ethics*, an ethics where we are developing skilled performances to meet *clear* challenges.

21. This section owes a great deal to the following articles by Charles Taylor: "Some Conditions of a Viable Democracy," manuscript, 6–7; "Invoking Civil Society," *Working Paper 31*, Center for Psychological Studies, pp. 4 and 11; and "Liberal Politics and the Public Sphere," in *Philosophical Arguments* (Cambridge, Mass.: Harvard University Press, 1995), 257–287.

22. The first to see the problem was Søren Kierkegaard, who attacked "The Public" in his book *The Present Age*, trans. Alexander Dru (New York: Harper & Row, 1962).

23. See Hubert and Stuart Dreyfus's discussion of the role of risk in acquiring expertise and the irrelevance of principles in *Mind Over Machine* (New York: Macmillan, 1986), 26–27.

24. This account of MADD is taken from news accounts. The details are meant to be suggestive and are not the result of exhaustive research.

25. California activists in favor of the death penalty during the 1970s are an example of this. Although strong laws were enacted, the judges on the state's supreme court did not come to see the death penalty differently and blocked death sentences.

26. Andrew Revkin, *The Burning of the Amazon* (Boston: Houghton Mifflin, 1990), 193.

27. Ibid., 194–195.

28. Ibid., 197.

29. Ibid., 205.

30. Ibid., 207.

31. Ibid., 217.

32. Ibid., 202–203.

33. Ibid., 201.

34. Ibid., 213.

35. Ibid., 218–219.

36. Ibid., 219. There were also alliances in opposition to the enemies of the rainforest. These enemies turned out to include the World Bank, which was financing the Brazilian government's building of roads into the rainforest. Mendes went to Washington to find allies in his attempt to stop the roads. He found such an ally in Senator Kasten, chair of the Subcommittee on Foreign Appropriations. Revkin reports: "Kasten thanked [Mendes] for his help. 'I can promise you that our subcommittee is going to continue to put pressure on the [Inter-American Development Bank] to withhold funds . . . if they are not cooperative,' he said. Kasten shook Mendes's hand, sealing the unlikeliest of alliances—between a staunch conservative from a state of rolling, treeless pasture that based its economy on cows and a Marxist forest dweller whose worst enemies were cattlemen" (p. 223).

37. Ibid., 226.

38. Ibid., 290.

Chapter 4

1. We do not attempt to give a scholarly account of Herder here. Rather, we focus on claims that have come to be associated with his name.

2. We are here examining what we suppose are the shared intuitions and experiences people have *when* they feel solidarity toward their fellows. We are not suggesting that people regularly feel this way in the West at present.

3. We hear today of MacJobs—temporary jobs like flipping hamburgers. Such jobs supposedly prevent people from exercising virtues. We suspect, however, that most jobs help people form identities that they care about. When critics see people as wage slaves, they are generally looking at work as a series of tasks rather than as a series of negotiations. True, many companies have mistakenly tried to standardize all negotiations so that work can become a series of tasks, but most companies have failed to bring about this disaster. Employees take the few opportunities these companies have left for negotiating and exercise some human virtue there. There are, unfortunately, low-virtue jobs (mechanical jobs that inhibit the exercise of the virtues we respect), but the sensitivity to how we produce cultural change should help us see why, given sufficient dissemination of entrepreneurial skill, such jobs could be eliminated.

4. Nothing we have said here should be taken to suggest that high-risk professionals such as firefighters would hesitate to take risks such as fighting fires in the homes of resident

aliens. Such a refusal is a logical possibility of our reasoning, but, in most nations, it is just one of the goods in the bundle that resident aliens are accorded most of the rights of citizens.

5. It follows that we think that the expectations we feel toward people living in different nations are of a different character from our expectations of our co-nationals. We calculatively come to learn what we may expect of people in various roles in foreign nations and even develop views on how people in various nations act in general. But unless we are truly bicultural, we do not see the world in terms of this alien way of acting. And when someone in a foreign nation acts in a way that surprises us but does not surprise her fellows, we change our calculations. When we deal with our own fellow nationals, however, we believe that we have a strong sense of the virtues that are attached to each role, given our shared set of goods. If someone does not live up to the virtue we expect of him, we feel cheated, and we will feel that way even if his fellows have grown inured to his behavior. Indeed, we will take these fellows to be partly to blame. Our expectations are not up for revision except in situations where goods are clearly being rearticulated by the courts, universities, or culture figures. (Universities, for example, have taken the lead in transforming the good of being a "melting pot" into being a "mosaic.")

6. In passing, we should point out that conscription and military law do not show that people usually risk their lives for their nations only under coercion any more than we should say that about any law. Most people are law abiding even when they recognize that they could violate the law without facing a penalty. For these people the law serves to reveal social expectations, and the penalty attached reveals the degree of seriousness attached to these expectations. Of course, a well-articulated and enforced law such as a conscription law should prevent a soldier from wondering if others are calculatively using him or her to die for them. Such calculativeness would, we have argued, dissolve solidarity.

7. In this section, we discuss those thinkers who try to save Herder's intuitions by focusing on one highest good or value. While these thinkers agree that the project of understanding solidarity ought to be engaged in the search for a good or value that all can and will identify themselves with, they disagree over whether this highest thing is a *good* or a *value*. Since we argue against both in the same way, we use the term *good* in this section to mean both a good and a value.

8. Richard Rorty, *Contingency, Irony, and Solidarity* (Cambridge: Cambridge University Press, 1989), 91.

9. Robert Bellah et al., *The Good Society* (New York: Vintage Books, 1992), 277.

10. Ibid., 285.

11. See section 5 below.

12. Benjamin Barber, *Strong Democracy: Participatory Politics for a New Age* (Berkeley: University of California Press, 1984), 182.

13. J. Habermas, "Justice and Solidarity: On the Discussion Concerning Stage 6," in Thomas E. Wren, ed., *The Moral Domain* (Cambridge, Mass.: MIT Press, 1990), 244.

14. Those who advocate an embrace of the proliferation of differences have already broken free of Herder's influence. For such thinkers, all that is shared in a democracy

is the agonism that comes with the dissemination, within the culture, of new concepts and meanings and therefore new ways of being. Recognizing this disseminating movement liberates us from conformism, the domination of tradition, and the dangers of authoritarian politics. Such a view is advanced by those influenced by Jacques Derrida. Chantal Mouffe, for instance, would substitute something like the mutual recognition of different parties conflicting with each other for national solidarity. We agree that such recognition produces a new openness, but we think that to live out of this experience, one would have to give up the sense of the stability of identities and institutions central to our tradition. If we gave up identity and embraced multiplying differences, we would not find ourselves living in democracies that had anything like the background of disclosing practices we now require for continuous history. Advocates of difference admit as much and claim that they are thinking about *radical* democracies, not liberal or civil democracies. We focus here, however, on the kind of solidarity that could sustain civil democracies and institutions that understand themselves in terms of their relatively continuous histories. Only time will tell if the West can give up these kinds of institutions. For more on versions of radical democracy, see Chantal Mouffe and Ernesto Laclau, *Hegemony and Socialist Strategy*, trans. Winston Moore and Paul Cammock (London: Verso, 1985); Chantal Mouffe, ed., *Dimensions of Radical Democracy* (London: Verso, 1992); Chantal Mouffe, *The Return of the Political* (London: Verso, 1993); and Roberto Mangabeira Unger, *False Necessity: Anti-Necessitarian Social Theory in the Service of Radical Democracy* (Cambridge: Cambridge University Press, 1987).

15. Vàclav Havel, "How Europe Could Fail," *New York Review of Books*, November 18, 1993, p. 3.

16. The ordering of goods is not a question of abstract, theoretical debate. *Goods*, as we are using the term, are meant to capture the situated choice of one way of doing things over another. Thus, if a community is deciding whether to build a dam that will reduce dwelling land but improve irrigation, the decision should be made on the basis of what the citizens feel best expresses their way of life in this situation. From an abstract point of view this can be put as the question of which value is higher for them, dwelling or farming, but their decision is not a desituated choice about how to rank these values in general but only how to rank them in this specific situation.

17. Sometimes political action consists in arguing over which model best predicts outcomes, and sometimes political action consists in balancing interests. But we believe that most of the time—when people dispute such things as whose model better predicts the effect of a new tax or whether the suffering involved in pursuing some goal will be equally shared—the concrete topic under discussion is a smoke screen for arguments about the ordering of goods. For example, people who argue for a model that predicts that a new tax will hurt the economy usually are really arguing that the good supported by the tax is not sufficiently high to displace the good of enjoying the fruits of one's labor, while those who argue for a model that shows that the new tax will help the economy generally are really arguing that the good supported by the new tax is higher than the good of enjoying the fruits of one's labor. This is not to deny that political argument can sometimes be about models; but when it is, technicians rather than politicians generally can better determine which model is appropriate.

18. To those who think that prolife and prochoice advocates do not mean the same thing when they speak of honoring either life or freedom, we would say that the fact that each group can have a wide range of agreement over what they detest on the basis of these two goods shows that they do mean the same thing and that the nub of their dispute really is abortion. Thus most prolife and prochoice people would feel strongly negative about those who, arguing the sanctity of their own lives, would not risk their life to save another and also those who, arguing freedom of choice, would use abortion to select the traits of their children.

19. When we speak of the collection of goods that a nation's citizens share, we do not claim that all citizens as citizens share precisely the same collection of goods. Some will have goods that others do not have. What we mean is that all citizens as citizens share a large number of important goods and that among those goods that are not shared, none are held by some citizens and detested by others. It is tempting to speak of a collection of core goods that are shared, but such an expression already moves in the direction of an ordering. One usually takes the core goods to be somehow higher than the other goods, and the goods constituting the core result in a rather short list. Our intuition is that, in most cases, the number of goods shared is quite large and that for this very reason different orderings can produce interesting political arguments.

20. We are indebted to Austin Sarat for drawing the following cases to our attention and for his analysis of what the court found in each of the cases. The Native American case is *Employment Div., Ore. Dept. of Human Resources v. Smith*, 494 U.S. 872 (1990). The Amish case is *Wisconsin v. Yoder*, 406 U.S. 205 (1972).

21. Although this case is real, we have abstracted it to avoid suggesting that the community involved shared the sense of honor imputed to it by the defendants. For our point we simply need to posit the possible existence of a community in which honor plays the role suggested by this case.

22. Modern scholars are discovering that such diffuse social movements are not so new. What had long been thought of as the organic Protestant movement in the early modern period was really made up of many different groups with different orderings of goods. Yet these groups all recognized the same set of goods and on that basis formed temporary coalitions with other groups. See, for instance, Stephen Greenblatt, *Renaissance Self-Fashioning* (Chicago: University of Chicago Press, 1980), 159.

23. For clarity's sake, we should point out that political leaders have four functions: to manage the political apparatus of a state that produces laws, adjudicates disputes, enforces decisions, and so forth; to act as a virtuous citizen defending the specific ordering of goods represented by a specific political party; to reconfigure a nation's practices and set up institutions that perpetuate this change (Franklin Roosevelt is a good example of this); and to function as a culture figure, holding up before a people the important shared goods embodied in their practices so that these goods become clear. Our focus is on the fourth function, but the fact that political leaders can act in all these ways may account for some of the confusion in people's attempts to evaluate them.

24. Our account is based on National Public Radio stories of King's life and on Taylor Branch's magisterial *Parting the Waters* (New York: Simon & Schuster, 1988). The analysis of King as a culture figure is our own.

25. Martin Luther King Jr. also engaged in both cross-appropriation and reconfiguration in subsidiary ways. He cross-appropriated the practice of nonviolent civil disobedience from Gandhi. Additionally, he used the nonviolent acts of civil disobedience to put European Americans in positions where they had to treat African Americans with new and unusual practices of respect.

26. Insofar as Martin Luther King Jr. asserted the importance of agape love as the defining aspect of his civil disobedience and as an important aspect of American life, he acted as a culture figure cultivating solidarity. Insofar as he argued that, on the basis of the good of agape love, the ordering of civil rights ought to change, he acted as a political leader. Americans celebrate him as both.

27. For more on social equilibrium, see Maurice Merleau-Ponty, *Phenomenology of Perception*, trans. Colin Smith (London: Routledge & Kegan Paul, 1962), 434–456.

28. See Friedrich Nietzsche, *On the Genealogy of Morals*, trans. Walter Kaufmann (New York: Vintage Books, 1967), 57–58.

29. Nietzsche engages in thought experiments along these lines. See Friedrich Nietzsche, *The Gay Science*, trans. Walter Kaufmann (New York: Vintage, 1974), 171–173, §§111–113.

30. We might think of this form of life as exemplifying the Nietzschean life of brief habits or of improvisation. See Nietzsche, *The Gay Science*, 236–237, §295, and 243, §303, respectively.

31. In suggesting that, for the sake of solidarity, judges account for their decisions in light of the continuing story of our developing understanding of the relevant law—the law of nuisance, in our instance—we are ignoring the role of moral and economic legal theorists. These theorists have influenced current legal thinking, but they have not given an accurate account of the nature of the bindingness of the law and therefore of the goods it embodies, and we would argue that their effect has been deleterious as far as solidarity is concerned. Economic theorists like Ronald H. Coase and his followers treat legal decisions as a substitute for optional bargains that would have been made under free-market conditions. The law then becomes (or ought to become) an imitation of market forces. Guido Calabresi and others with compensation programs treat the law as a tool of social planning whose success is determined by how adequately it distributes goods. The law then is understood as no more binding than the notion of distribution it embodies. Moral theorists like Richard Epstein treat the law as analyzable from the perspective of atomic individuals forming a social contract, but such theorists fail to explain how a law can be binding if it cannot be rationalized as something to which a precontractual subject would oblige herself. In short, all these theorists develop accounts of human behavior as it exists outside the law and offer them as perspectives in terms of which to evaluate and rationalize the law. Since the way these kinds of behavior are binding on us is nonlegal, they miss the way the goods supported by the law and the law itself are binding on us.

For an account of how these theoretical proposals miss the binding quality of the law of torts and thus necessarily run into dilemmas, see Nancy A. Weston, "The Metaphysics of Modern Tort Theory," *Valparaiso University Law Review* 28 (1994): 919–1006. Although we endorse Weston's criticism of the theorists' understandings of the bindingness of tort law (and believe that these criticisms may be extended to other branches of the law), we do not share her sense of the law as always embodying a shared duty that ought to be mitigated only in light of other shared duties. Instead, we hold that the penalties attached to laws articulate the relative bindingness of the publicly shared goods embodied in the laws to one's idiosyncratic ordering of goods. (That is, we believe that for most members of a society the shared public ordering of goods and the individual ordering of goods are largely the same but that various unusual experiences lead to personal differences in the ordering of goods concerning particular aspects of life.) In matters where the penalty for legal transgression is death, societies do not allow any personal inflection of the public ordering of goods. Where penalties are less than death, however, the community prescribes by the size of the penalty how much it tolerates individuals acting according to their own different orderings of goods.

For us, then, the law is neither economic (i.e., discretionary) nor moral (i.e., absolutely compulsory). The status of the law shows up, for us, most clearly in the case of the individual who loves the public ordering of goods embodied in the law of the community and does not seek their change whenever they deviate from her own personal ordering of goods, but who acts against the law when her own ordering of goods differs from the public ordering and pays any resulting penalty without complaining. This individual regrets that her own goods do not line up more closely with the public goods, which she recognizes as binding, and therefore also regrets violating the law, but she is thankful to the community that the penalties assigned for this violation of community standards do not deny her the possibility of being true to her way of handling her identity and life. Our individual, then, is not like the individual postulated by the economic theorists, who is outside a law that is optional in the sense that she can always choose to pay the costs of violating it just as she can choose to pay the cost of going to a Bach concert. And unlike the individual postulated by moral theorists, she is not so constrained by the shared public standards that she feels obliged always either to act in accordance with them or to change them. The law, then, does not have the character of moral principles that leave no leeway in one's duty to abide by them. Within the law as the embodiment of a community's ordering of goods, the personally necessary thing may be the publicly wrong thing, and this need not indicate that something is wrong with the public ordering of goods. Penalties, short of absolute penalties, articulate how much one's own ordering of goods ought to match the public ordering, and those who have, in other productive dimensions of communal activity, acquired sufficient resources to pay the cost of a violation are left enabled to do so by the community's law. Of course, the law will not tolerate repeated or casual violation, and that is why penalties rise for repeat offenders.

This view is not meant to suggest that the law is or should be optional for the rich and binding for the poor. We believe, however, that our account is an accurate reflection of how people actually experience the law as what is essential about the law. If we look at the whole range of cases that appear for adjudication, we find that in many areas of the law it is the poorer members of a society who are often "judgment free," whereas people with assets are often targets of litigation for seemingly minor infringements. In the middle class, the fact is that people do at times find themselves in situations where they suffer legal penalties with regret but no moral guilt, and this experience seems to us to be worth exploring and not a moral glitch.

32. Gerald Graff, *Beyond the Culture Wars* (New York: Norton, 1992), 128 and 130.

33. Ibid., 151.

34. Ibid., 152.

35. Ibid., 144–170. See also Charles Taylor, "The Politics of Recognition," in Arthur and Amy Shapiro, eds., *Campus Wars* (Boulder: Westview Press, 1995), 256–261; Taylor claims that we can accept that all groups should be treated with the presumption that their concerns deserve equal respect and opportunity for public articulation but that ultimately horizons ought to be fused so that competing concerns can be assessed.

36. See John Searle, "Postmodernism and the Western Rationalist Tradition," in Arthur and Shapiro, eds., *Campus Wars*, 28–48, for an argument in favor of intellectual excellence as the main criterion in curriculum formation.

37. Alasdair MacIntyre, *Three Rival Versions of Moral Enquiry* (Notre Dame: University of Notre Dame Press, 1990), 7.

38. For more on this weak form of incommensurability, see Charles Spinosa and Hubert L. Dreyfus, "Two Kinds of Anti-Essentialism," *Critical Inquiry* 22 (1996): 735–763.

39. See Graff, *Beyond the Culture Wars*, 171–196.

40. MacIntyre, *Three Rival Versions of Moral Enquiry*, 228–229.

41. Ibid., 230.

42. Ibid., 215.

43. In matters of higher education, what we say of Searle's position, except insofar as Searle sees consequences for religion, holds as well for William J. Bennett's and Diane Ravitch's positions. Searle, Bennett, and Ravitch understand the humanities in terms of an expanded version of Matthew Arnold's notion that the humanities consist in "the best that has been said, thought, written, and otherwise expressed about human experience (William J. Bennett, "To Reclaim a Legacy" [Washington, D.C.: National Endowment for the Humanities, 1984], 3) and assume that the best that has been thought and so forth has at least a rough internal coherence. See Diane Ravitch, "Multiculturalism: *E Pluribus Plures*," *The American Scholar* 59 (1990): 337–354.

44. Robert N. Bellah, "Conflicting Roles of the Intellectual Today, or What I Am Doing Here on Good Friday," paper presented at the symposium "Fin-de-Siècle Intellectuals: Looking Back and Looking Forward," University of California at Berkeley, April 5, 1996, 10–11.

45. Ibid., 13–14.

46. E. D. Hirsch Jr., *Cultural Literacy* (New York: Vintage, 1988), 14, 102.

47. Ibid., 100.

48. Searle, "Postmodernism and the Western Rationalist Tradition," 46–47.

49. bell hooks, *Teaching to Transgress* (New York: Routledge, 1994), 29.

50. Ibid., 28. hooks lists some of the lies to which our culture of domination tends to addict us. Of the lying she writes: "That lying takes the presumably innocent form of many white people (and even some black folks) suggesting that racism does not exist anymore, and that conditions of social equality are solidly in place that would enable any

black person who works hard to achieve economic self-sufficiency. Forget about the fact that capitalism requires the existence of a mass underclass of surplus labor. Lying takes the form of mass media creating the myth that [the] feminist movement has completely transformed society, so much so that the politics of patriarchal power has been inverted and that men, particularly white men, just like emasculated black men, have become the victims of dominating women. So, it goes, all men (especially black men) must pull together . . . to support and reaffirm patriarchal domination. Add to this the widely held assumptions that blacks, other minorities, and white women are taking jobs from white men, and that people are poor and unemployed because they want to be, and it becomes most evident that part of our contemporary crisis is created by a lack of meaningful access to truth. That is to say, individuals are not just presented untruths, but are told them in a manner that enables most effective communication" (ibid., 29). The point hooks is making, however, does not depend on our believing this list of lies or even that they are lies. hooks thinks that learning requires, first, that we test claims against our own experience to see if the claims make sense and, second, that we do not take our own experience as normative but seek to see if claims make sense according to the experience of others. The first claim runs against the attractively packaged truths of the media and certain educators. The second explains her requirement that cultural diversity inform every aspect of learning (ibid., 33).

51. Ibid., 33.

52. Ibid., 207.

53. hooks's view of education as criticism of what we take for granted is close to the one Hilary Putnam endorses and describes as John Dewey's. See Hilary Putnam, "Pragmatism, Relativism, and the Justification of Democracy," in Arthur and Shapiro, eds., *Campus Wars*, 264–273. To see how close Putnam is to hooks, we need only cite his claim that "for Dewey education plays the role that revolution plays in the philosophy of Karl Marx" (272).

54. Hirsch also thinks that claims for diversity and for social unity produce contention, but he imagines that this contention takes place in a middle area between the concerns of civil religion that we all acknowledge as highest and the concerns that we all share simply as part of our historical legacy. See Hirsch, *Cultural Literacy*, 102–103.

55. We have certainly noted the same ignorance of pervasive and comprehensive differences in cases of nationality, race, class, and religion, but we may feel, in those cases, that our ignorance of the differences came from lack of thoughtful exposure to people of other nationalities, races, classes, and religions. Once we excuse our ignorance on these grounds, we can assume that more study will reveal these others as having categories that are either like ours or hopelessly confused. But it seems ludicrous, for example, to defend men's ignorance of the way women have understood being and truth on grounds of unfamiliarity. Indeed, the fact that men have been fooling themselves into believing that women saw things pretty much as men did, except when the women were behaving in nonserious ways, ought to make us think twice about relying on any method such as fusion of horizons or debate for coming to a genuine recognition of difference.

For a persuasive account of how Western middle-class women's ethical thinking differs from Western middle-class men's ethical thinking see Carol Gilligan, *In a Different*

Voice: Psychological Theory and Women's Development (Cambridge, Mass.: Harvard University Press, 1982). For an account of the phenomenological presuppositions of this book, see Hubert L. Dreyfus and Stuart E. Dreyfus, "What Is Morality? A Phenomenological Account of the Development of Ethical Expertise," in David Rasmussen, ed., *Universalism vs. Communitarianism* (Cambridge, Mass.: MIT Press, 1990). See also Seyla Benhabib and Ducilla Cornell, eds., *Feminism as Critique* (Minneapolis: University of Minnesota Press, 1987). For an account of how men and women misunderstand each other, see Deborah Tannen, *You Just Don't Understand: Women and Men in Conversation* (New York: Morrow, 1990).

56. Nietzsche, *On the Genealogy of Morals*, 157–163.

57. Nietzsche, *The Gay Science*, 232–233, §290 (developing a unified style); 236–237, §295 (leading a life of brief habits); 243–244, §303 (engaging in constant improvisation).

58. Ibid., 347, §382.

59. Although Graff is alone in making this argument for education, Michel Foucault makes it more generally. In *The Uses of Pleasure*, trans. Robert Hurley (New York: Vintage, 1985), he writes: "This project, whose goal is a history of truth, . . . was a matter of analyzing, not behaviors or ideas, nor societies and their 'ideologies,' but the *problematizations* through which being offers itself as having to be thought—and the practices on which these problematizations are formed" (11). For Foucault, then, as well as for Graff, problems or difficulties or incoherencies in our everyday practices are not a mere adventitious matter but are part of the nature of human social being. Foucault, of course, tries to show that social practices in the West have always been vexed in this way.

60. Whenever Heidegger tries to understand another philosopher, he seeks to determine the everyday practices to which the philosopher was sensitive and that therefore reveal the core experience the philosopher was clarifying. While extended examples of this way of proceeding can be found throughout Heidegger's writings, we list a few short ones. First, Heidegger unpacks the relations among Platonic notions by setting them out in terms of basic craftsmanly comportments in *The Basic Problems of Phenomenology*, trans. Albert Hofstadter (Bloomington: Indiana University Press), 106–117. He does the same for Aristotle's four causes in "The Question Concerning Technology," in *The Question Concerning Technology and Other Essays*, trans. William Lovitt (New York: Harper & Row, 1977), 7–12. To see how Heidegger does this for a modern philosopher, see how he explains Nietzsche's crucial notion of the "eternal recurrence of the same" in terms of the fledgling practices of technology to which Heidegger thinks Nietzsche was sensitive and that are endlessly disaggregating and reaggregating everything. See *What Is Called Thinking*, trans. Fred D. Wieck and J. Glenn Gray (New York: Harper & Row, 1968), 100–110.

Conclusion

1. We distinguish our defense of democracies with market economies from Francis Fukuyama's account in his *The End of History and the Last Man* (New York: Free Press, 1992). Fukuyama bases most of his account on a Hegelian understanding of human

beings seeking recognition from other human beings. He argues that seeking a stable form of recognition has driven human history and that liberal democracies grant a stable form in that citizens recognize each other as having equal dignity. So for Fukuyama liberal democracy is the political form that ends history. All that remains for liberal democracies to do is to find a way of channeling those few who seek more than equal recognition into market, athletic, or aesthetic competition. In contrast, we argue that a civil democracy with a market economy is the best political construction *so far* because it best allows people to act as history makers. But we do not argue against the possibility that some future anomaly might lead to a political construction that enables people to respond to anomalies even more meaningfully and sharply. Those who argue for radical democratic forms claim that they have a better way than ours of responding to anomalies because they do not require that responding to anomalies produce *meaningful* change. We respond that such a requirement is the only way of keeping change *as* change.

2. We are using the term *commitments* to capture a set of insights in the speech-act tradition. *Commitments* is a general term for all the ways in which human beings can become obliged to one another. For more on communication seen in this vein, see Terry Winograd and Fernando Flores, *Understanding Computers and Cognition: A New Foundation for Design* (Reading, Mass.: Addison-Wesley, 1987), 76–77.

3. For more on the limitations of theory, see Hubert L. Dreyfus, "Why Studies of Human Capacities Modeled on Ideal Natural Science Can Never Achieve Their Goal," in J. Margolis, M. Krausz, and R. M. Burian, eds., *Rationality, Relativism and the Human Sciences* (Dordrecht: Martinus Nijhoff, 1986), 3–22.

A Philosophical Appendix

1. For our fully developed answer to the charge of essentialism, see Charles Spinosa and Hubert L. Dreyfus, "Two Kind of Essentialism and Their Consequences," *Critical Inquiry* 22 (Summer, 1996): 735–763.

2. In saying that life is lived at its best when human beings are sensitive to one or another of these features does not mean that one feature or another is merely thematized or admired. It cannot simply mean either that one of the formal features such as background style becomes a foreground focus of concern. By definition, style, like the other formal features, must normally remain in the background, like the illumination in the room that allows things to appear to us. Yet human beings are especially sensitive to one or another formal aspect of skillful coping. For example, on occasion and to a certain extent the members of a culture can become sensitive to their style *as* a style. We gave the example of the husband and wife who found that life was more than working, investing, and playing. When they held on to this anomaly, they discovered that, if they focused on having a child, their fast-track style was transformed into a baby-nurturing style. Not only did everything appear in a new light, but at the time of transformation, they became sensitive to their style *as* a style. Cultures work the same way. A culture sensitive to its receptivity and style would not normally focus on its style. However, like our couple, the members of the culture would be receptive to holding on to anomalies and so to producing moments of transformation of their style in which it *was* salient *as* a style.

Insofar as such sensitivity to anomalies exists, we could say that in such a culture the receptive practices for *dealing with its style* are highly developed.

3. Whether a particular good is an ontological good or an ontic one is not a question of generality or specificity. Any disclosive space from that of a whole culture to that of the business world will be structured by ontological goods, and its members will admire an appropriate set of substantive-ontic goods.

4. Our example of the pack of teenagers gives the flavor of what skillful coping with receptivity as its end would look like more or less. In our example, the teenagers would probably see themselves as seeking intense experiences. But Søren Kierkegaard describes the purest case of this marginal possibility (in the West) of a life lived with receptivity as the only ontological good. In his *Concluding Unscientific Postscript*, trans. David F. Swenson and Walter Lowrie (Princeton: Princeton University Press, 1941), Kierkegaard names such a life Religiousness A, in which the immanent telos is "self-annihilation before God." Such a life leaves one receptively responding to whatever happens, like the birds of the air and the lilies of the field. Kierkegaard describes such a life in detail in his *Edifying Discourses*. See, for example, Søren Kierkegaard, *Edifying Discourses: A Selection*, trans. David F. and Lillian Marvin Swenson (New York: Harper & Row, 1958).

5. To make matters clearer, we consider how our general response to the charge of formalism applies to the same charge when leveled against Fernando Flores's account of work and against our account of the entrepreneur in general. Many claim that the external good of work is the product and coordination is only an internal good. Consequently, any work should be evaluated by its products. We, in contrast, claim that work goes through important historical changes in the ontological goods that structure the space of work. The underlying activity of work may always involve products, but it also involves tasks, negotiation, coordination, and so on. The notion that the point of work is to produce a product is, to us, as false as the notion that the point of work is to undertake tasks. Until one finds that one's products and services will be sought after by others, one is undertaking tasks or producing products as a hobby. For a product or service to play a useful part in the lives of others, the producer's concerns must be coordinated with the purchaser's and user's concerns. Today's entrepreneurs and even today's average businesspeople make such coordination the goal of their focused activity. Hence, we have marketing divisions that focus on quality, where quality does not simply mean how well the product meets its engineering specifications but the quality of the purchaser's or user's experience with the product.

We could argue endlessly over whether the point of work is to undertake tasks, to produce a product, or to sell a product that customers find useful. What is interesting to us is that work changes historically as one or another of the above aspects (tasks, products, coordinating activities) becomes dominant—that is, when one or another of these aspects becomes the ontological good that determines the space in which we attend to work as a whole. As these different disclosive spaces change, so does the nature of work, and so do the goods on the basis of which work or its products could be evaluated.

For instance, today the space in which we attend to work is shifting. The product is becoming increasing hard to define as products come to require services as well. Thus, when people purchase software packages for their computers, they no longer simply get something that is guaranteed to live up to certain technical specifications. They also receive the right to use a software support line. They are not just purchasing a widget; they are purchasing help to make the widget useful. Successful companies have their software support technicians not simply answer questions but suggest new uses as well. When businesses purchase software, they enter into a relationship with the software provider for training, support, updates, customization, and consulting. The only sensible good for criticizing work now is thus the quality of the relationships it produces between vendor and client, not the quality of the product.

6. We use Athens and Sparta as our exemplary cases here and later because Thucydides' interpretation of these two different cultures is widely known and has few opponents. See his *History of the Peloponnesian War*, trans. Benjamin Jowett (New York: Bantam, 1960).

7. Disclosive spaces structured with either gathering or style as their top ontological good have the same difficulty as those structured by disclosing since all three of these ontological goods produce a tendency toward a unity that passes over rather than exploits and integrates seemingly insignificant differences until crisis moments are reached. If we turn to affective appearance, we find the opposite problem. On the micro-level of skillful performance, affective appearance captures the way in which things and people appear for us. They always appear with an affect. They are attractive or repulsive. This goes for people, but it also goes for things, as, for example, a chess master's possible chess moves. In a disclosive space where affective appearance was the top ontological good, skillful coping would be governed by conflicting affective impulses. (Athenians in the Golden Age of Pericles were receptive and successful, but, under the pressure of the plague, they came to privilege affective appearance as their ontological good. They then became ripe victims for demagogues and adventurers.) Moreover, under the regime of affective appearance, various modes of life are not receptive enough to each other to cross-appropriate. (Indeed, in Athens after the death of Pericles, new ideas became rallying points for party opposition rather than possibilities for adaptation.) But in the receptive, disclosive Periclean space, as different praxes branch off, they also remain receptive to each other as well. That is what enables the disclosive space with receptivity as its top ontological good to remain efficiently coordinated as well as open to anomalies.

8. It follows from our description of skilled behavior that ontic ethics must always be practice-based. See H. L. Dreyfus and S. E. Dreyfus, "What Is Morality? A Phenomenological Account of the Development of Ethical Expertise," in David Rasmussen, ed., *Universalism vs. Communitarianism* (Cambridge, Mass.: MIT Press, 1990).

9. Heidegger's notion of a "gentle law" inspires what we say here. What follows derives from an interpretation of how Heideggerian sending (the other side of the coin of receptivity) acts as a gentle law. See Martin Heidegger, "The Way to Language," *On the Way to Language*, trans. Peter D. Hertz (New York: Harper & Row, 1971), 128–129.

Index

Abortion, 4–5, 100–101, 131, 200n18
Ackerman, Bruce, 196n15
Activism. *See* Citizen virtue; Civic activism; Political action groups
Affective appearances, 179, 180, 208n7
Agreement, democratic, 108–109
Amazonia, preservation of, 110–115, 197n36
American Indian cultures, 132, 133, 189n1, 200n20
Amish, education, 78–79, 132–133, 200n20
Anomaly. *See also* Disharmony
  in civil democracies, 109, 168–169, 206n1
  defined, 193n25
  disharmony vs., 193n25
  holding on to, 46, 50, 54, 59, 62–63, 66–68, 193n26
  innovation as sensitivity to, 50, 54, 66–67, 173
  Kuhn on, 193n25
  normalizing, 54, 68
  in polytheistic cultures, 178–179
  in receptive cultures, 206–207n2, 183, 208n7
  scientific, 193n25
  universal standards vs., 145–146
Anti-Semitism, 81–82
Apathy, 127

Apple Computer, 14, 47, 53, 55
Arendt, Hannah, 70
Aristotelians, 153, 191n6
Aristotle, 60, 178, 205n60
Arnold, Matthew, 203n43
Articulation, 187. *See also* Culture figures
  of concerns in higher education, 159–161, 198n5
  cultural, 140, 142–143, 146
  by culture figures, 2–3, 164, 165–166
  defined, 3, 24–25
  in entrepreneurship, 51
  forms of, 25
  as gathering from dispersion, 25
  generation-based, 15
  of goods in democracy, 77–78, 80–83
  institutions necessary for, 168–171
  by judges, 149–151
  literary, 81–82
  needs experienced through, 37
  reconfiguration vs., 26
  as retrieval from dispersion, 25, 164, 165–166
Assassinations, 139
Associations, free. *See* Political action groups
Athens, culture of, 183, 187–188, 208n6, 208n7
Augustinians. *See* Religious thinkers, on education